DAYS OF VALOR

DAYS
OF
VALOR

An Inside Account of the Bloodiest Six Months of the Vietnam War

By
ROBERT L. TONSETIC

CASEMATE
Philadelphia

Published by
CASEMATE

ISBN: 1-932033-52-1

Cataloging-in-Publication Data is available from the
Library of Congress.

10 9 8 7 6 5 4 3 2 1

MANUFACTURED IN THE UNITED STATES OF AMERICA

CONTENTS

For the brave men of the 199th Light Infantry Brigade who gave their lives for their country, and for the men who shared their foxholes during 1967–1968.

PREFACE

This book is about acts of courage and valor, and the men who performed them. Few, if any, of the men described in this book consider themselves heroes. Among them, this accolade is reserved for those who made the ultimate sacrifice. Most of the veterans who contributed their stories to this book attempt to downplay their experiences and deeds. Nonetheless, it is important that their stories be told. For as the Greek poet Pindar wrote, "Unsung, the noblest deed will die." The intent of the author is not to glamorize war or justify it, but rather to preserve the stories of heroism and sacrifice. Since the experience of war—the fighting, the dying, the surviving—is all but impossible to comprehend unless one has experienced it, those who may be called upon to take up arms in defense of the nation must have role models for proper behavior in war.

As we begin our fifth year in the war against terror, we face a prolonged conflict that may test our national will as never before. There exists a possibility that a catastrophic attack will be launched against the US homeland, or against our deployed forces that will make the 9-11 attacks pale in comparison. The generation of men and women coming of age today face challenges not unlike those that confronted the much heralded "greatest generation."

The heroic deeds, selfless sacrifice, and valor demonstrated by our fighting men in past wars provide necessary models for the youth of America as they assume responsibility for the nation's security. Sadly, the deeds of valor from our most prolonged conflict, the Vietnam War, remain mostly unreported and forgotten. Unlike the almost legendary stories of heroism that evolved from World War II, such as the Army Rangers' assault on the cliffs of Pointe Du Hoc or the Marines' capture of Iwo Jima, the number of stories emerging form the Vietnam War are few. The reasons are complex and rooted in the political and strategic miscalculations of that war. Perhaps the most odious reason is that the opponents of that war unjustly focused their anger and frustration with the conflict on those who fought it. Despite the fact that there were far more heroes than miscreants in the ranks, stories of atrocities and abuses far outnumbered the reports of American valor and sacrifice. Unfortunately, the anti-war movement's efforts to discredit the rank and file who fought the war was abetted by the media. Stories of atrocities and criminal conduct perpetrated by members of the armed forces, like airline crashes, are rare, but make front-page and prime-time news. A similar trend is beginning to emerge in Iraq and the war on terror. Reports of prisoner abuse and other discreditable acts should be reported, but equal attention should be paid to the numerous individual and unit acts of valor and sacrifice. The latter far outnumber the former.

Days of Valor covers a six-month slice of time during the Vietnam War from December 1967 through May of 1968. These months, which encompassed both the Tet Offensive and the May Offensive of 1968, were the bloodiest months of the war for US forces. Most of the book is focused on the infantry battalions of the 199th Light Infantry Brigade as they struggled to disrupt the enemy's build-up and subsequent attacks on the strategic installations in and around Saigon, Bien Hoa and Long Binh. Though the author's experiences are included in the book, they are written in the third person format. The book is not intended to be a personal memoir. There were many other US units that played key roles in defeating these attacks, and similar acts of heroism and valor occurred in all of these units. The narrow focus of this book allows the author to tell the stories of the men who performed the deeds of valor through their own eyes and words. There is much to learn from the experiences of Vietnam combat veterans, and they deserve a chance to contribute to the history that is written about the Vietnam War.

The majority of this book focuses on battle, even though the number of days spent in battle during a one-year tour in Vietnam was a small percentage of the average twelve-month tour. Most days for the average combat soldier consisted of exhausting marches and tedious searches for an elusive enemy. The physical and mental demands on the combatants during these periods were exceeded only by the relatively short periods of actual battle. Full descriptions of the everyday life of a combat soldier in Vietnam can be found in the many fine personal memoirs of the war.

Few of the men who provided details of their Vietnam experience for this book had discussed their service with anyone outside the veteran community since the war. In some cases, the men who related their stories to the author were personal acquaintances. Others were introduced during reunions, or contacted by telephone or email. As a fellow veteran, there was an element of trust between the author and the men who related their experiences. Shared combat experience generates a sense of camaraderie and brotherhood that withstands the tests of time. In some cases, the author gained a new perspective of his own experiences after talking with other veterans. Without exception, the men with whom the author communicated were remarkably honest and forthright about their combat experience and the effect it had on their lives. Their recollections of combat are corroborated by other sources such as official records and documents held by the National Archives.

It is hoped that the reader will gain a new appreciation for the men who fought in Vietnam. The stoicism that they demonstrated in the midst of an unpopular war is impressive. Their ability to endure under the most difficult conditions and continue on with the mission, even though worn out and exhausted, and fighting for a cause they little understood, is remarkable. Those who gave their lives, as well as those who survived, should serve as an inspiration for all those called upon to defend the nation in current and future wars.

* * *

The author thanks the many veterans of the 199th Light Infantry Brigade who over the past several years shared their memories and recollections of the events described in *Days of Valor*. In particular, I appreciate the insight and encouragement provided by Colonel

William Schroeder, who was at the center of many of the events described in this book, both as a battalion commander and later as a key staff officer at II Field Force Headquarters. While the research for this book was in progress, it was brought to his attention that two members of his battalion never received the Silver Stars that he had recommended. Bill Schroeder reinitiated the award recommendations, spending days of his personal time to insure that his men received the awards, and then organized an appropriate ceremony for the presentation of the awards in 2005.

Additionally, the author thanks and commends the efforts of Bill Hill of Columbus, Georgia who provided copies of many of the documents used as sources for this book. Bill was also the primary organizer of a 2005 reunion at Fort Benning, Georgia for veterans of the 4/12th Infantry, many of whom contributed their stories to this book. Bill is a tireless worker who has assisted many veterans in preparing the necessary documentation for their disability claims.

Also, I would like to thank and commend Peter Joannides and George Holmes, co-founders of the Redcatcher Association, for their efforts to locate hundreds of veterans of the 199th Light Infantry Brigade and reunite them with their former comrades-in-arms. Larry McDougal, historian of the 199th Light Infantry Brigade Association, is also deserving of special recognition for his efforts to document the history of the brigade over the past decades. Clifford Snyder, military archivist at the National Archives, was also extremely helpful in identifying and locating after-action reports, unit orders, and daily staff journals of the units involved in this book. A special thanks is also given to Mike Podolny of MP Cartographics for his preparation of the maps found in this book. My sincere appreciation is also extended to David Farnsworth of Casemate Publishers, who thought this book worthy of publication, and to my editor, Steven Smith.

Last but not least, I offer my gratitude and thanks to my wife, Polly Tonsetic, for her love, encouragement, and support during the many months that it took to research and write this book.

GLOSSARY

ACAV   An armored cavalry assault vehicle: a modified M113 armored personnel carrier
ACR   Armored Cavalry Regiment
Agent Orange A defoliant/herbicide used to kill vegetation
AK-47   A shoulder-fired Russian or Chinese manufactured assault rifle, standard weapon carried by Viet Cong and North Vietnamese soldiers
AO   Area of operations
APC   Armored Personnel Carrier
ARVN   Army of the Republic of (South) Vietnam

Beehive round A round fired from a recoilless rifle containing dart like flechettes
B40   A Communist shaped charge projectile fired by the RPG2 or RPG7
BMB   Brigade main base

C4   Plastic explosive used for demolition work
C&C ship   Command and control helicopter
Canopy   The uppermost spreading branchy layer of a jungle or forest
CAR15   A short barreled version of the M16 with a collapsible stock
CAS   Close air support by tactical fixed wing aircraft
CG   Commanding general

Checkfire	Artillery command that causes an immediate temporary halt in firing
Chi-Com	Chinese Communist
Chinook	The CH-47 heavy lift helicopter used by Army aviation
CIB	Combat Infantry Badge
Claymore	A US anti-personnel mine
Click	Slang for kilometer
CMD	Capital Military District (Saigon)
CO	Commanding officer
Cobra	AH-1 helicopter gunship
Cold LZ	A helicopter landing zone having no enemy opposition
Commo	Communications
Concertina	Coils of barbed wire used in defensive positions
CONEX	A steel shipping container
CP	Command post
COSVN	Central office for South Vietnam: the central command for North Vietnam=s operations in South Vietnam
CP	Command post
Cottonbalers	The nickname of the 7th Infantry Regiment
C rations	Combat field rations issued to U.S. forces
DEFCON	A defensive concentration of artillery or mortar fire
Direct fire	Fire aimed by line of sight
Door gunner	A soldier who fires a machine gun from a helicopter
DSC	Distinguished Service Cross, the nation's second highest award for heroism
Duster	The M42 combat vehicle with twin 40mm cannons, used for ground defense in Vietnam
Dust-off	Medical evacuation by helicopter
Elephant grass	Tall coarse grass with sharp edges that grows in open uncultivated areas
EOD	Explosive ordnance disposal

FAC	Forward air controller
FDC	Fire direction center
Fire base	A temporary forward base from which artillery and mortars fire in support of deployed infantry units
Fire mission	A formatted request for artillery or mortar fires from forward deployed troops
FO	Forward observer for artillery
FSB	Fire support base
Grunt	Infantryman
Gunship	An armed helicopter that provides fire support for ground forces
HE	High explosive
H&I	Harassment and interdiction fire (artillery fire)
Hooch	Vietnamese hut or house
Hot LZ	A helicopter landing zone held by enemy troops
Howitzer	An artillery piece capable of firing projectiles at medium muzzle velocity with relatively high trajectories
Huey	UH-1 helicopter
I&R	Intelligence and reconnaissance
Indirect fire	Fire not directly aimed at a target by line of sight
Infusion	Transferring soldiers from one unit to another to balance combat experienced soldiers with new arrivals
KIA	Killed in action
Kit Carson Scout	A North Vietnamese soldier who defected and agreed to scout for US troops
LAW	The M72 light anti-tank weapon, fired from the shoulder
LIB	Light infantry brigade (Army)
Local Force	Viet Cong forces who generally stayed in the same geographical area and usually employed guerilla tactics when engaging U.S., ARVN, and Allied forces
LP	Listening post

LRP	Long range patrol
LRRP	Long range reconnaissance patrol
LZ	Landing zone for helicopter(s)
M16	U.S. 5.56mm rifle, standard rifle used by U.S. troops in Vietnam
M60	U.S. 7.62mm machine gun, standard light machine gun used by U.S. troops in Vietnam
M79	U.S. 40mm grenade launcher
MACV	Military Assistance Command Vietnam
Main Force	Viet Cong units that were better armed, trained and equipped to conduct major attacks against U.S., South Vietnamese forces, and Allied forces
Mechanized unit	An infantry unit that moves by armored personnel carriers
Medevac	Medical evacuation of wounded from the battlefield usually by helicopter
MIA	Missing in action
Military crest	The area on the forward slope of a hill or ridge from which maximum observation covering the slope down to the base can be obtained
Mortar	a high trajectory indirect fire infantry weapon
MOS	Military occupational speciality
MP	Military Police
Napalm	An incendiary mixture of thickened petroleum dropped by aircraft in canisters
NCO	Noncommissioned officer or sergeant
NDP	Night defensive position
NVA	North Vietnamese Army
OCS	Officer Candidate School
Old Guard	The nickname of the 3d Infantry Regiment
People Sniffer	A device sensitive to ammonia in urine that could be mounted on a helicopter, usually a UH-1 or variant, flying low over the jungle

PF	Popular Forces (South Vietnamese local militia forces)
PIO	Public Information Officer
Point man	The forward most man in an infantry maneuvering unit who leads the way
POW	Prisoner of war
PSP	Pierced steel planking: used for makeshift runways and helipads
PX	Post exchange
PZ	Pick-up zone, an area where helicopters land to pick-up troops
Quad-50	Four .50 caliber machine guns mounted on a truck chasis
RAG boat	Riverine Assault Group watercraft
R&R	Rest and recreation, a five-day leave period granted U.S. soldiers and usually taken outside Vietnam
Recon by fire	To fire into an area where an enemy may be hiding before entering the area
Redcatchers	The nickname of the 199th Light Infantry Brigade
RF	Regional Forces (South Vietnamese)
ROTC	Reserve Officers Training Corps
RPD	Communist 7.62 light machine gun
RPG	Soviet or Chinese made rocket propelled grenade with a shaped charge
RTO	Radio Telephone Operator
Rucksack	Backpack in which a soldier carries his field equipment and rations
S1	Staff personnel officer
S2	Staff intelligence officer
S3	Staff operations officer
S3 Air	Staff officer responsible for planning and coordinating airmobile and air support of a unit's operations
S4	Staff logistics officer
Sapper	A VC or NVA soldier specially trained in infiltration and demolitions

Satchel charge An explosive charge carried by sappers that can be placed or hurled into bunkers and other facilities

Shrapnel Metal shards or fragments from an exploding shell, bomb, or mine

SITREP Situation report

Slick UH-1 troop carrying or supply helicopter

Spooky U.S. Air Force fixed-wing gunship/flareship, either an AC-47 or AC-130

Stand to A period of time when the troops in a defensive position are at 100 percent alert in their assigned fighting positions

Starlight scope An optical night vision scope

TAC air U.S. Air Force fixed-wing tactical air support

TF Task Force

TOC Tactical Operations Center

Top First Sergeant

Tracer Ammunition containing a chemical composition to mark the flight of the projectile

Track Armored personnel carrier or armored cavalry vehicle

USARV U.S. Army Vietnam

USMA United States Military Academy (West Point)

VC Viet Cong

VNAF Vietnamese Air Force (South)

Warriors Nickname of the 12th Infantry

Web gear Suspender like harness attached to a pistol belt from which a soldiers equipment is attached

WIA Wounded in action

WO Warrant Officer

WP White phosphorous

XO Executive officer

PROLOGUE

A mantle of pre-dawn darkness enshrouded the jungle around the fire base. Only the faintest streaks of light brightened the sky to the east. Specialist Cliff Kaylor of Charlie Company was on radio watch at his platoon command post (CP). The 20-year-old Ohio native finished heating his C-ration coffee in his canteen cup, and leaned against the sandbagged bunker to sip the brew and watch the day rise. Suddenly, mortar rounds began to fall near the helicopter landing pad on the far side of the battalion perimeter. He recalled, "It was like watching a thunderstorm from a distance." Charlie Company and Alpha Company manned the outer perimeter of Fire Support Base (FSB) Nashua while Bravo Company manned the inner perimeter that protected the battalion headquarters and the howitzers of Charlie Battery, 2nd Battalion, 40th Artillery. FSB Nashua was still a work in progress. Lieutenant Colonel (LTC) Bill Schroeder's "Warriors" of the 4th Battalion, 12th Infantry had established the base only two days earlier, December 4, 1967.

The shelling was not heavy and did minimal damage. Twenty to twenty-five mortar rounds, probably meant for the helicopters or the battalion CP bunker, missed their targets and exploded in the Alpha and Bravo Company defensive sectors. Like his counterpart in Charlie Company, PFC John Sayers of Alpha Company was standing radio watch outside his bunker when the barrage began. He had no time to reach the bunker. A mortar round impacted a few meters away from him, and searing hot shrapnel tore into his arm and hand. A tree that he was standing beside protected most of his body. PFC John Nawrot,

1

also a member of Alpha Company, was dozing on top of his bunker and was not as fortunate. Nawrot was seriously wounded by the blast and was evacuated to a hospital in Japan for treatment of his wounds. Sayer's and Nawrot's platoon leader was more fortunate. Newly assigned First Lieutenant Wayne Morris was asleep on the ground ten meters from his bunker. He had been warned by his platoon sergeant Dan Garrison not to sleep in the open, but ignored the advice. It nearly cost him his life. As the first rounds impacted in his platoon's area, Morris dashed to his bunker just ahead of the next salvo, narrowly escaping the blasts.

Captain Eaton's Bravo Company on the inner perimeter had just finished "stand-to" when the mortars rounds began to explode. Eaton stood outside his CP bunker as he prepared to make his rounds of the company perimeter. He took cover after the first round exploded. Specialist-four Allen Phillips followed the Captain's lead and sprinted toward his bunker, but never got there. He was hit in the legs with multiple pieces of white-hot shrapnel.

Five minutes after the mortar attack began it was over. Bleary-eyed cannoneers from the 2/40th Artillery, and mortar crews of the 4/12th ran to their sandbagged gun pits and began sighting their M102 towed howitzers and 81mm mortars on the suspected location of the enemy mortars. Captain Grinnel, the Charlie Battery commander, requested radar surveillance for the counter-battery mission, but there was none available. The artillery fire direction center computed the firing data for the counter-battery fire mission using a back azimuth to the target and an estimated range. At best, it would take a lucky shot to nail the enemy mortars and their crews, since they moved quickly to alternate firing locations after each mission.

The howitzer crews loaded the 33-pound 105mm shells, slammed the breeches closed, and awaited the command to fire. Seconds later, the howitzers belched flame and smoke as the rounds left the tubes. The mortar crews dropped round after round into their mortar tubes adding to the crescendo. The explosions of impacting howitzer and mortar rounds reverberated through the jungle, shattering the morning calm. All told, the enemy drew three or four times the fire he delivered, but it was impossible to know if the counter-battery fires had destroyed their target.

The commander of the 4/12th Infantry, LTC Bill Schroeder, USMA 1952, had five months of command behind him on the morning of December 6, 1967. The lean and fit 36-year-old was no stranger to Vietnam, having been one of the first US military advisers assigned to the country. When he arrived in Saigon in 1961, Schroeder was assigned as senior advisor to the Vietnamese Airborne Division's 6th Battalion at Vung Tau. He understood the Vietnamese including their culture and language, and this coupled with his tactical acumen made him a highly effective battalion commander. The present author, who was the Charlie Company commander in Schroeder's battalion, recalls that he had a very professional, calm demeanor. Roberto Eaton, Bravo Company commander, described him as "Absolutely the best. He was a fighting commander who knew his stuff. . . . He understood the strain and danger that the common soldier lived on, especially when on point." It was not out of character for LTC Schroder to land his C&C helicopter and walk with a line company on a mission. His men would follow him to hell and back if he asked.

The mortar attack did not disturb Schroeder's calm and deliberate demeanor. As the battalion radio operator, Specialist Pancho Ramirez, took the casualty reports from the rifle companies, Schroeder huddled with his S-3 Operations Officer, Major Ed King, and his S-2 Intelligence Officer, Captain Stone, readjusting the rifle company missions for the day. The officers had no inkling that 6 December 1967 would be the bloodiest day of the war for the Warrior battalion, and a prelude for the nationwide carnage to come.

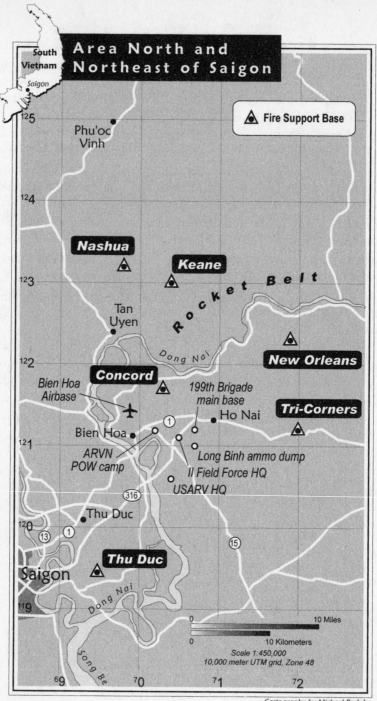

Area North and Northeast of Saigon

South Vietnam

Saigon

△ Fire Support Base

125

Phu'oc Vinh

124

123 *Nashua* △

Keane △

R o c k e t   B e l t

Tan Uyen

122 *Dong Nai*

Concord △

△ *New Orleans*

Bien Hoa Airbase

199th Brigade main base

Ho Nai

△ *Tri-Corners*

Bien Hoa

① 1

121

ARVN POW camp

Long Binh ammo dump

II Field Force HQ

USARV HQ

③16

Thu Duc

120 ⑬ ① 1

⑮

Saigon

119 *Dong Nai*

Thu Duc △

Song Be

0 _____ 10 Miles
0 _____ 10 Kilometers
Scale 1:450,000
10,000 meter UTM grid, Zone 48

69   70   71   72

Cartography by Michael Podolny

CHAPTER 1

WHAT CAME BEFORE

The 4/12th Infantry was assigned to the 199th Light Infantry Brigade (LIB). The battalion's regimental affiliation was with the storied 12th Infantry Regiment, nicknamed the "Warriors." The men who served in the 4/12th in Vietnam shared a revered heritage with other brave men who had fought with the regiment in previous wars. The 12th Infantry traced its lineage back to the Civil War during which the regiment participated in twelve campaigns with the Army of the Potomac. The Warrior regiment fought with distinction at Antietam, Fredericksburg, Chancellorsville, and Gettysburg, and finished the war in the blood-soaked trenches of Petersburg. Following the Civil War, the 12th Infantry participated in the Indian Wars, the Spanish American War, and more recently in World War II.

On D-Day, the Warriors of the 12th Infantry landed on Utah Beach with the 4th Infantry Division, and then fought their way through five European campaigns. During the Battle of the Bulge, the regiment was awarded the Presidential Unit Citation, the highest award for a unit participating in combat. During the Vietnam War, the 12th Infantry had more battalions deployed than any other infantry regiment. Two of its battalions, the 4th and 5th, were assigned to the 199th Light Infantry Brigade (LIB), while three other 12th Infantry battalions served with the 4th and 25th Infantry Divisions.

The 4/12th Infantry joined the 199th LIB when the brigade was activated at Fort Benning, Georgia in June of 1966. It was one of three infantry battalions assigned to the brigade. The 2/3d Infantry, nicknamed the "Old Guard," and the 3/7th Infantry, the "Cottonbalers," were also assigned to the 199th LIB upon its activation. Six months later the brigade shipped out for Vietnam, arriving at Vung Tau on December 10, 1966.

The 199th LIB spent most of its first year in-country securing and pacifying the area surrounding Saigon. When LTC Schroeder assumed command of the 4/12th in July of 1967, the battalion was in the closing phase of Operation Fairfax/Rang Dong, a joint Revolutionary Development and Pacification program in which US and Army of Republic of Vietnam (ARVN) forces were intermixed to form a combined forces team. The objective of the operation was to secure and pacify the countryside surrounding the sprawling city of Saigon and its environs. Schroeder's battalion was teamed with the 30th Vietnamese Ranger Battalion, and was assigned an area of operations (AO) centered on Thu Duc, north of Saigon. It was the type of mission that Bill Schroeder was well prepared for given his previous tour as an advisor to Vietnamese forces and his considerable skills as a trainer.

LTC Bill Schroeder was a second generation Army officer who grew up on Army posts around the world. He was born in Tientsin, China in 1929, the son of Army sergeant in the 15th Infantry Regiment. Schroeder's father had joined the Army at 15 and served in World War I. At the outbreak of World War II, Schroeder's father was commissioned in the Army Air Corps, and retired after the war with the rank of Lieutenant Colonel. There was never much doubt about which career Bill Schroeder would pursue. After graduating from high school he joined the Army, took the US Military Academy admissions test, and received an appointment to West Point. He graduated in the class of 1952. With an airborne infantry and Special Forces background, and a previous tour as an advisor to ARVN forces, Bill Schroeder was well qualified to command an infantry battalion in combat.

LTC Schroeder turned each operation into a learning experience for his troops. He never missed an opportunity to make on-the-spot corrections when he saw something he didn't like, but he always made them in a calm and even-tempered manner. On one occasion, when a company commander was having difficulty navigating in some rough terrain, Schroeder landed his helicopter, and gave the Captain a quick course on how to properly "shoot an azimuth," and move on a compass heading. Schroeder also debriefed his officers and NCOs on a regular basis, and distributed a series of "Commanders Notes" on subjects like ambush procedures, marking of helicopter landing zones, booby traps, treatment of POWs, communication procedures, and daylight and night movement. His purpose was to save as many lives as possible. Soon after he took command, his subordinates and superiors alike recognized that his leadership was making a difference in the battalion.

Schroeder's battalion was highly successful during Operation Fairfax. Viet Cong influence over the villages and hamlets surrounding Thu Duc began to decline as a result of the joint operations conducted by the 4/12th Warriors and the ARVN Rangers. By August 1967, the 4th VC Local Battalion was assessed as ineffective in the Thu Duc District, and intelligence reports suggested that it had departed the district for training and refitting.

On August 7th, Schroeder's Echo Company and a company from the 30th ARVN Ranger Battalion conducted an integrated airmobile assault in the Hoc Mon District, engaging an estimated VC Company on the landing zone (LZ). Five UH-1D helicopters were shot down during the combat assault and the Echo Company Commander was killed. After a tough fight to secure the LZ, Schroeder's mixed force regrouped and attacked the dug- in enemy force driving them from their positions. Twenty-two VC were killed and nine were taken prisoner by Schroeder's men. Another casualty of this battle was the 199th Brigade Commander, Brigadier General "Fritz" Freund, who was severely wounded when he landed his C&C ship on the "hot" LZ to evacuate casualties. Freund was evacuated to the States, and Lieutenant General Fred Weyand, the II Field Force Commander, looked around for a replacement. Fortunately, he had a qualified candidate close at hand.

Brigadier General Robert C. Forbes was General Weyand's Chief of Staff at II Field Force Headquarters. Forbes had held the position since February 1967, and had earned Weyand's trust and confidence. Prior to his assignment to II Field Force, Forbes was the Assistant Division Commander of the 9th Infantry Division, one of three divisions under Weyand's command. Without question, Forbes' reputation in Vietnam was firmly established. He was also well connected with the Army's hierarchy. Forbes joined the Army in 1939 after graduation from the University of Pennsylvania. He served with distinction in World War II and Korea, and later served multiple tours in the Pentagon. Forbes was known personally by a number of the Army's four star generals. There was no one close at hand who surpassed Forbes qualifications for the job, and he assumed command of the 199th LIB on 4 September 1967.

Later that month, Schroeder's men killed the battalion commander of the Viet Cong's 4th Local Force Battalion in Thu Duc effectively breaking the back of that unit's operations in the district. By mid-October, the 30th Ranger Battalion was declared fully combat ready by the new 199th LIB commander, Brigadier General Forbes, and Schroeder's 4/12th Infantry began to phase out of Operation Fairfax.

Forbes was anxious to conclude Operation Fairfax. He sincerely believed that the ARVN Rangers were completely competent, and were ready to be cut loose from their American support in order to assume full responsibility for the defense of Saigon. Moreover, he was concerned that his combat brigade was being tied down in a relatively inactive area and was gradually losing its combat edge.

After a series of briefings and discussions with his superiors, including General Westmoreland, Forbes gained approval for a plan to move the center of gravity of the 199th LIB north into the southwestern portion of War Zone D. There was, however, one proviso. The 199th LIB had to remain close enough to the Saigon defensive area to respond if the city was threatened.

War Zone D was a large, sparsely populated area north of Saigon, Long Binh, and Bien Hoa. The area was used by the Communists to train, rest, and stage troops through. Additionally, it was a significant logistical base area for the enemy. During the late summer and early fall of 1967, intelligence reports indicated that enemy activity in the area was on the increase. Aerial observers reported numerous enemy sightings, including the movement of 2-1/2-ton Russian-made trucks through the area. The enemy was clearly up to something, but at the time, no one realized that the build-up was in preparation for a major nationwide offensive scheduled to take place during the Tet holiday at the end of January 1968.

In fact, the decision to launch a nationwide offensive during the Tet holiday period was made by the Communist leadership in Hanoi in July 1967. The following six months were spent preparing for the general offensive. Military preparations were in high gear by the fall of 1967.

Replacements, many newly arrived from North Vietnam, were assigned to Viet Cong Main Force battalions and regiments, and local units. Communist plans for the Tet Offensive called for these units to be the first wave "shock troops" in the attacks on the population centers of Saigon and Bien Hoa, and the US base camps and logistic centers at Long Binh. A reorganization of the communication and transportation networks stretching from the Cambodian border to the Saigon, Bien Hoa, and Long Binh areas was also underway. A vital part of these networks stretched eastward from the Cambodian border through War Zone C and on to War Zone D. Rest stations were established every four to eight hours' march along these infiltration routes. A steady stream of supplies, small arms ammunition, 122 mm rockets and mortar shells, and men flowed along these routes throughout the fall of 1967. Every indigenous means of transportation was called into service including bicycles, ox carts, and civilian and military trucks to preposition supplies within striking distance of the enemy's objectives for the Tet Offensive.

Brigadier General Forbes selected an area north and northeast of Tan Uyen between the Song Be and Song Dong Nai Rivers, as the first area to be searched. That area had been under the control of the Communists since 1948. From firing sites in the southern portion of this area, the VC and NVA could launch 122mm rockets into the strategically important Bien Hoa airbase, and the huge Army base and logistic complex at Long Binh. More worrisome was the fact that enemy ground troops staging from this area could reach the same targets in a day or two.

Although the U.S. 1st Infantry Division spent a limited period of time in the area, it was never thoroughly searched by U.S. troops. Forbes wanted to move in and destroy any enemy forces operating in the area. He also wanted to find and destroy enemy weapons and ammunition caches, particularly the 122mm rockets and their launchers that were used to bombard the U.S. Long Binh/Bien Hoa base complex. The 199th LIB's rear base installation, Camp Frenzell-Jones, was located within this complex along with the II Field Force Headquarters, USARV Headquarters, and a number of other unit headquarters.

To accomplish this new mission, the 199th Commander planned to establish a fire support base (FSB) in the area of operations (AO) to support the ground troops as they searched the area. A 105mm artillery battery and a 155mm artillery battery would displace to the base. Forbes believed that by putting infantry on the ground in the enemy sanctuary, he could interdict the enemy's infiltration routes and inflict major damage on their logistical support.

Brigadier General Forbes selected the 4/12th Infantry to be the first of his three infantry battalions to relocate to War Zone D. Once Schroeder's "Warriors" established a fire base in the area, they would be followed by LTC Gibler's 3/7th Infantry. The 2/3d Infantry under the command of LTC Poage was to remain in the Nha Be District south of Saigon until mid-December, when the 199th LIB would complete the final phase of Operation Fairfax/Rang Dong.

Forbes chose Schroeder's battalion for the new mission because the battalion had significantly reduced enemy activity in Thu Duc District. He was also impressed with Schroeder's calm, imperturbable manner and his professionalism. With five months of battalion command behind him, he was Forbes' most battle-tested battalion commander. Both men knew that this new mission posed significant challenges and risks for the troops and their leaders.

The initial deployment of only a single infantry battalion to the area was especially dangerous. Six weeks earlier, the 2/28th Infantry, the "Black Lions," from the 1st Infantry Division were pounced on by an enemy regiment and lost the better part of two infantry companies and most of the battalion command group in an area less than twenty miles to the northwest of the AO selected by Forbes. The "Black Lions" fought bravely, but were badly outnumbered by a regiment of the 9th VC Division. Lieutenant Colonel Terry Allen Jr., the battalion commander and son of the famed World War II general, was killed along with fifty-seven of his men. Bill Schroeder and Terry Allen were classmates at West Point and later at the Army's Command and

General Staff College. Schroeder was well aware of what had happened to the "Black Lions" and his former classmate, and he knew that he was about to confront the same determined enemy.

The 199th LIB Intelligence Officer briefed Forbes and Schroeder that the VC Dong Nai Regiment, a unit that traced its lineage to 1948, was based in War Zone D. The Dong Nai Regiment was composed of three maneuver battalions, designated K1, K2, and K3. The K1 and K3 were formerly local force battalions; however, the K2 was formerly the 7th Battalion, 568th Regiment, 330th NVA Division. Enemy troops wearing NVA uniforms and helmets were spotted in the new AO by aerial observers. It was highly probable that these troops were members of the Dong Nai Regiment's K2 battalion.

The troops of the Dong Nai Regiment were very familiar with the dense jungle terrain and the trail network that crisscrossed it. In addition to using the area to train for major operations, the Dong Nai Regiment was responsible for defending the logistical base areas and camps scattered throughout the region. The Dong Nai Regiment would not of relinquish control of their stronghold without a fight.

War Zone D was a vastly different environment from the one the Warriors were accustomed to. The area around Thu Duc where the battalion had operated for the prior eleven months was made up of open rice paddy fields, canals, streams, marshes, and nipa palm bogs. Immersion foot was more of a drain on manpower than wounds sustained in combat. The terrain in the new Area of Operations, just barely 20 kilometers to the north, was strikingly different. In the former area, the mean elevation averaged eight meters above sea level, while in the new AO the average was 22 meters with rolling hills up to 54 meters high. Instead of flat open terrain cultivated with rice paddies, the troops would be operating in continuous double and triple canopy jungle. Beneath the canopy was an understory of small trees, patches of bamboo, and weedy grasses that hindered cross-country movement and limited observation to a few meters. The area was ideal for the establishment of fortified enemy base camps and supply depots that could not be easily spotted from the air. Due to the differences in terrain and vegetation, the tactics developed by Schroeder's men over the past year were of limited use in the new AO.

Brigadier General Forbes and LTC Schroeder were also concerned that the troops of the Warrior battalion had become, in a sense, victims of their own success. By November 1967, it was a rare occasion when the infantrymen encountered more than a squad of VC. A lack of contact with the enemy led, in some cases, to carelessness, lack of alertness, and overconfidence. Schroeder was concerned about this, and convinced Forbes to let the outfit operate just north of the Bien Hoa/Long Binh area for a couple of weeks before moving into the heart of War Zone D. This area was the responsibility of the US 9th Infantry Division, and his battalion would be operating under 9th Infantry command, but he didn't give a damn. He wanted to give his men a chance to re-hone their combat skills in a different environment.

Although there were no large main force enemy units operating in the area, there were a number of guerrilla squads charged with reconnaissance, tax collection, propaganda, and communication missions. There was also a support unit charged with establishing and guarding numerous supply and arms caches. It was one of the former units that Schroeder's men brought to bay on 29 November 1967.

Staging out of Fire Support Base Concord just east of Bien Hoa, Schroeder ordered his Charlie Company to conduct an airmobile assault into the southernmost part of War Zone D just north of the Dong Nai River. Charlie Company landed on three separate landing zones (LZs), and began to sweep south toward the river. As the troops advanced on parallel axis, Schroeder, orbiting overhead in an OH-23 Light Observation Helicopter, spotted a squad of VC. He directed the ground troops to intercept the enemy.

Charlie Company's 3d Platoon was first to make enemy contact. The point man, backed- up by PFC Jim Pittman of Saranac, Michigan, spotted ten guerillas advancing toward their position. Reacting aggressively, the two grunts tossed four grenades at the enemy and then cut loose with their M-16s, killing five of the VC, and capturing two more. Third platoon then began to pursue the remaining VC. Pittman was again in the lead. Suddenly he found himself on the edge of a 15-foot bank overlooking the river. The bank was overgrown with a choked assortment of vines and weeds, and below was a flat piece of ground some ten feet from the water's edge.

As Pittman surveyed the scene, Schroeder's helicopter returned and hovered thirty feet over the river. All at once, the bubble-nosed chopper began taking fire from VC concealed in spider holes dug into the bank. Schroeder's pilot tilted the blade toward the bank to separate the vegetation and expose the VC to the Charlie Company grunts standing above. Schroeder leaned out the door of the ship and fired his .45 caliber pistol downward at one of the VC, killing him. Taking their cue from their commander, the grunts fired down the bank at the VC positions.

Anxious to finish the fight, Pittman leapt down the15-foot drop, landing beside the river's edge, and began spraying the bushes with his M16. After finishing off two VC, he looked up at Schroeder's helicopter still hovering 25 to 30 feet above, and moved his hand across his throat to signal that the VC were dead. He was only partially right. Three diehard VC popped up from their camouflaged spider holes and opened fire on Pittman. He stiffened as he was hit, staggered forward, and collapsed into the river. Bleeding profusely, he crawled through the knee-deep water to the shore before collapsing again. Schroeder's pilot attempted get low enough to pull the wounded man onto the chopper's skids, but he was driven off by more hostile fire. The pilot pulled pitch and as he gained altitude he radioed for a dust-off.

The grunts on top of the bank again opened fire on the VC, driving them back into their holes. The platoon medic, George Hauer, a stalwart Alabaman, stripped off his web gear and weapon and, with only his medical bag, leapt the 15 feet down the bank, landing next to PFC Pittman. The VC opened fire on the pair, but Hauer ignored the rounds impacting around him and continued to work on the wounded man. Inspired by Hauer's actions, several more Charlie Company grunts jumped down the bank and finished off the remaining VC with hand grenades and rifle fire.

Moments later, a medevac chopper arrived and hovered a few yards offshore. Doc Hauer and Sergeant Louis Warmack, known to his men as "Mobile," carried Pittman into the fast moving current until they were able, with the crew's help, to hoist the severely wounded Pittman into the chopper. Pittman was kept alive until he reached the 93d Evac Hospital, but his wounds were so extensive that he was flown to Japan for extensive treatment, and then on to the States. He was paralyzed from the waist down.

While Schroeder was impressed with Pittman's and Hauer's bravery, he was concerned with Charlie Company's overall performance during the fight. The company commander had been slow to react when his men made contact, and only one platoon was able to reach the area in time to engage the enemy. The Warrior commander resolved to provide closer guidance to the Captain in the future.

While 4/12th continued operations along the Song Dong Nai, planning was underway for a deeper incursion into War Zone D. Brigadier General Forbes wanted a thorough air and ground reconnaissance of the new area, but he didn't own the assets to accomplish this mission. Fortunately, there were other units available. The 3d Squadron, 17th Cavalry, 12th Aviation Group was assigned the mission of aerial reconnaissance, while the mission of ground reconnaissance was assigned to F Company, 51st Long Range Patrol. Forbes convinced his boss, General Fred Weyand, the II Field Force Commander, to give operational control of F Company, 51st Long Range Patrol to the 199th Brigade. F Company, a ground reconnaissance unit, was commanded by Major William C. Maus, a six foot two, highly respected West Pointer with prior combat experience in the 1st Infantry Division. All of the soldiers assigned to the LRP Company were volunteers and they were anxious for a mission.

F Company was activated two months earlier, and its members spent their first two months in training at the 5th Special Forces Recondo School at Nha Trang, where they learned the techniques of long range patrolling and survival skills while operating deep in enemy controlled territory. Maus was eager to give his teams a final shakedown mission in support of the 4/12th Infantry. They were given the mission of infiltrating into the Warrior battalion's new area of operations ahead of the ground troops to locate enemy base camps and supply dumps.

The site chosen by LTC Schroeder for the new fire base in War Zone D was nine kilometers north of the Song Dong Nai in the Tan Uyen District of Bien Hoa Province, just one kilometer south of the Binh Duong-Bien Hoa Province boundary. The base was given the name Fire Support Base Nashua. The exact location was in a large cleared area that was once the location of a Vietnamese "Strategic Hamlet" that had been abandoned several years before. The site was accessible by a dirt road that branched to the northeast off Highway 16 about six kilometers north of Tan Uyen. The Song Be River flowed west to east in a serpentine path some six kilometers to the north. Schroeder selected the site after an aerial reconnaissance of the area, but had to convince his boss that it was the best site. Brigadier General Forbes was concerned that the site selected by the Warrior commander was too far north, and that it could not be easily reinforced. Forbes wanted the firebase established further to the south, but Schroeder convinced him otherwise.

The site chosen by LTC Schroeder had several advantages. It had clear fields of fire out to several hundred meters around the perimeter, and it was accessible to tracked and wheeled vehicles. A platoon from Delta Troop, 17th Armored Cavalry was attached to Schroeder's battalion, and its nine M113 ACAV vehicles would escort the battalion trains to the new firebase after the rifle companies air assaulted into the area to secure it. Schroeder didn't think the Cav's tracked vehicles would be of much use in the heavy jungle of War Zone D, but their .50 caliber and 7.62 machine guns would bolster the defensive fires along the firebase's perimeter. He was also promised a battery of 155mm howitzers that would also have to be towed in. Schroeder wanted the firebase established as quickly as possible so that the Warrior battalion's rifle companies could begin operations in the new AO. He was unaware that the site selected for Fire Support Base Nashua was in the center of a Vietcong regimental area with well-concealed base camps all around. The enemy would not abandon their stronghold without a fight.

Major Ed King, the battalion S-3 operations officer, developed the plan for the Warrior battalion's incursion into War Zone D. King, a Citadel graduate, joined the Warrior battalion a month prior, and quickly gained the confidence of LTC Schroeder. King was a natural for the job, an expert planner and a quick thinker, who could quickly adjust tactical plans to adapt to any changing situation. Like Schroeder, Ed King never "lost his cool."

King coordinated with Major Maus, the A Company, 51st LRP Commander, to insert five Long Range Patrols into the AO beginning on 3 December. The LRP teams would prowl the areas in a five-kilo-meter circle around the proposed fire base location, and watch the trails for enemy movement. The Warrior battalion commander did not want any surprises when his men air-assaulted into the area. A few days earlier an aero scout team from 3/17 Cav had spotted an enemy soldier in a tree near one of the proposed LZs. Schroeder and King both knew that the enemy routinely employed LZ watchers.

After Major Maus' LRP teams conducted their reconnaissance missions, 4/12th's four infantry companies would air assault into the area on the morning of 4 December, and establish the perimeter of Fire Support Base Nashua. Once the infantry companies secured the perimeter, Charlie Battery, 40th Artillery would sling load it's 105mm howitzers in by CH-47, Chinook helicopters. Simultaneously, the bat-talion's tactical operations center (TOC) would be airlifted in, fol-lowed by other support units. A combat engineer squad from the 87th Engineer Company would also join the battalion to clear any mines in the area and operate the D7 bulldozer and ditch digger that were to be airlifted in.

While the massive airmobile operation was in progress, an armored cavalry platoon from D Troop, 17th Cavalry and support vehicles would depart Fire Support Base Hanover just north of Tan Uyen for the new location. The 3/17th Air Cavalry operating out of Hanover would provide convoy cover and security on the route, and conduct reconnaissance in the new area. Artillery support would be provided by Bravo Battery, 2/40th Artillery located at Fire Base Hanover. King and Schroeder hoped that the speed and size of the operation would surprise the enemy and buy enough time to get the firebase established before nightfall. The first twelve hours of the oper-ation were critical.

CHAPTER 2

ACROSS THE SONG DONG NAI

3–4 December 1967

The first of Major Maus' six-man LRP teams was on the helipad at 1700 hours on the afternoon of 3 December. The men wore camouflage fatigues and bush hats with their faces painted to match the camouflage pattern of their uniforms. Their rucksacks each weighed up to 75 pounds, and were loaded with extra ammunition, Claymore mines, LAWs, and an assortment of other survival equipment. This was their first real mission and the men were pumped. Their adrenalin began to flow as they clambered aboard the Huey that would insert them into the jungles of War Zone D. The pilot pulled pitch and the ship lifted off the helipad bound for the LZ. Flying low level, the UH-1D skimmed over the fast flowing waters of the Song Dong Nai and then continued north over the jungle canopy toward a tiny remote landing zone selected for the insertion. The LZ was five kilometers southwest of the area where Schroeder's infantrymen would land the following morning. Five minutes after they took off, the pilot yelled over the roar of the Huey's engines that they were 30 seconds out of the LZ.

The LRPs, seated on the floor of the slick with their legs dangling over the side, stepped out onto the skids, and prepared to leap to the ground as the ship touched down. Three feet off the ground the men jumped and ran toward the tree line, while the ship took off over the trees. It was a perfect insertion. After moving into the jungle, the patrol formed a tight perimeter and listened for any movement toward their location. Before moving out, the patrol members used branches and other flora to complete their camouflage.

Fifteen minutes later, a second LRP team was inserted three kilometers to the east. Both teams moved to pre-selected night positions as darkness fell. The LRPs sensed the enemy's presence around them, and they occasionally heard the sound of movement amid the cacophony of sounds in the darkened jungle. They hunkered down in the thick undergrowth hoping not to be discovered. Their job was to watch, listen, and report enemy sightings and movement.

A third LRP team was inserted at 0630 hours on the morning of 4 December. Their AO was four kilometers southeast of 4/12th's designated LZs. While the LRPs began to prowl the jungle looking for the enemy, Schroeder's infantry companies began to line up on their pick-up zones (PZs) for the airmobile assaults. Ed King and the airmobile company commanders planned the operation with clockwork precision. King had requested enough aviation support to lift all four of the battalion's rifle companies simultaneously. He also flew a reconnaissance of all the pick-up and landing zones with each company commander the day before, and he was confident that the battalion would be firmly established in the new AO by sunset.

At 0730, thirty minutes before the 4/12th airmobile operation was to commence, LRP Team 12 made contact with a VC platoon, less than four kilometers away from one of the Warrior battalion's LZs. The firefight lasted less than ten minutes and the LRPs managed to kill two VC and wound four others. Outnumbered and outgunned, they called for artillery support, broke contact, and sprinted toward one of their prearranged PZs with the enemy in hot pursuit. Their job was not to stand and fight. At 0755, the LRPs jumped aboard the extraction ship, while Major Maus orbited overhead in a C&C chopper, directing a pair of gunships that pounded the surrounding jungle with rockets and machine gun fire. The Huey lifted off amid a hail of gunfire from the surrounding jungle.

LTC Schroeder and Major King monitored the LRP extraction from their C&C ship, as they prepared for the battalion's airmobile insertion. They were concerned. In addition to the LRP contact, Delta Troop, 3/17th Cavalry scouts had reported numerous sightings of enemy bunkers, trenches, and tunnel entrances near the Warrior battalion's LZs. The scouts also reported small groups of enemy soldiers moving throughout the AO. Some wore NVA uniforms. The commander and his operations officer were also worried about a report they received from a forward air controller (FAC) the evening prior. Three Russian made enemy trucks were spotted driving on a secondary road about eight kilometers north of the LZs. The trucks disappeared before a flareship and gunships could arrive on the scene. Both Schroeder and King were apprehensive about the level of enemy activity in the area.

As the LRPs flew back to their base at Bien Hoa, the sky around them began to fill with helicopters. The airmobile operation began shortly after 0800 hours. Alpha and Bravo companies were picked up just outside the perimeter of Fire Base Concord, while Charlie and Echo Companies moved to PZ s north and east of the Song Dong Nai. As artillery and gunships pounded the LZs with preparatory fires, the lift ships made their final approaches. The men were briefed to expect a "hot" LZ.

The airmobile assault achieved tactical surprise, and all LZs were "cold." By 0905 hours all four rifle companies were on the ground. The battalion's prior experience conducting airmobile assaults paid off, and this one was performed with precision. Bob Eaton, Bravo Company CO, wrote, "There was no confusion, no problem. We went in fast. Set up security. Cleared fields of fire, and dug in. We expected to be hit immediately."

LTC Schroeder breathed a sigh of relief as he directed his company commanders to search and secure the areas surrounding the LZs before forming a battalion perimeter. He was not surprised when the grunts found unoccupied enemy bunkers, trenches, caches of rice, and other evidence of enemy presence within a few hundred meters of the LZs.

As the rifle companies began to dig in to form the battalion perimeter, CH-47s from the 478th Heavy Helicopter Company began to arrive with the artillery. Charlie Battery, 2/40th Artillery's howitzers were sling loaded beneath the giant cargo helicopters. The rotor wash of the hovering CH-47s kicked up swirling clouds of dust and dirt as the Chinooks hovered downward until their loads were on the ground. The cargo straps were then released from the hooks dangling from beneath the bellies of the ships, and free of their loads, the powerful two-engine Chinooks gained altitude and flew off to pick up additional loads. As the Chinooks lifted off, artillerymen ran through the maelstrom of swirling sand and dust and quickly manhandled their howitzers into firing positions. Red and white aiming stakes were then placed in front of each howitzer, laying them in for registration.

Additional CH-47 sorties lifted in coiled rolls of concertina wire, steel engineer stakes, bundles of sandbags, and pre-fabricated bunkers. As Lieutenant Wayne Morris of Alpha Company described the scene, "With the Flying Crane [CH-54] lifting in a bulldozer and other heavy equipment, Hueys and gunships everywhere, soldiers swarming in all directions in the dust . . . I remember my amazement at the organized confusion underway." The Warrior battalion soon had over 500 men on the ground at Firebase Nashua, and more were on the way. Everyone wanted to be dug in with overhead cover by nightfall.

Around 1500 hours, a platoon of Delta Troop, 17th Cav rumbled into the FSB Nashua with a portion of the battalion trains. The convoy had moved by unpaved road from Fire Support Base Hanover, a distance of some twelve kilometers, without incident. During the days that followed, the cavalrymen would have to fight to keep the overland route to Fire Base Nashua open.

The grunts were glad to see Delta Troop's ACAVs, as they pulled into firing positions around the perimeter. With their high silhouettes, the armored vehicles were tempting targets for enemy RPGs, but each track's .50 caliber machine gun and two 7.62 machine guns added a significant amount of firepower to the battalion perimeter. As the Cav troopers strung concertina wire in front of their positions, the infantrymen continued to improve their fighting positions. The Warrior platoon leaders checked and re-checked their platoons' defensive preparations. They insured that their M60 machine guns were positioned to provide interlocking fields of fire across their platoon frontages. Additionally, they made sure that each fighting position had two Claymore mines positioned at least 16 meters to the front of the position.

The Claymore was detonated by a handheld electrical firing device. When fired, the mine blasted the area to its front with 700 spherical steel balls. It was 100 percent lethal to anyone within a 50 meter range, and it was moderately effective out to a range of 100 meters. Further to the front, the grunts rigged trip flares in the wire entanglements. Beyond the wire, in front of most platoon positions, there was fifty to a hundred meters of relatively open area with some low scrub brush and weeds. Fire Base Nashua was not an easy objective for an enemy ground assault, but it was not unassailable, particularly to enemy sappers who were adept at slipping through firebase perimeters with satchel charges and destroying artillery pieces and command bunkers.

As a precautionary measure, LTC Schroeder directed Captain Bob Eaton's Bravo Company to establish an inner perimeter to protect the artillery, mortars and battalion TOC. Eaton's company was also designated battalion reserve with the mission of counterattacking and destroying any enemy that managed to penetrate the FSB's outer defenses.

As twilight approached, the Charlie battery's howitzers and the battalion's mortar platoons completed firing their registrations. On-call defensive concentrations were plotted all around the perimeter. FSB Nashua was as well prepared as it could be for a new firebase.

LTC Schroeder decided to have one last walk around the battalion perimeter before darkness fell. The firebase was still a work in progress, but his men were well dug in on the outer perimeter. In the Alpha Company sector on the southeast side of the firebase, a new lieutenant in a clean set of jungle fatigues and shined boots saluted him. Schroeder reminded the lieutenant that it was "downright dangerous" to salute an officer in the field, since enemy snipers were on the lookout for high-value targets. Lieutenant Morris was embarrassed, but he would not make the same mistake again.

After walking the perimeter and satisfying himself that adequate preparations had been made for the night's defense, Schroeder and King met with the company commanders to update them on the most recent intelligence, and the plan of operations for the following day. The Warrior commander wanted his battalion to maintain an offensive posture.

LTC Schroeder had a number of concerns. First, he felt that he wasn't getting timely information from the LRP teams that were under his operational control. He asked the LRP commander, Major Maus, to meet with him at Fire Base Nashua the following morning. He was also concerned about a bunker complex found by A Troop 3/17th Cav less than two kilometers northeast of Nashua. The Cav troopers did not find any enemy at the site, but the area looked suspicious. Schroeder gave his Echo Company CO, Captain Stan McLaughlin, the mission of checking the area out further on the next day.

While McLaughlin's company patrolled north of Nashua, Captain Donald Drees' Alpha Company was to reconnoiter to the south. Charlie Company, commanded by Captain Ronald Jones (not his real name), was instructed by Schroeder to complete work on their sector of the perimeter and patrol northwest of the firebase. Schroeder then instructed Captain Eaton to complete work on the inner perimeter and provide security for the combat engineers who were constructing a trench and berm. Schroeder reminded his commanders that he'd ordered a stand-to for 0600 hours the next morning. At stand-to, all of the men on the perimeter were required to be in full battle dress manning their fighting positions.

LTC Schroeder and Major King planned to continue saturation patrolling in the area around Fire Base Nashua, pushing out farther each day. When the immediate area around the base was cleared, he planned to initiate company-size airmobile operations throughout the AO to interdict enemy movement and to destroy major VC/NVA forces that were operating in this portion of War Zone D. After receiving their missions for the following day, Schroeder's battle captains returned to their companies.

The Warrior battalion commander was pleased with the professionalism that his battalion displayed that day. The battalion-sized airmobile insertion had gone like clockwork without a hitch, and work on the new firebase was progressing well. He knew that 4/12th Infantry ranked among the best combat battalions in Vietnam, and was confident that they would meet any challenge they faced with courage and fortitude. He had no idea, however, that in the next 48 hours, the Warrior battalion would face its greatest challenge since landing at Vung Tau some twelve months prior.

All was quiet along the perimeter of Fire Base Nashua that night. The rifle company night ambush patrols and listening posts (LPs) were positioned on the likely avenues of approach to the perimeter to provide early warning of an attack. The patrols and LPs remained alert, uneasy in their new environment. All they heard were the night sounds of the jungle.

Things were not so quiet for the LRPs. Four kilometers south of Nashua, Major Maus' LRP Team 13 reported that an enemy unit, estimated at company size, had settled around them for the night. The news was unsettling to RTOs Mangai and Dowd manning the battalion radios in the TOC. They informed the duty officer who in turn informed the battalion S3, Major Ed King. King took the report and instructed the duty officer to report the information to Brigade. He was not alarmed, since the LRPs had not called for assistance or extraction. If they were in serious trouble, they would call for artillery and gunship support and haul ass for the nearest extraction LZ. In this case they had not. The remainder of the night was uneventful.

5 December 1967

At first light, LRP Team 13 slipped quietly out of their night position and moved slowly southward. The six-man team moved stealthily through the vines and bushes along an intermittent streambed, moving ten meters, then stopping and listening before moving again. The jungle air was heavy and no breeze was stirring. Meanwhile, two additional LRP teams were about to be inserted to the north and northwest of the fire base. Team 23 was inserted shortly after 0630, followed by Team 27 at 0700 hours. With these insertions, Major Maus had four teams on the ground looking for the enemy. It did not take long to find them.

LRP team 13 was the first to report a sighting. They saw four armed VC moving east to west in front of their position some four kilometers south of Fire Base Nashua. The team leader reported the sighting, then continued moving south.

At 0845 hours, LRP Team 25, led by Sergeant Alexander, made contact with a platoon-size enemy force two kilometers east of Team 13's location. While moving through the dense jungle the point man, Specialist Four Dan Lindsey, spotted six VC advancing in line formation toward the patrol's location. Lindsey knew that the team's mission was to monitor and report enemy movement, not to engage in a firefight, but it was too late. The VC had spotted him. Recognizing the need for immediate action, he opened fire, killing two of the enemy. The remainder of the VC platoon returned the fire, and Lindsey went down with a serious leg wound. Dropping to the ground, he crawled back to his patrol's position where, along with his teammates, he continued to fire on the advancing enemy while the patrol leader, Sergeant Alexander, radioed for artillery, air support, and a medevac. The LRP team was outnumbered and in serious trouble.

Five minutes after he received the report, Major Maus was aboard his C&C ship headed for the LRPs' location. The team had to be extracted before they were overrun. Under the cover of artillery fire, the patrol broke contact and began to move toward an extraction zone carrying the badly wounded Specialist Lindsey. As the LRPs made their way toward the LZ, an extraction ship flew at max speed over the triple canopy jungle. After reaching the LZ, Alexander's team popped a smoke grenade to signal the UH-1D that they were prepared for extraction. Artillery fire kept the VC at bay. When the Huey dropped down into the tiny LZ, the team raced for the ship carrying their wounded comrade just as the VC arrived and began to fire. As the slick lifted off, the M60 door gunners blazed away at the enemy, hitting two. AK-47 rounds riddled the UH-1 as it lifted off. Gaining altitude, the pilot headed for the 93th Evacuation Hospital at Long Binh at maximum speed. It was a race against time. Dan Lindsey did not complete the race. He'd lost too much blood and died before the helicopter touched down on the hospital's landing pad. F Company, 51st LRP lost their first man, and he was one of their best.

Captain Stan McLaughlin's Echo Company headed north out of the fire base perimeter at around 0800 hours. McLaughlin, USMA 1964, was in his fourth month of command. He took command of Echo Company after the previous commander was killed on a hot LZ the previous August. His impact on Echo Company was soon noticeable. By the time the Company arrived at FSB Nashua it was arguably the best rifle company in the Warrior battalion.

A combat tracker team consisting of a dog and handler from the 49th Scout Dog Platoon accompanied McLaughlin's patrol. If there were enemy in the area, he wanted to find them before they found

Echo Company. He knew that the Air Cav and LRPs had spotted enemy soldiers and bunkers north of Nashua, and the risk of an enemy ambush weighed heavily on his mind.

Working their way cautiously northward, McLaughlin's lead platoons stayed east of a stream called Suoi Dia paralleling a trail. Every hundred meters the rifle platoons halted and sent out cloverleaf patrols in all directions to insure that they were not marching into an ambush. The point men carefully skirted cleared areas that were overgrown with waist-high elephant grass, and spotted with huge chest-high anthills. The enemy usually posted spotters to observe such areas, and they were perfect locations for L-shaped ambushes. Typically the enemy would conceal themselves along tree lines forming the long and short axis of the "L," with the clearing in the middle. Any unit crossing the clearing would be caught in the open and exposed to both frontal and flanking fire, a deadly situation.

Shortly after noon, Echo Company found a newly cut trail through the jungle and began to follow it. A point man and the combat tracker team moved cautiously forward. The dog sensed the presence of the VC before the point man and alerted on the enemy. Six VC were walking on the trail directly toward Echo Company. The company's lead squad opened up on the VC to cover the withdrawal of the point man and the tracker team. One of the VC managed to throw an armed 82mm mortar round, rigged as a hand grenade, at the handler and his dog. The round exploded, showering both with shrapnel. The handler survived, but the dog did not. The VC then melted back into the jungle while Echo Company called for a dust-off. McLaughlin was convinced that there must be an enemy base camp nearby. He would continue to patrol the area, but moved with extreme caution.

Fortified enemy base camps and bunker complexes were common in VC/NVA controlled areas. The enemy tended to move from base camp to base camp to exert their control over an area and to facilitate their offensive and defensive operations. Battalion-size units tended to be nomadic, moving at night from one camp to another every few days. When not occupied by a main force unit, the enemy sometimes left a few caretakers at the unoccupied base camps. The units of the Dong Nai Regiment operating in War Zone D generally adhered to this doctrine.

Enemy sightings continued throughout the afternoon of 5 December. LRP Team 27 reported finding a company size bunker complex northwest of Fire Base Nashua, and a ground element from 3/17th Cav reported finding bunkers, tunnels, and spider holes near where Sergeant Alexander's LRP team had made contact earlier in the day. Even more disturbing was an intelligence report disseminated by the Brigade TOC which indicated that a force of 250 VC armed with three 82mm mortars, a .50 caliber machine gun, two 60mm mortars, and a 75mm recoilless rifle had been spotted about six kilometers southeast of Nashua. According to an agent report, the enemy formation planned to attack the South Vietnamese Tan Uyen District Headquarters. There was no doubt that Schroeder's battalion was positioned right in the middle of an enemy-controlled area. The next 24 hours would determine if Schroeder's Warriors or the enemy's Dong Nai Regiment would control that area.

Shortly after 1500 hours on 5 December, Major Maus extracted the last of his five LRP teams from the AO. An hour later an air strike was called in on a company-size base camp they'd found northwest of Nashua. Only one VC was spotted in the vicinity of the camp; nevertheless, it was deemed prudent to deny its future use to the enemy. The Air Force F-100s dropped eight 750-pound bombs, destroying the bunkers, and then followed up with 20mm cannon fire.

The LRPs had done their job, locating two enemy bunker complexes and reporting over 40 enemy sightings, but they missed the biggest prize of all. An enemy battalion sat undetected in a base camp under triple canopy jungle only two kilometers southeast of FSB Nashua. While the grunts of the 4/12th Infantry prepared for their second night at Nashua, the enemy battalion finalized its plans for the day to follow. The mortar attack on Nashua on the morning of December 6 was the invitation to the Warrior battalion to come find them. The enemy commander knew that the Americans would do a shell crater analysis at the points of impact, and determine the direction from where they'd been fired. The enemy battalion was ready for a fight.

CHAPTER 3

THE BLOODIEST DAY

---

6 December 1967

The VC unit occupying the fortified base camp near Firebase Nashua was a battalion of the Viet Cong main force Dong Nai Regiment. The regiment was composed of three maneuver battalions, designated K1, K2, and K3. In December 1967, the regiment's strength was estimated at 2,200 men. In addition to preparing for the Tet Offensive scheduled for the end of January 1968, the regiment was also responsible for safeguarding storage and base areas in the vicinity of FSB Nashua. It was augmented by local VC organized into a Rear Service Group. Since some of the enemy soldiers spotted and engaged by the LRPs and 3/17th Cav were clad in khaki uniforms, it is very probable that the Dong Nai Regiment was receiving NVA regulars to fill its ranks. Malnutrition and malaria, along with US air attacks, had taken a toll on the regiment over the preceding months. By early December, the battle-tested Dong Nai Regiment was undergoing a rapid build-up of men and supplies in War Zone D in preparation for a major offensive. An active defense of their base areas around FSB Nashua was a top priority.

The 105mm artillery and 81mm mortar counterbattery fires had little if any effect on the enemy. Hunkered down in bunkers dug deep below ground with overhead cover consisting of logs and dirt up to two feet thick, the enemy soldiers were at minimum risk from the counterbattery fires. Their bunkers could take a direct hit from a mortar or 105mm round without killing those inside. Some of the rounds detonated overhead in the trees, resulting in even less damage.

The enemy base camp near FSB Nashua, like most VC and NVA jungle base camps, was constructed to withstand a ground assault, and the site was selected with great care. There was a dense overhead foliage in the form of double or triple canopy jungle to conceal the fortifications from the air. On the ground, the terrain clearly favored the defenders with excellent cover and concealment. The site also afforded the defenders some observation of an approaching force. This was accomplished by cutting one- or two-foot-wide lanes in the jungle that could also be used as firing lanes in front of the enemy bunkers and trenches. These paths were often mistaken by US soldiers for trails worn by small animals moving through the jungle. The base camp was constructed to allow for a 360 degree defense with an outer and inner ring of bunkers all connected by fighting trenches deep enough to provide cover and concealment to a crawling or crouching soldier. The trenches were dug in a zigzag or Z pattern to facilitate their defense even if the attackers managed to infiltrate them.

The bunkers varied in size, but the typical individual fighting position was slightly more than a meter long with an open trench on one end, about one meter deep, and about a half-meter wide. Crew-served weapon bunkers (machine guns, recoilless rifles) and the command bunker located inside the perimeter were considerably larger. Overhead cover consisted of roughhewn logs covered with a meter of dirt. Dirt from the excavation was piled in front of the position to form a parapet to deflect incoming rounds from the bunker's firing port. All fighting positions and bunkers were elaborately camouflaged with vegetation that was replaced daily. Cooking stoves were dug into the larger bunkers with underground chimneys dug horizontal for 50 or more meters, fanning out in several directions to dissipate the heat and smoke, making detection from the air almost impossible.

The fortified camp was also well protected with booby traps, mines, and improvised explosive devices that could be command detonated from the fighting positions and trenches. The VC were particularly adept at rigging undetonated US artillery rounds and bombs with explosives. These explosive devices were buried along likely avenues of approach and hung from trees to inflict maximum casualties from airbursts. The devices were triggered by electrical firing wires from the enemy's bunkers. The VC also employed homemade Claymore-type mines that were filled with nails, scrap metal, and bits of concrete. Sighted along likely avenues of approach, the Claymores were devastating, often killing and wounding dozens of troops caught in the open.

By December of 1967, almost all members of the Dong Nai Regiment had been issued the AK-47 assault rifle. The weapon was particularly effective and reliable at close range, making it highly suitable for the jungle terrain of War Zone D. Crew served weapons included the RPD machine gun, the .57 recoilless rifle, and the B40 rocket launcher. The VC also had on hand a number of DH-10s, a Communist-manufactured version of the Claymore. The DH-10 was three times larger than a U.S. Claymore with more than 200 fragments packed inside. In terms of small arms, crew-served weapons, and munitions, the Dong Nai Regiment was as well armed as the Warriors of the 4/12th Infantry.

The enemy wanted the combat to occur at as close a range as possible. By "hugging" the attackers, the VC made it difficult for US troops to call in artillery or air strikes without risking friendly casualties. The VC were also trained to emerge from their fighting positions to launch limited counterattacks or flank attacks when the US troops were disorganized, or when it was necessary to cover a withdrawal of their own troops.

Attacking a fortified enemy base camp was the bete noir for US commanders even under the most favorable of circumstances, and the camp manned by the Dong Nai Regiment just two kilometers south of FSB Nashua was no exception. Some would later say it was like entering a tiger's den armed only with a stick.

LTC Schroeder was not overly concerned by the mortar attack against FSB Nashua. Such attacks were anticipated, and not particularly lethal since the troops were well dug in with overhead cover. Ground attacks were of greater concern. The Warrior commander's priority was to complete defensive preparations around the base to insure it could withstand a ground assault. There was still much work to be done constructing a berm around the base and laying more defensive wire. Nevertheless, Schroeder decided he could spare two platoons from

Alpha Company to patrol to the southeast in the direction of the enemy mortar site. The Warrior commander believed that the best defense was a strong offense.

Schroeder also ordered Captain Jones' Charlie Company to patrol to the west of Nashua. With Echo Company still patrolling north of the firebase, Schroeder thought that his patrols would detect any major enemy units staging for a ground attack on Nashua. Bravo Company, two platoons from Alpha Company, and a portion of Charlie Company remained at FSB Nashua where they continued to work on the fortifications.

While the company commanders briefed their platoon leaders on their missions for the day, the grunts readied their equipment, loaded their rucksacks with extra ammunition and grenades, and gave their weapons a final cleaning. Most were still uneasy in their new surroundings. The mortar attack was an ominous sign.

At 0912 hours, two platoons of Alpha Company departed FSB Nashua to locate the enemy mortar site. Captain Donald Drees, the company commander, accompanied the two platoons with his command group. Drees had previous command experience with Bravo Company 3/7th Infantry, and was in his second month of command of Alpha Company. Altogether, the two platoons and command group numbered around 75 men. Captain Drees knew how to maneuver his rifle company in the swampy areas and rice paddies that surrounded Saigon, but this was his first trek in the thick jungle terrain that surrounded Firebase Nashua.

Alpha Company's artillery forward observer (FO), Lieutenant Wayne McKirdy, and Sergeant Baker, his recon sergeant, accompanied the Alpha Company command group. McKirdy, a 23-year-old artillery officer, had been in Vietnam for five weeks, and had spent most of that time as an FO with Alpha Company. His experience in adjusting artillery fire was limited to the firing ranges at Fort Sill, and the relatively open terrain around Thu Duc. Adjusting artillery in the dense jungle around Nashua was much more difficult. Before the day was over, McKirdy would have to learn how to adjust artillery fire by sound rather than sight.

Also accompanying Alpha Company was the 37-year-old Catholic Chaplain, Captain Angelo Liteky. The rugged and deeply tanned priest had already earned a reputation among the grunts of the 199th Light Infantry Brigade as an infantryman's type of chaplain. He wasn't afraid to get his boots muddy, and spent the majority of his time in the field with infantry companies. He held field services when the opportunity arose, but spent most of his time talking to the troops as he slogged along beside them. The troops loved and respected him. The padre always carried extra water and cigarettes, and volunteered to carry extra gear and equipment such as the chainsaws and gas containers that each platoon carried to cut emergency LZs for dust-offs. Though nearly twice the age of most of the men, the chaplain had no trouble keeping pace with the troops even when he was lugging heavy equipment. On occasion, he carried extra ammunition for the troops, but drew the line at carrying or firing a weapon. Standing over six feet tall with a lanky frame and closely cropped hair, Liteky could have easily passed for an infantry battalion commander rather than a Catholic priest. Before the day ended, Chaplain Liteky would be faced with the brutalities and inhumanities of war at the extreme.

First Lieutenant Wayne Morris of Oak Ridge, Tennessee, 25 years-old, led Alpha Company's 4th Platoon. The career NCO, Sergeant First Class Dan Garrison, was his platoon sergeant. Morris had earned his commission through the ROTC program at Tennessee Technological University, and had three years experience in the Tennessee Army National Guard before that. Both men were solid professionals, but Morris was a newcomer to Alpha Company. He had joined the company two weeks earlier on Thanksgiving Day. As the senior lieutenant in the company, Morris was put in charge of 4th Platoon. The platoon was technically an 81mm mortar platoon, but it was also equipped to fight as a rifle platoon. Because of their weight, the 81mm mortars were not carried on patrols, but were often flown in to bolster night defensive positions. The men of the 4th Platoon were still sizing up their new platoon leader, but most thought the six-foot-two Tennessean was a fast learner; an officer they would follow.

Thirty-six enlisted men were present for duty in 4th Platoon on the morning of 6 December, while the 2nd Platoon led by Sergeant Jones started the day with 30 men. Morris' 4th Platoon took the lead as the patrol left FSB Nashua. They followed a compass heading of 130 degrees. That direction was based on the crater analysis of the mortar rounds that impacted on the base earlier that morning.

A few minutes after Drees' platoons crossed through FSB Nashua's perimeter wire, a scout dog accompanying the 4th Platoon alerted as the platoon approached a cleared area. After speaking with the dog's handler, Captain Drees radioed the battalion TOC to request a combat tracker team. Thirty minutes later, two Labrador Retrievers and their handlers arrived and began to work the area. The Labs did not detect a scent so the two Alpha Company platoons moved out across the clearing with 4th Platoon still in the lead.

Once across the clearing, the grunts headed into a dense patch of jungle where progress slowed almost to a halt. The area had been defoliated the year before, but the vegetation had grown back into an impenetrable tangle of vines, saplings, and bushes some ten to10 to 12 feet high. Morris wrote that he "put three men with machetes in the lead to hack a path through the tangle. . . . undergrowth snagged each and every part of our bodies and equipment."

For over an hour, the grunts cut through the undergrowth, covering only 100 to 125 meters. The troops moved in single file, stopping every few meters while the cutting teams were rotated. Thorny bushes and "wait-a-minute" vines slowed each man's progress by catching on their rifles and web gear. Annoying insects buzzed around the sweat-soaked men. The temperature was well over 90 degrees. At each short halt, the men bent forward at the waist readjusting their loaded rucksacks. Some removed their helmets to mop their brows while others took sips of water from their canteens. Most of the grunts carried at least fifty pounds of equipment and ammunition distributed between their rucksacks and web gear. Radio operators carried their own gear as well as the PRC-25 radios. When the column moved out, the morning's calm was again disturbed by the hacking of machetes and the crackling of radios as sergeants reported their squads' progress.

While Alpha Company searched for the enemy mortar site southeast of Nashua, Echo Company patrolled to the north. At 1120 hours, an Echo Company patrol detonated an anti-personnel mine, wounding several members of the patrol. A battalion resupply slick that was in the area picked up the wounded men and flew them to the 93d Evacuation Hospital at Long Binh. The remainder of the morning passed without incident.

Shortly after noon, five ACAVs from Delta Troop, 17th Cavalry departed FSB Hanover headed for FSB Nashua. It was a routine road clearing operation for the Cav. After completion of the mission the Cav platoon was under orders to return to Hanover. Anticipating vehicular movement along the road, the VC buried anti-tank mines on a stretch of the road some five kilometers southwest of Nashua. The road was mined at a point where the road left a large clearing, and entered an area with heavy growth on both sides. At that point, the five ACAVs had to follow the road in single file. VC machine gunners were zeroed in on the ambush site.

At 1230, the tracks rumbled across the clearing and then moved onto the road in single file. Seconds later, command-detonated anti-tank mines exploded under the first and fifth tracks in the column. The lead ACAV was flipped completely over on its command cupola by the explosion and its engine block was thrown fifty meters. The platoon sergeant seated in the open command cupola hatch was crushed to death under the vehicle. The ACAV that brought up the rear of the column was lifted off the road by the force of the explosion and landed on its side. After the explosions, both ACAVs were engulfed in flames and the ammunition began to cook off.

Delta Troop's ACAVs were an older variant of the M113 Armored Personnel Carrier. The vehicles had supplemental armor modifications to increase crew protection. Armor gun shields were installed around the .50 caliber machine gun and two pintle-mounted M60 machine guns, but the armor shields offered no protection from anti-tank mines that exploded beneath the vehicles. Unlike the newer ACAVs that had diesel engines, Delta Troop's ACAVs were gasoline powered, increasing the risk of fire and explosion.

After detonating the anti-tank mines, enemy machine gunners opened up on the column from across the field that the vehicles had just crossed. The cavalrymen in the undamaged ACAVs returned fire, while others dismounted to assist their wounded comrades. All told, the platoon had two KIAs and seven men badly wounded with shrapnel, burns, broken bones, and contusions. Fearing that more mines were buried in the road, the Cav platoon leader did not move his undamaged ACAVs. The survivors fought for their lives as their platoon leader radioed Firebase Nashua for immediate assistance.

LTC Schroder responded quickly. He ordered his Bravo Company commander, Captain Roberto Eaton, to prepare his company for an immediate airmobile assault into the area of the ambush. Then he dispatched the battalion resupply UH-1 to the scene to medevac the wounded. Eaton's company was in battalion reserve, and had been working on the defensive perimeter of Fire Base Nashua.

Captain Eaton was a seasoned Regular Army infantry officer. Born in Paraguay, and educated in the US, the 29-year-old Captain was a graduate of the University of Vermont where he had been commissioned in the Regular Army through the ROTC program. As a graduate of the Army's Airborne, Ranger, Special Forces, and Jungle Warfare Courses, he was more than qualified to command a light infantry company. As a lieutenant, he had served in every position a line officer could hold, and his reputation was that of a fighting commander who knew his stuff.

When LTC Schroeder radioed Brigadier General Forbes to request an aviation company to lift Bravo Company, the general quickly diverted a lift company from another mission. Eaton and his CP group lined up on the PZ with the lead platoons. Two platoons were going in on the first lift to secure the ambush site. The other half of the company was scheduled to follow on a second lift.

As soon as Captain Eaton's first lift was airborne, another firefight broke out north of Nashua. One of Echo Company's patrols was ambushed by an estimated enemy squad. As PFC Robert Buckner, the patrol's point man, followed a trail ahead of a combat tracker team, he was fired upon by the concealed VC squad. Buckner spotted the enemy position and charged the VC. An enemy machine gunner fired a burst that mortally wounded Buckner before he reached their position. The remainder of the patrol then flanked the VC, forcing them to flee into the dense jungle. Captain Stan McLaughlin, the Echo CO, maneuvered his dispersed platoons in an attempt to cut them off.

In the air, five minutes out of the LZ, Eaton and his Bravo Company men spotted a pall of thick black smoke from the burning ACAVs at the ambush site. Both badly damaged vehicles were still afire, and the cavalrymen were under machine-gun fire. As the lift ships made their final approach to the LZ, Eaton's men standing on the skids could hear the battle. Their LZ was between the enemy and the beleaguered Cav platoon. Leaping from the lift ships as they settled to the ground, Bravo Company's grunts spread out in an assault formation and quickly moved toward the wood line where the enemy machine gunners were positioned. As Eaton's men advanced, a gunship team blasted the tree line with rockets and machine-gun fire. Outnumbered and outgunned, the VC machine gun teams withdrew into the jungle.

After clearing the tree line, Captain Eaton left one platoon to secure the LZ for the second lift while the second platoon formed a perimeter around the ACAVs. The Captain had the foresight to bring mine dectectors in with the first lift, and his men began to sweep the area for additional mines. Several undetonated mines were found on the road. The mines were blown in place before a dust-off arrived to evacuate the wounded and dead cavalrymen. When the dust-off was complete, Schroeder ordered Captain Eaton to escort the undamaged ACAVs back to FSB Hanover. Bravo's second airmobile lift was scrubbed by Schroeder, since the rescue mission had been successfully completed.

With Captain Eaton's men providing front, flank, and rear guard for the ACAVs, the column moved out. It was a slow cautious road march, but the column reached Hanover by dusk without further incident. However, the rescue and recovery mission took Schroeder's most experienced commander and two of his platoons out of what was to be the major battle of that day.

While Captain Eaton and his men rescued the ambushed Cav platoon, the Alpha Company patrol continued to move southeast of Nashua. The combat tracker team found a "hot" VC trail and followed it. At around 1330 hours, the point man, Sergeant Norman Tinker, broke through the undergrowth onto a rough trail running in a northeast direction. He immediately spotted two enemy soldiers who ran up the trail. The point man opened up on the pair as they ran. The VC left that trail and ran into jungle. Lieutenant Morris radioed Captain Drees and asked for instructions.

Captain Drees called for gunship support, and directed Morris to move 4th Platoon on-line, wait for the 2nd Platoon to move in behind, and then sweep through the jungle to the west to establish contact with the enemy. A gunship team arrived on the scene and began to work over the heavily wooded area, while Morris maneuvered his men into position to begin the sweep. At 1400 hours, Captain Drees ordered his platoons forward. All was quiet again except for the swishing of jungle fatigues moving through the dense undergrowth and the occasional snapping of a twig. The quiet didn't last for long.

In Lieutenant Morris' words, "We moved into the woods and within minutes all hell broke loose." The jungle erupted in a tremendous roar as Chinese Claymores bellowed out thousands of steel pellets and tracer rounds from heavy machine guns seared through tree leaves and elephant grass. The two VC trail watchers had led Morris' platoon directly to a heavily fortified base area. Alpha Company was nose-to-nose with an entrenched enemy battalion of the Dong Nai Regiment.

The enemy fortifications ran several hundred meters parallel to the trail on its west side. They were laid out in NVA textbook fashion for all around defense. Lieutenant Morris' 4th Platoon approached the enemy position dead-on, just slightly left of the center. The enemy opened up with everything they had against Morris' platoon. Interlocking machine gun and AK-47 fire from camouflaged bunkers raked the platoon's line. Several of Morris' men were hit and dropped as enemy rounds tore their flesh. Simultaneously, a series of deafening explosions from command-detonated mines inflicted even more casualties. Enfilading fire along the length Morris' battle line pinned his men down as they tried to regroup. The screams and moans of the wounded were heard above the sound of gunfire and explosions. The 4th Platoon battle line was less than thirty meters from the enemy bunker line, and the grunts were pinned down.

Dennis Castaldo was a 20-year-old rifleman with 4th Platoon. He recalled that, "The firepower of that Vietnamese camp was absolutely incredible . . . but no one ran. Everyone stood their ground as they were told." He further recalled seeing "men walking around with half their faces blown off from tree-mounted Claymores." Despite the incredible volume of close-range fire directed at the grunts, they held their ground and fought back in a stunning display of personal courage, unit cohesion, and discipline.

Lieutenant Morris, the only officer west of the trail, encouraged his men to assault the enemy fortifications, unaware that he was heavily outgunned and outnumbered. He was assisted by his platoon sergeant Dan Garrison. During the initial contact, Garrison sustained wounds to his left hand. Ignoring his wounds, Garrison continued to push his men forward. When he saw his men fall, he rushed forward and pulled the wounded to the rear. As he moved from position to position, he was wounded again, this time by a Claymore mine blast. When he saw his platoon sergeant go down in the blast, PFC Norm Reeves, the platoon RTO, rushed forward to administer first aid. As he was trying to stem the flow of blood from Garrison's shoulder, Reeves was wounded by a burst of machine-gun fire. The rounds also knocked out his radio. Despite his wounds, Reeves managed to drag his platoon sergeant forty meters to the LZ for medical evacuation. PFC Reeves then refused evacuation himself, and volunteered to replace the company commander's RTO who was more seriously wounded. Reeves calmly and efficiently assisted Captain Drees in coordinating fire support and communicating with the various elements in the battle.

As Lieutenant Morris' platoon laid down a base of fire, 2nd Platoon moved in directly behind 4th Platoon, and began to mix in with Morris' men. In Morris' words, "It became rather unimportant who belonged to who that afternoon . . . the soldiers just fought with whoever was there to support or needed help." The devastating enemy fire took a heavy toll on the grunts, particularly on the squad leaders and fire team leaders.

Squad leader Sergeant Ray Kelley led his men toward the concealed bunkers, throwing hand grenades as he advanced. He moved to within fifteen meters of the enemy bunker line when he was hit with a burst of machine-gun fire. Kelley's squad was caught in interlocking machine-gun fire from two bunkers. He shouted to his men to move back to the trail while he provided covering fire.

On the 4th Platoon flank, squad leader Sergeant Gary Hahn courageously led his men through the dense undergrowth in an attempt to flank the enemy fortifications. Moving in from the flank, the 24-year-old Californian was hit in the arm with small arms fire and thrown to the ground. Despite his wound, he got to his feet and hobbled forward, firing his weapon with his one good hand while urging his men to continue their attack. He spotted an enemy bunker and attempted to get close enough to toss a grenade into the aperture. As he ran toward the bunker, he was hit again by enemy automatic weapons fire and knocked off his feet. Unable to rise, Hahn crawled forward toward the bunker and was shot again and mortally wounded.

Twenty-one-year-old Sergeant William Pruitt maneuvered his squad forward toward the enemy bunker line. The entrenched enemy unleashed a furious blast of small arms fire that cut through Pruitt's squad, wounding several grunts. As the attack stalled, Sergeant Pruitt turned his attention to the wounded that were still in the line of fire. After ordering his men to take cover and lay down a base of fire, Pruitt started to evacuate his wounded men. He was mortally wounded himself as he was carrying one of his squad members away from the heaviest concentration of enemy fire.

As the squad leaders fell, fire team leaders took over the close-quarter fighting. When 23-year-old Specialist Four Eugene Zeigler realized that the lead elements of his platoon were pinned down, unable to advance or withdraw, he maneuvered his fire team forward until he reached his beleaguered comrades. He then shouted to his men to lay down a base of fire to cover the evacuation of the wounded and dead. Ziegler then rallied the remaining men and assaulted the trench line to their front. While aggressively leading the assault, Zeigler was mortally wounded.

The loss of these key leaders was taking its toll on Alpha Company. Wounded and dying men were scattered all along the shrinking line. As the battle raged on, combat medics moved from man to man to render life saving first aid and drag the men out of the line of fire.

PFC Durward Limbacher, an Alpha Company medic, was one of the lifesavers that the grunts depended on. The 20-year-old Iowa native moved forward immediately after contact was made to administer first aid to two seriously wounded soldiers. After he treated the two, he spotted a third soldier several yards forward of his position. Without hesitation, Limbacher exposed himself to incoming fire and dashed forward to aid the seriously wounded man. Enemy machine gun fire erupted from a bunker less than ten meters away, killing Limbacher instantly. He was not the last medic die in the battle.

Lieutenant Morris continued to press the attack with his remaining men. Morris was in radio contact with his CO, Captain Drees, whose command group was some fifty meters east of the trail. While the men assigned to the command group started to cut a one-ship LZ to bring in medevac choppers, Drees radioed Lieutenant Colonel Schroeder with a desperate request for gunship and air support for his heavily engaged platoons. Schroeder told Drees that fire support was on the way.

When the helicopter gunships arrived on station, Drees instructed the pilots to switch to Morris' platoon radio frequency. The gunship team leader's voice crackled over the platoon's PRC-25 radio, requesting Morris to "pop" a smoke grenade to mark the forward position of his platoon. The lieutenant removed a yellow smoke grenade from his web harness, pulled the pin, and tossed it a few meters to his front. The grenade burst and hissed on the ground as it spewed a billowing cloud of yellow smoke from its nozzle. Morris' subordinates monitoring the radio net popped their own smoke grenades. Observing the smoke, the enemy threw smoke grenades as well, hoping to confuse the gunship pilots. Soon a mix of multi-colored smoke hung over the battlefield like a fog. As a result, the gunship pilots had great difficulty identifying the location of all friendlies on the ground, and on two runs their 2.75mm rockets screeched overhead and detonated on Morris' men with shattering blasts. Morris yelled into the handset of his radio to call off the strikes. The dense foliage and jungle canopy hid the enemy positions, and it was difficult to identify friend from foe from the air. Alpha Company's men, some wounded, some dead, and others still fighting were scattered across the terrain in front of the enemy positions.

The number of dead and wounded in the 2nd and 4th Platoons limited Alpha Company's capability to sustain the fight. The assault on the superbly concealed VC bunker complex was repulsed by overwhelming enemy firepower. Gunship and artillery support was unable to break the stalemate. The final outcome of the battle remained in doubt as small groups of enemy soldiers began to emerge from their bunkers and trenches in attempts to roll up Alpha Company's flanks. The embattled Warriors of Alpha Company were in desperate need of reinforcements and heavy fire support.

Orbiting overhead in his C&C ship, LTC Schroeder informed the Alpha CO that he was requesting TAC air support. Captain Drees ordered his platoons to withdraw with their dead and wounded to the small LZ that his CP group had cut in the jungle. After the errant gunship strikes, he was concerned about the possibility of friendly casualties from the incoming TAC air strikes.

Despite the heavy volume of incoming fire, and lack of able-bodied men to carry the wounded, Morris and his men began to pull back. In fact, the evacuation of the wounded was already underway.

Like the men around him, Chaplain Liteky was stunned when the enemy battalion opened fire on Alpha Company. He'd been under sniper fire before, but never intense close-range fire. Liteky was in the center of the column with Captain Drees and his RTOs when the battle began. The Chaplain hit the dirt and hugged the ground as enemy rounds snapped off twigs and branches a few inches above his head. Claymore mines exploded and blasted the area around him with hundreds of pieces of lethal shrapnel. Trying to make himself heard over the deafening roar of gunfire and explosions Liteky shouted to Drees, "Is there anything you want me to do?" but the Captain was on his radio requesting gunship support. Nothing in his chaplain training had prepared Liteky for this moment.

Father Angelo Liteky had entered the Army in July 1966 and arrived in Vietnam in March of 1967. Born in Norfolk, Virginia in 1931, Liteky grew up in a Navy family. His father served 32 years and retired as a Chief Petty Officer. During an interview with the brigade information officer, Liteky recalled that when he decided to become a priest his father "was a little more than surprised after some of the things I had done in my younger days." After graduating from high school, Liteky was accepted at the University of Florida with a football scholarship. Injured in pre-season practice, he sat out the season, and later transferred to Chipola Junior College in Mariana, Florida on another scholarship for a year. During his second year, he related that he read the book entitled "The Red Hat," about a man who became a priest and later a cardinal, and that book started him thinking about becoming a priest. He later entered the seminary and was ordained a priest in a religious order, the Missionary Servants of the Most Holy Trinity, in Winchester, Virginia. After his ordination, Father Liteky worked at the Shrine of St. Joseph Mission in Sterling, New Jersey, until he volunteered for military service. Entering the Army, he completed the Chaplain School at Fort Hamilton, New York, and was subsequently assigned to the Basic Training Command at Fort Benning, Georgia. Six months later, Chaplain Liteky volunteered for Vietnam where many of the trainees he counseled were headed. Upon his arrival in Vietnam, he was assigned to the 199th LIB as the brigade Catholic chaplain.

Father Liteky soon earned a reputation for going out on operations as often as he could. He indicated that "he just wanted to be with the men." That feeling was reciprocal among the grunts who didn't mind having a Chaplain along, especially Father Liteky. This was especially true on December 6, 1967.

Chaplain Liteky could not ignore the screams and cries of the wounded and dying men all around him. His compassion and love for his fellow man inspired him to take action. Prayer alone was not enough. Ignoring the incoming fire, he stood up and moved off the path into the jungle, following the route taken by 4th Platoon. The first man he encountered was a young medic named McElroy. The medic had propped himself up against a blackened tree with one leg seemingly curled up under him. Only it wasn't his leg, it was a bloody stump.

Senior Medical Corpsman Everett McElroy was with the Alpha Company command group when the fight began. Reacting quickly, he rushed forward with his aid bag to the hard hit left flank of the assault formation. As he treated the most seriously injured, the enemy detonated a mine a few yards from his position, shattering his leg at the knee. Waving off several grunts who moved forward to assist him, he crawled back out of the line of fire and propped himself up against the tree. Looking at Liteky with a smile, the 20-year-old medic said, "Did you say a prayer for me, Padre?" "Of course I did . . . you'll be all right." McElroy told the Chaplain that he thought he could make it back to the LZ on his own after he caught his breath, but there were three other men a few yards ahead that needed his help more than he did. "You'll make it," Father Liteky told him, and then the padre moved on further into the jungle following the route that 4th Platoon had taken. After pushing his way through the brush for several meters, he came upon three GI s lying face down on the jungle floor. They looked as if they were asleep. He checked their pulses and found that they were dead. Rolling them over he saw that they all had deep chest wounds. After administering last rites to the fallen Warriors, he moved on until he reached 4th Platoon's front line of troops just as another enemy Claymore exploded with a quaking roar.

The men around the padre reported that while everyone crawled or sprinted from cover to cover, Chaplain Liteky walked calmly from one wounded man to the next administering last rites to the dying and assisting others to the rear. One of the wounded men fell in a particularly dense patch of undergrowth and Liteky was forced to break through a network of thorny vines to reach him. After he administered first aid, he lifted the man out of the thicket and lugged him to safety. Time after time, the Chaplain returned to the forward platoons to evacuate more wounded. When he found wounded men who were not ambulatory, he laid them atop his own body and crawled the men back to the rear. While administering last rites or first aid, one observer reported that he always put his own body between the enemy fire and the injured man.

On one of his trips to the front lines, Liteky found a Z-shaped trench where Lieutenant Morris and his platoon sergeant, Dan Garrison, had dragged half a dozen of the dead and wounded. The trench was part of the enemy's outer perimeter fortifications. The priest dove into the trench just as an enemy mortar round exploded nearby, sending up a blizzard of shrapnel.

"Let's try to get these men out of here to the LZ," the lieutenant shouted. "They sure ain't going to make it here." The trio lifted the wounded out of the trench and crawled back toward the landing zone with the hurt men in tow. Knee-high enemy fire cracked overhead. Dragging the wounded, they somehow made it to the LZ.

Lieutenant Wayne Morris, among others, reported that he "never saw the Chaplain try to protect himself . . . and he seemed to be everywhere and his presence inspired awed and inspired myself and my men." Norman Reeves, Morris' wounded RTO, recalled that he saw Liteky carrying the wounded and dead on his back and in his arms time and again. "He was without benefit of a steel helmet, and had donated his fatigue jacket to a wounded soldier." Dennis Castaldo, who earned a Bronze Star for Valor that day, remembered seeing Liteky "in the middle of chaos pulling men to safety." Castaldo and Bill Clayford joined Liteky and pulled a couple of men to safety. Before the day was over, Chaplain Liteky was credited with personally extracting twenty wounded men while under continuous enemy fire. His bravery led to his recommendation and receipt of the nation's highest award for bravery, the Medal of Honor.

As Alpha Company's forward platoons began to withdraw from the killing zone, covering fire was provided by a pair of intrepid M60 machine gunners. PFCs Jose Acevedo, who joined the Army in Puerto Rico, and Allen Oakes from Syracuse, New York, were in the fight from the beginning. Oakes and Acevedo moved forward with their platoon until they reached the forward elements that were pinned down. Enemy automatic weapons fire and explosive devices had leveled a number of trees to their front, and they lacked clear fields of fire for their machine gun. Lieutenant Morris described what happened.

"I found myself behind an anthill with R.D. Jones and Sergeant Dan Kelley. Kelly was shot several times. . . . Jones and I wanted to drag Dan out of this position but the RPD50 machine gunner in the dug in positions about 10 meters beyond had other plans. He was ever so slowly reducing the size of the anthill with his machine gun, and our M16 return fire and several grenades were having no effect to suppress his fire. The situation did not look too promising until out of the smoke and haze of the battlefield appeared two young soldiers running at a crouch with their M60 machine gun. They were heading straight into the RPD's field of fire in the open. I yelled for them to get down but they were oblivious to anything but getting their gun in operation and taking out the RPD50 position. The enemy gunner realized what was about to happen and moved his fire from the anthill towards Allen and Jose. Allen was the gunner and Jose the ammo bearer and they were good at their job. As the RPD50 fire stitched the ground towards them they threw themselves to the ground, loaded and began firing in a fluid maneuver right out of a John Wayne movie. The RPD50 fire ceased. Jones and I grabbed Kelly and ran like hell, dragging him like a sack of potatoes. As we cleared the area adjacent to Allen and Jose they simply disappeared in a tremendous roar and a black cloud of smoke and shrapnel."

Acevedo and Oakes had unknowingly set up their machine gun just a few meters from a buried mine. The mine was detonated by the enemy just as Morris and Jones dragged the wounded man Kelly from behind the anthill. After Kelly was dragged to the relative safety of the LZ, Lieutenant Morris made his way back to where the mine had detonated to find out if Acevedo and Oakes survived the blast. He recalled, "They were tied together in a tangle of shredded soldier, machine gun and gear. Both had horrific and massive gaping head wounds and torn body parts." Morris was unable to detect a pulse in either man. Chaplain Liteky arrived on the scene and administered last rites to the two soldiers. Both the lieutenant and the chaplain assumed the men were dead.

Lieutenant Morris returned later in the afternoon to recover the bodies of the two machine gunners. He was amazed when he found that the men were alive and semi-conscious. He radioed his CO and requested a dust-off. The men were too seriously wounded to be carried to the LZ. When the medevac chopper arrived, the crew lowered a basket down through the canopy.

Morris recalled, "The dirt and debris flying around; and the din of the machine guns, the explosions and other weapons firing made it seem like the twirling basket would never get down. I remember being cut by shards of something as I was reaching for the basket. Just as I got my hands on the basket, it jerked straight up and was gone."

Enemy fire shattered the plexiglass windshield of the medevac chopper, and the pilot had to pull pitch and leave the area, aborting the medevac. The only option left for Morris and his men was to carry the men back to the LZ. No one thought that Avecedo and Oakes would make it. They were wrong. Both of the wounded machine gunners were still alive when they were carried onto the LZ and put on the dust-off ship. Both men survived despite their grievous wounds.

Lieutenant Colonel Schroeder continued to orbit above the Alpha Company fight in his C&C ship. He knew that the two Alpha Company platoons were in serious trouble. Since there was almost no wind, the smoke and dust hanging over the battlefield made it difficult to identify his unit's positions. He wanted to put in an airstrike, but he was reluctant to use heavy ordnance so close to friendly troops. On the ground, Captain Drees was in no better position to direct fires due to the dense vegetation. Both men had to be sure that the forward platoons were a safe distance before the airstrike. There was also an urgent need to evacuate Alpha Company's numerous casualties.

Lieutenant Wayne McKirdy, the Alpha Company FO, was wounded by shrapnel from an enemy Claymore mine about thirty minutes into the fight. His recon sergeant, Baker, was severely wounded in the same blast. Baker's left foot had been blown off just above the top of his boot. After, summoning a medic to treat Bakers wounds, McKirdy grabbed the team's PRC-25 radio, and rejoined Captain Drees. McKirdy wrote, "There was some delay in calling in artillery fire for several reasons. . . . We really didn't any idea what we were up against . . . and our men were so close to the base camp we didn't want to risk friendly casualties from the fire." In fact, most of the Alpha Company grunts were within the "danger close" distance for artillery fires, and there was a high risk of accidental casualties. McKirdy held off calling for artillery until he and Captain Drees were satisfied that most of the wounded and KIAs were evacuated to an area where an LZ was being cut. Once he began calling in fire missions, McKirdy recalled that he never actually saw a round hit. He adjusted fires, "primarily by sound and gut instinct." He "prayed a lot" that no rounds dropped on friendly troops.

Most of the artillery rounds fired by Charlie Battery 2/40th Artillery were 105mm High Explosive (HE) rounds. These rounds fired by Charlie Battery's howitzers were nearly totally ineffective on the enemy's well constructed bunkers. Delayed fuse artillery rounds were effective, but they were in limited supply at fire base Nashua on December 6.

Lieutenant Colonel Schroeder knew that he needed more troops in the fight. It was obvious that Alpha Company was engaged with a large, well entrenched enemy force. However, reinforcements posed a problem for the 4/12th commander. Echo Company was in sporadic contact with the enemy north of Fire Base Nashua, and half of Bravo Company was deployed to assist the beleaguered armored Cav platoon. Neither was Charlie Company immediately available, for its line platoons were patrolling west of Nashua. Consequently, Schroeder decided to request the release of the brigade ready reaction force to his control. Concurrently, he ordered Bravo Company's two uncommitted platoons to move with all possible speed to Alpha Company's location along with a platoon of Delta Troop, 17th Cav. He also ordered the Charlie Company commander to pull all of his platoon patrols back to FSB Nashua. It was almost mid-afternoon and the fighting was far from over.

First Lieutenant Henderson Garnett was the senior offficer in charge of the two Bravo Company platoons at FSB Nashua. Lieutenant Philip Baynum led Bravo's 4th Platoon, and Staff Sergeant James Pius was in charge of 2nd Platoon. Less than thirty minutes after the alert, Bravo's platoons mounted the five ACAVs from Delta Troop that would carry them to the scene of the battle. At 1515 hours, Lieutenant Delbert Ehler, the Cav platoon leader, gave the word and the armored tracks rumbled out of the FSB Nashua perimeter headed for the hard pressed Alpha Company.

Brigadier General Forbes approved Schroeder's request for deployment of the brigade's ready reaction force company. The 199th Light Infantry Brigade's Standing Operating Procedure (SOP) specified that one infantry company from the brigade always be on 30-minute stand-by to respond to a tactical emergency. This on-call tasking rotated between the brigade's three infantry battalions. On 6 December, 1967, Alpha Company, 3/7th Infantry was the on-call force.

Alpha Company, 3/7th was located at Fire Support Base Concord a few kilometers northeast of Bien Hoa. The CO of Alpha Company, Captain Antonio (Tony) Smaldone, of Cohoes, New York, was the type of company commander the general could rely on in a tough situation. Forbes later described Smaldone as one of the best company commanders he'd ever known.

Tony Smaldone was no stranger to Vietnam, and he had already earned a reputation as a Warrrior before he was assigned to the 199th LIB. Prior to his assignment to the brigade, he had spent six months with the 5th Special Forces Group, and another 24 months as an adviser to a Vietnamese Ranger battalion and a Vietnamese Airborne battalion. Smaldone volunteered for three tours in Vietnam, and was wounded four separate times. The most serious was a wound in the chest that collapsed his right lung. In another firefight he was shot in the right hand and refused to be evacuated until the fight was over. He went AWOL from the hospital after treatment of this wound, and returned to his unit in the field before his doctors gave their OK. After interviewing him, a reporter for the Army Times described Smaldone as "the kind of guy who would walk around for 20 hours with a bullet hole through his right hand and a leg full of shrapnel rather than give up command of his company while the enemy is still engaged." The war correspondent wasn't far off the mark.

Smaldone's Alpha Company stood at the ready on the pick-up zone (PZ) by 1500 hours. The 187th Assault Helicopter Company was the Ready Reaction lift company tasked to support the airmobile assault. The assault helicopter pilots knew the potential for a hot LZ was high, but were reassured that their gunship team, the "Rat Pack," would prep the LZ with rockets and machine-gun fire.

Clouds of brown dust swirled around the Alpha 3/7th grunts as they ran toward the helicopters on the PZ. Smaldone and his command group loaded up with the first lift. With their engines roaring, the lift ships were airborne at 1525 hours. LTC Schroeder selected an LZ north of the enemy base camp. His choices were few in the dense jungle terrain. The LZ was within small arms range of the enemy base camp, but Schroeder was counting on the element of surprise.

As the lift ships flew toward the LZ, volleys of high-explosive artillery shells pounded the jungle surrounding the LZ. When the troop-carrying helicopters were five minutes out, the "Rat Pack" gunships pounced upon the enemy positions, firing their 2.75 rockets and mini-guns. As the lift ships were on their short final approach to the LZ, they took automatic weapons fire, but the gunships suppressed the enemy fire with a torrent of their own. As the helicopters touched down, Smaldone's men leapt into the waist-high elephant grass and sprinted to their assembly areas around the LZ.

Schroeder landed on Smaldone's LZ immediately after the lift ships cleared the LZ. Jumping out of his C&C ship, Schroeder ran toward Captain Smaldone's location just off the LZ. He gave the Captain an update on the situation and ordered him to move his company to an attack position north of the enemy base camp. Alpha Company's situation was too serious to wait for Smaldone's second lift to land. Schroeder recalled telling the Captain to make sure that his men moved forward in a low crouch as they assaulted the enemy bunker line. All indications were that the VC had sighted their weapons a bit high. After briefing the Captain, LTC Schroeder returned to his C&C ship to take control of the battle from the air.

While Smaldone's grunts moved to join the fight, Lieutenant Ehler's ACAVs, carrying Bravo's 2nd and 4th Platoons, smashed their way through the jungle en route to the battle area. Ehler knew his mission was to reach Alpha Company's position in the shortest possible time. He only hoped that his column would not be ambushed on the way in.

CHAPTER 4

VICTORY AT NIGHT

The scene at Alpha Company's LZ was horrific. The small jungle clearing was littered with the debris and carnage of combat. Discarded rucksacks, damaged weapons, smashed ammo crates, and empty metal ammo boxes lay strewn about the ground. The mangled bodies of dead and wounded men were scattered about the CP area. A bomb crater served as the LZ. Most of the trees around the LZ were blown apart and toppled as if chewed up by a giant chainsaw. Some of the wounded were unconscious while others lay moaning on the ground around the makeshift LZ. Those who were still able to hold a rifle were given one, and told to help man the defensive perimeter. As the afternoon wore on, more wounded and dead were carried into the perimeter. The wounded were "triaged" by the medics as they were carried in. Those who had a better chance of surviving were worked on first, while those who were unlikely to live were made as comfortable as possible and set aside.

Dust-off helicopters dropped into the small LZ, risking a tricky touchdown amid ground fire aimed at shooting off their tail rotors. The wounded were quickly stacked on board the medevacs, and the intrepid dust-off pilots pulled pitch to lift off before the enemy mortar crews began dropping rounds on the LZ.

Medic George Hauer treated the wounded as they arrived at the makeshift clearing. His jungle fatigues were covered with blood. He later recalled that as soon as he "patched up" one group, Father Litkey would arrive with more. Phil Tovin, who arrived at the LZ with the Cav and Bravo platoons, recalled, "They were carrying them out

49

one by one, between the respite in the fire. Each one was dead, their bodies riddled with bullet holes and mangled by high explosive booby traps." Medics and members of Drees' command group applied dressings to torn flesh, injected morphine into those writhing in pain, and gave water and smokes to those who could handle it. When he expended all the morphine in his own aid bag, George "Doc" Hauer replenished his supply from the aid bags of those medics who were killed in the fight. Chaplain Liteky circulated among the most critically injured, offering encouragement and administering last rites to the dying.

Since 2nd Platoon's sergeant was wounded and out of the action, Captain Drees gave Morris the remaining men from the platoon. With the additional men, Morris' 4th Platoon was almost up to its original strength. The men were exhausted, but knew that they would have to attack again. The remaining ammunition, C-rations, and water were redistributed, and those who had cigarettes shared them with their buddies. Most of the grunts had buddies who were killed, wounded, or missing, and they were determined to recover those who still had not been evacuated.

At 1620 hours, a Forward Air Controller (FAC) arrived over the battlefield. Schroeder radioed Captain Smaldone, giving him instructions to hold in place until the air strike was complete. He planned to launch a coordinated ground assault with Smaldone's company attacking from the north and his own units attacking from the east after the air strike.

The FAC orbited the area, trying to spot the precise location of the enemy fortifications. He also had to identify all of the friendly ground unit locations. It was not an easy task. The thick jungle canopy hid the enemy fortifications, and when he asked for smoke to identify the friendlies, there were smoke grenades popped in several areas around the strike area. Schroeder did his best to identify the targets for the FAC. The FAC decided that 20mm cannon fire would be the safest type of ordnance to use, due to the proximity of friendly troops on the ground.

After the FAC marked the target with rockets, two F-100s swooped down from the cloudless sky and strafed the target with 20 mm cannon fire. Kicking in their after-burners after each run, the F-

100s returned for more passes until they had expended all their 20mm ordnance. The air strike boosted the morale of the troops, but even though it was right on target, the overall damage to the enemy hunkered down in their bunkers was negligible.

Frank Paoicelli, a member of Alpha 3/7th's 4th Platoon, landed with the second lift of Smaldone's Alpha Company. Part of his platoon landed with the first lift, and he was surprised that there were no friendly troops securing the LZ when the second lift landed. He recalled seeing the air strike commence moments after he came in. As he watched the jets strafing the base camp, he knew his company was in for it.

As the Air Force F-100s strafed the determined enemy, Ehler's armored Cav platoon arrived at Alpha Company's location with Bravo's two platoons. Captain Drees, as the senior officer on the ground, took command of these forces and organized them for a second assault on the dug-in enemy battalion. He quickly outlined his plan to the platoon leaders and their sergeants. The ACAVs were to attack on the left flank of Alpha Company's two platoons. Their attack was to be supported by one platoon from Bravo Company. The second Bravo Company platoon led by Lieutenant Baynum would support Alpha Company's two platoons led by Lt. Morris on the right. While Captain Drees' force attacked the enemy base camp from the east, Captain Tony Smaldone's Alpha Company was to launch an attack the enemy position from the north. Everyone hoped that the combined weight of these two attacks would overrun the enemy defenses.

The plan of attack was dependent on close coordination between the maneuver units working together in tandem. Captain Drees and Captain Smaldone were in radio contact, but there was no physical contact between their respective units. At platoon level there was only minimal time for platoon leaders to prepare their men for the assault. Morris and his men knew all too well what they were going up against, but the others did not.

The attacking platoons moved out at 1700 hours. The grunts were pumped with adrenaline and nicotine. There was less than two hours of daylight remaining. Sunset was around 1830, and by 1900 the troops would be operating in total darkness. It was a high risk attack, but there were still wounded men near the enemy fortifications to recover. There was also a strong likelihood that the enemy would attempt a breakout during the hours of darkness.

Sergeant Jim Pius' Bravo platoon attacked on the left with the platoon of ACAVs from D/17th Cav. Pius worked out a plan with the Cav platoon leader, Lieutenant Ehler. Pius and his men were to move dismounted behind Ehler's ACAVs as they rolled forward toward the enemy position. In Pius' words, "My platoon would move in behind his APCs and while he smoked the area with 50 caliber machine gun, we would follow him in. Once they stopped, we would move out and set up a base of fire and try to cover him and Alpha Company."

As Sergeant Pius and his men moved out with Ehler's tracks, Morris led his platoon forward on the right. He thought that Lieutenant Baynum's Bravo platoon was moving directly to his rear. He was wrong. Baynum's platoon halted at the trail and contact between the two units was broken. Morris wrote, "The B Company platoon was directly behind my unit as we moved to contact. Or so I thought. As we reengaged the enemy we were again being cut to pieces and were pinned down again . . . the supporting platoon had not moved from the ready line." Morris was furious and radioed Captain Drees, shouting into his radio handset over the din of battle and told him, "If he didn't get us some help soon there would be nobody left at the end of the day." After Morris' radio call, Drees moved to the ready line along the trail, and got the Bravo platoon moving forward again. The situation on the left was going no better.

As the Cav tracks rumbled forward in the attack, one of them was blasted by an explosive device that was hanging from a tree. The track commander was seriously wounded along with the other members of the crew. Specialist John Noel, a crew member, quickly took command of the disabled vehicle. Although Noel's arm was nearly severed from the blast, he continued to deliver fire on the enemy until he received another severe wound in the abdomen.

Jim Choquette was an M79 gunner on the Cav platoon's Track 12. Choquette's ACAV was moving right beside Noel's track. Choquette recalled that Russ Anderson was behind the .50 caliber machine gun on his track. When the enemy opened up, Anderson returned fire with the .50 caliber, depressing the butterfly trigger and firing up an entire belt of ammo before releasing it. The barrel was red hot, so Anderson poured a can of oil over it before loading a second belt. Seconds later Choquette received multiple shrapnel wounds from another Claymore blast. Despite his wounds, he continued to place effective fire on the enemy until his platoon leader ordered him to take cover and treat his wounds. Since there was no medic nearby, Choquette bandaged his bleeding left arm, and then moved to man one of the track's machine guns.

Bravo Company's Sergeant Jim Pius saw that Noel's ACAV and its crew were in serious trouble, and quickly went into action. He grabbed four men nearest his position along with two medics, Specialists Albert Bohrer and Teddy Whitton, and rushed under intense fire to the burning ACAV. He positioned two men on each side of the vehicle and then climbed onto the track with the two medics. While the medics pulled the wounded from the crew compartment, Sergeant Pius attempted to fire the ACAV's .50 caliber at an enemy RPG team that was rushing forward to finish off the disabled track. When he couldn't get the damaged gun to fire, Pius muscled the .50 caliber from its cradle mount and ordered the medics to get the wounded off the vehicle. After getting the wounded men and the machine gun off the ACAV, Pius and his men took cover nearby. Pius later wrote:

"I only remember the seriously wounded driver, who was riddled with shrapnel and his arm was missing. I can recall him because he asked me if I got the birthday cake his mother sent him and he thought the fire ants were all over the one side of his body. I don't believe he knew his arm was gone while the medics worked frantically on him."

Specialist John Noel survived his ordeal, and was subsequently awarded the nation's second highest award for valor, the Army's Distinguished Service Cross, for his extraordinary heroism.

After rescuing the wounded cavalrymen, Pius redeployed his men in time to counter a group of NVA who had left their fortifications and moved to flank his platoon's position. After directing his machine gunner, Bill Hill, and his M79 gunners to keep the attackers pinned down, Sergeant Pius took four men and rushed to reinforce the platoon's endangered left flank. Pius later wrote, "The same four men and I moved to take out the NVA I saw moving to flank us on the left. With hand grenades and automatic weapons we were able to take out the three positions they had set up." By his aggressive action, Pius stopped an enemy counterattack from rolling up Bravo's exposed left flank.

Medics Bohrer and Whitton evacuated Noel and the other casualties to the LZ, and made their way back to battle area where they went their separate ways. After providing medical assistance to several soldiers, Whitton spotted another ACAV with wounded men on board. Whitton had less than two weeks to go on his 12-month tour. Since he had risked his life on numerous occasions, the Bravo Company Commander, Captain Eaton, directed him earlier in the day to remain at FSB Nashua. Eaton wanted to insure that Whitton made it home for Christmas. Ignoring Eaton's instructions, Whitton had moved out with the Cav and Bravo platoons to support Alpha Company. Whitton knew that medics were badly needed on that day.

Having done all he could for the wounded soldiers he was treating on the ground, Whitton picked up his aid bag and sprinted toward the ACAV. He climbed aboard and began to treat a severely wounded cavalryman. Moments later, yet another large explosive device, probably a command-detonated mine, exploded near the ACAV. The blast mortally wounded Specialist Whitton who was standing upright in the open crew hatch as he treated a wounded trooper. William Hill from Jim Pius' platoon was nearby, and recalled that another five men were killed by the blast. Whitton's friend and fellow medic, Albert Bohrer, rushed to the scene when he heard Whitton was down and tried to resuscitate his friend, but was unsuccessful. Teddy Whitton was the third medic to die that day.

Lieutenant Philip Baynum's Bravo Company platoon, once it got moving forward, also ran into stubborn resistance. Phil Tolvin described the action. "We began to move laterally in reference to the enemy encampment, with the Lt. at the point. He then stopped and directed those behind me, Reid, Dr. Bopp, and Browley, directly into the bunker complex, with me at the point, the Lt. and his radio man now at the rear. . . . As I began to move forward again, all hell broke loose. We were opened up upon with automatic weapon fire. My steel pot was ripped from my head, as I hit the dirt with all my strength."

Tolvin thought he was headshot, but was only stunned by the concussion shock of an explosion. He lost most of his hearing and had a persistent ringing in his ears. The two men behind him, Reid and Bopp, were not as lucky. Reid caught one in the arm and Bopp was hit from debris from a booby trap explosion. Tolvin and the two wounded men crawled back to several anthills where Lt. Baynum, his RTO and another man, Browley, took cover. Tolvin picked up several M16s dropped by wounded men earlier in the day along the way. The six men were now about 15 meters from the enemy fortifications and 30 meters to the front of the rest of their platoon. Tolvin wrote, "All we could do was to keep at a low angle to the earth, to prevent ourselves from being riddled by the hail of lead traversing our position from the two forces that straddled us."

Seconds later, Lieutenant Baynum took a round in the back, probably from friendly fire. Realizing their untenable position, Tolvin grabbed the lieutenant shoulder to shoulder and shouted to the other four men to start falling back, hoping all the while not to be mistaken for a group of enemy soldiers. As the men fell back through the thick foliage, Tolvin shouted, "We're coming in, we're coming in!" Upon reaching the friendly lines under intense enemy fire, Tolvin and his party took cover in a bomb crater. Somehow Tolvin, in addition to carrying his wounded platoon leader to safety, managed to carry his own M16 and two he had recovered from the battlefield. After catching his breath, Tolvin felt a stinging in his thigh. He'd landed right on a bunch of large ants. Brushing them off, Tolvin again grabbed hold of the lieutenant, and directed the other two wounded men, Reid and Dr. Bopp, to follow him to the LZ where they were dusted off. With sunset fast approaching and their platoon leader evacuated, the Bravo platoon was spent.

On the right, the firestorm erupted again as Lieutenant Morris and his men pushed forward stubbornly in a renewed assault on the enemy bunker line. Morris was now practically deaf from the concussion of several grenade and mine blasts, and his RTO sustained additional shrapnel wounds. As sunset approached, Morris had only 17 men left in the fight. Those 17 of the original 78 were all that remained from the two Alpha Company platoons. PFC R.D. Jones was acting platoon sergeant. He was the highest ranking enlisted soldier left in Alpha Company who could still function. With Bravo Company's attack stalled on his left and his own men exhausted, Morris knew there was no possibility that his meager force could overrun the enemy base camp. He began the evacuation of his casualties to the LZ. For his extraordinary heroism that day, Lieutenant Morris was awarded the Army's Distinguished Service Cross.

Alpha Company, 3/7th Infantry, under Captain Smaldone's command, jumped off on the attack a few minutes after the joint Alpha and Bravo Company, 4/12th attack. His two platoons that had landed on the second lift had yet to make it to the scene. With less than two hours of daylight remaining, Smaldone and his platoon leaders had no time to conduct a reconnaissance, or wait on his other platoons. His men moved forward through the unfamiliar terrain, not knowing the precise location or layout of the VC fortified base camp. It was risky business, but Smaldone was an aggressive commander and master tactician, and he wanted to close with the enemy as quickly as possible.

Alerted by the airmobile assault, the enemy knew that another US unit was moving toward their fortifications from the north. The defenders prepared to meet Smaldone's attack by rushing men to the bunkers and trenches on the base camp's northern side. The VC could hear the Americans moving through the thick jungle, but held their fire waiting until Smaldone's men were only a few meters away.

Second Lieutenants John Sognier, of Savannah, Georgia, and Gary Clark, from San Francisco, led Smaldone's two platoons in the attack. Both men were "gung ho" infantry platoon leaders. Tony Smaldone accepted no less from his lieutenants. However, both men were relative newcomers, and this was their first experience with the terrain of War Zone D. Nevertheless, the lieutenants pushed their men hard toward the Communist fortifications.

Sognier's and Clark's platoons made contact with the enemy's outer perimeter before they were deployed in attack formation. The enemy blasted the two platoons with homemade Claymores filled with pieces of cement, nails, rocks, and anything else they could find that would be lethal projectiles. Then they opened up with machine guns, AK-47s, and grenades at near pointblank range. Among those hit were PFC Jerald Payton and PFC Chris Kimbel. Payton was hit in the face by shrapnel from a grenade, and was also wounded in the leg. The shrapnel broke his nose and blurred his vision. Kimbel took a round in the ankle. He was in intense pain and could barely walk. The two wounded grunts helped each other back to safety. They were more fortunate than most. Dozens of men in the lead platoons were killed or mortally wounded in the fusillade, but the survivors managed to hold their ground and return fire.

As dusk approached, the firestorm increased in intensity as Captain Smaldone pushed more men forward to reinforce his lead elements. Twenty-two year old Lt. Sognier rallied a group of soldiers nearest him and moved to overrun an enemy bunker. He was struck by a burst of automatic weapons fire and fell mortally wounded.

Lieutenant Clark was hit in the leg in the initial encounter but remained in the fight, guiding the forward movement of his men while his platoon sergeant, Guy Finley, rendered first aid to his platoon's seriously wounded and directed their evacuation to his company's reserve position. Several of Smaldone's men who were wounded in the initial exchange stayed in the fight until they were killed in the follow-on fighting. Among these were Specialist Mario Moreu-Leon, and PFCs Thomas Harper, Robert Bawal, Daniel Puhi, Solomon Dehart, and Douglas McCloud.

After evacuating his most seriously wounded, Lieutenant Clark launched another attack on the enemy perimeter. He managed to penetrate the outer defenses with a group of his men, but when the VC detonated another Claymore from the inner perimeter, he suffered more wounds to the leg and thigh. More of Clark's men fell in the same blast, but he pressed on with the survivors, tossing hand grenades into bunkers as they fought their way deeper into the enemy complex. As the small group reached the center of the enemy base camp, Clark was struck by a burst of fire and mortally wounded. Incapacitated and in deep pain he urged his men to leave him behind and fight their way out of the camp. Lieutenant Clark's platoon sergeant, Guy Finley, and his radio operator, Robert Pretty, refused to leave their dying platoon leader. The pair died at his side. All three men were found the following day lying shoulder to shoulder near the middle of the enemy base camp. More US bodies were found the next day, strewn from where they first broke through the northern perimeter all the way to the center of the base camp where the lieutenant, his platoon sergeant, and radio operator were killed.

Darkness fell before Smaldone ordered his men to withdraw with as many of their casualties as they could carry. Nine men who fell inside the enemy base camp were not retrieved until the following morning. The enemy battalion still held their camp as night fell, and they quickly set about organizing an evacuation on preplanned escape routes, carrying their wounded and as many of their dead as possible with them. Before they left, however, they took time to finish off several wounded Alpha Company soldiers who lay inside their perimeter, a senseless act of cruelty that the Americans would not soon forget.

While the battle raged for control of the enemy base camp, Captain Stan McLaughlin's Echo Company caught up with a group of NVA soldiers that they had stalked most of the afternoon. In a short but bloody firefight, Echo Company killed two enemy soldiers and wounded several others. It was, however, a costly fight for the grunts. Echo Company lost two soldiers killed and seven wounded in the fight. McLaughlin began a pursuit of the fleeing NVA until he received an order to return to FSB Nashua. Colonel Fred Davison, the brigade deputy commander, radioed LTC Schroeder, and directed him to extract McLaughlin's company and return them to Firebase Nashua. Davison wanted the 4/12th to launch an all out attack on the enemy base camp with all available forces the following morning.

The only airmobile asset available to extract Echo Company was an Australian Navy helicopter company, nicknamed the Emu's. LTC Schroeder and the Aussie commander, Commander Ralph, rendezvoused at Nashua, and took-off to find an LZ to extract Echo Company. As darkness fell, their C&C ship flew at low level over the jungle, scouring the terrain for an LZ. The only LZ in the immediate area was in a dry streambed, and it would accommodate only four ships. Schroeder directed Mclaughlin to move his company to the LZ, and the dangerous night extraction began.

The desperate battle for control of the enemy base camp subsided as darkness descended, but sporadic firing continued into the night. The 4/12th and 3/7th LZs were set up for night operations, and the dust-offs of the wounded continued well into the hours of darkness.

A flare ship arrived shortly after 1900 hours to illuminate the area, and gunships and artillery continued to pound the enemy base camp. At 1915 hours, one of the "Rat Pack" gunships piloted by Warrant Officer William Britt began to experience engine problems. Britt tried to make it back to Bien Hoa, but the gunship experienced a complete engine failure and he had to auto-rotate his ship into an unsecured area about two kilometers north of the Dong Nai River. Britt and his crew plus equipment were picked up almost immediately, leaving the downed aircraft in place. A platoon from Echo Company 3/7th Infantry conducted a night insertion into a narrow LZ to secure the downed gunship overnight. The platoon was inserted at 2130 hours, and immediately set up a defensive perimeter around the disabled aircraft. Defensive artillery fires were called for when the enemy began to probe the platoon's perimeter, but no ground attack was initiated by the enemy.

Captains Drees and Smaldone anticipated an enemy counterattack against their positions during the hours of darkness, so they ordered their men to dig in. The grunts, many of whom were wounded, scraped out fighting positions in the dirt. A few still had their entrenching tools, but most had to use their steel pots and bayonets. No one seemed to panic, but everyone knew it was going to be a long night.

Lieutenant Morris recalled settling into his foxhole, prepared to fight off a night attack, when he received an unexpected visitor. King, the attack dog, which had first alerted on the enemy that day, suddenly pounced into Morris' foxhole, landing on top of him. The shock was too much for the lieutenant's digestive system. He tried to leave the hole to relieve himself, but the dog thought otherwise, and the lieutenant had a "very distasteful accident" with the dog lying on top of him. According to Morris, the dog soon "decided to move in with someone else." Morris was later told by his men that they saw King during the battle charging enemy positions and being driven off by enemy bullets. The dog did, in fact, receive multiple wounds during the battle and died very soon after December 6th.

Lieutenant McKirdy, the Alpha Company FO, who had sustained shrapnel wounds early in the fight, refused medical evacuation that night, and stayed on as a member of Captain Drees' command group. He wrote that the company command post (CP) was set up in an old bomb crater. "I think I have ever been so scared in all my life . . . especially when about 0200 hours we heard a great crashing through the jungle. Somebody said they thought we were surrounded. The crashing kept getting closer until all of a sudden, a deer came loping through the crater, in one side and out the other. We had been surrounded by a deer. Needless to say, everyone became unglued, but not for long. Because we still didn't know what to expect, no one slept that night . . . one very long night."

As the night wore on, the commanders and their first sergeants began to tally up their losses. It had been the bloodiest single day in the history of the 199th Light Infantry Brigade. Captain Smaldone's Company, Alpha 3/7th, lost 11 killed and 21 wounded. Captain Drees' Company, Alpha 4/12th lost nine dead and 36 wounded. Captain Eaton's, Bravo 4/12th lost one dead and 19 wounded, and Troop D, 17th Cav suffered three dead and nine wounded. Captain McLaughlin's Echo Company, 4/12th lost two dead and seven WIA in its separate firefights north of Fire Base Nashua.

After Echo Company's night extraction, Lieutenant Colonel Schroeder returned to Fire Base Nashua determined to continue the attack the following morning. There were still nine men missing that had to be accounted for, and he wanted his battalion to finish the job. Brigadier General Forbes flew into Nashua shortly after Schroeder's arrival. The two commanders conferred at the Warrior TOC. It was clear to Schroeder and Brigadier General Forbes that the VC and NVA were not ready to relinquish control of this area of War Zone D. Schroeder told the general that it would take more than just his battalion to establish control of the area. Forbes had already asked the II Field Force Commander for more troops, and a battle-hardened Vietnamese Marine battalion was ordered to reinforce the Warrior battalion at Nashua on the following morning along with the 2/27th Infantry from the 25th Infantry Division. Schroeder began to outline his plan for a continuation of the attack for the next day while the general lit his trademark meerschaum pipe.

Charlie and Echo Companies of the battalion would move to reinforce Alpha and Bravo Companies on the morning of 7 December . After preparatory air strikes on the enemy positions, LTC Schroeder planned to lead a ground attack to overrun the enemy position. He decided to lead the attack himself from the ground. Schroeder's intent was to fly into the Alpha Company night defensive position as soon as his meeting with Forbes was concluded. General Forbes discouraged Schroeder from returning to the scene of the battle that night. He thought it was too risky for the battalion commander to be on the ground. A night counterattack on the thinly manned US perimeter was still considered a possibility, and Forbes did not want to lose a battalion commander unnecessarily. The two reached a compromise. Schroeder would spend the night at Nashua, and fly in to lead the attack on the following morning.

The Aftermath—7 December 1967

On the morning of December 7, 1967, the enemy base camp was targeted with two separate air strikes. Air Force fighter-bombers roared across the sky, dropping their bombs on the enemy positions. The enemy camp was hit by numerous M117, 750-pound bombs that blasted the enemy fortifications and surrounding jungle. It was early afternoon before the bombardment lifted. LTC Schroeder then moved forward on foot with Alpha, Bravo, Charlie, and Echo Companies toward the enemy base camp.

Lieutenant Morris of Alpha Company led his men toward the bunker line. He recalled that "Most of the saplings and other vegetation that had a diameter of around 2" or less were sheared off clean at about chest height." He was also surprised to see many of the hundreds of 40mm M79 rounds that his men had fired "laying all over the ground unexploded." The M79 grenade launcher, often referred to by the grunts as the "blooper," was fired from the shoulder and launched a single 40-millimeter high explosive round that spiraled in an arc toward its intended target. At its maximum range it could reach a target at 400 meters, but it was most often employed at much shorter ranges. The weapon covered the gap between the distance a hand grenade could be tossed, and the safe distance that mortars and artillery fire could be fired near friendly troops. There was, however, one problem when the weapon was fired in dense jungle. The spiral rotation of the 40-millimeter round causes it to arm, but only after it travels a minimum of 30 meters. It was apparent to Lieutenant Morris that during most of the battle he and his men were less than 30 meters from the enemy fortifications.

As Schroeder's rifle companies entered the enemy base camp, Captain Smaldone leading Alpha 3/7th moved in from the opposite side, and the two forces linked up in the center of the base camp. There was no enemy resistance. The survivors of the enemy battalion had faded away with the night shadows.

The air was acrid, and the smell of death permeated the area. The whole place was like a scene out of Dante's Inferno. Nothing moved among the caved-in bunkers and hootches. Bomb craters were still smoking and reeked of cordite. Trees were toppled or scarred by shrapnel, their once leafy branches pruned by withering small arms fire and explosions. Enemy rucksacks and equipment lay scattered about the camp.

Lieutenant Marv Stiles was an artillery officer who arrived at the scene of the battle that morning as a replacement for a wounded FO. Describing himself as a "newbie" that December, morning, Stiles recalled seeing "grotesquely mis-shaped steel helmets, burned out APCs, and debris all around." He further recalled that, "The smell of blood and flesh hung in the air." Stiles went on to spend ten and a half months in the field as a FO with various Warrior rifle companies, but this one scene, among the many he witnessed, remains indelibly etched in his memory.

Lieutenant Wayne Morris recalled that he and his men found dead US soldiers who "were laying where they had been killed as they fought their way into the base camp, along with enemy soldiers who were hastily buried in shallow graves" Arms and legs protruded from the dirt of these hasty graves. Blood soaked clothing and equipment and unexploded ordnance were scattered throughout the camp. As he made his way toward the center of the camp, Lieutenant Morris found a US platoon sergeant with a lieutenant lying next to him. It was apparent that the two had died in what must have been an epic struggle. Morris wrote, "It looked as if someone had emptied an entire machine gun belt into the platoon sergeant's belly."

Cliff Kaylor, a Charlie Company grunt, was also among those who walked through the enemy base camp that same morning. Kaylor recalled seeing "lots of American bodies lying dead in the trenches. . . . Many were shot between the eyes with a single round, as if executed. These were the first dead GI's I had seen and there were many of them."

Lieutenants Clark and Sognier were dead. Platoon Sergeants Dugger and Finley were dead. Squad and Team Leaders Hahn, Pruitt, and Ziegler were dead. Corporal Robert Pretty was dead two weeks before his 21st birthday. Medics Limbacher, Pultz, and Whitton were dead. Specialists McGovern, Moreu-Leon, and Hammerstrom were dead. PFCs Bawal, Brown, Buckner, DeHart, Fillipi, Harper, McLoud, Midcap, Puhi, Reynolds, Spainhower were all dead. The youngest among the dead was Clayton Marqui Spainhower of Fort Myers, Florida, 18 years of age, and the oldest was Guy Marvin Finley of Norfolk, Virginia, age 39. Four of the fallen heroes were native sons of the state of Ohio. Half regular army, half draftees, white, black, brown, representing nineteen states—all dead.

The 4/12th After Action Report for the battle near Fire Base Nashua lists enemy losses at: 67 enemy killed in action as determined by body count, along with an additional 85 enemy dead possible. As a result of the heavy artillery barrages and air strikes directed against the enemy positions, it was virtually impossible to verify the accuracy of the numbers of enemy casualties. Documents found on several enemy bodies identified the men as members of the D-800 Battalion (K1) of the Dong Nai Regiment.

Large quantities of mortar rounds, explosive devices, and small arms ammunition, along with stocks of medical supplies and unissued uniforms were also recovered from the camp. Remarkably, however, the enemy left no wounded or serviceable weapons on the battlefield. It was obvious to all that the enemy battalion, though battered during the fight, conducted a near perfect night withdrawal, perhaps the most difficult of all maneuvers in combat. The VC battalion, though bloodied, would continue to struggle for control of its territory.

After recovering and evacuating the US KIAs, and destroying the enemy bunkers with demolitions, Lieutenant Colonel Schroeder ordered his companies to return to FSB Nashua. Lieutenant Morris recalled, "Our uniforms were filthy and caked with mud and blood. Most had been snagged and ripped in several places. Our Load Bearing Equipment (LBE) was a mishmash of gear we had scrounged from the battlefield. Jones (PFC and acting platoon sergeant) held up his pants with twine he had picked up somewhere. But as we approached Nashua on the trail, each man straightened himself up as much as possible and we moved into a perfect tactical patrol formation and walked into the FSB as a solid and cohesive unit."

The fighting on 6 December significantly reduced the "foxhole" strength of the Warrior battalion. Alpha Company alone lost forty percent of its men, and LTC Schroeder planned to temporarily deactivate the unit. With losses exceeding the number of replacements arriving in the battalion, Schroeder knew it would take weeks, if not months, to rebuild the company. When the men of Alpha Company learned of the battalion commander's plan, a group of the company's NCOs asked to speak with him. They talked him out of it.

Several days later General William Westmoreland, the MACV Commander, visited FSB Nashua. After he was briefed on current operations and intelligence, the General wanted to talk to the Alpha Company soldiers who had fought the 6 December battle. Escorted by Brigadier General Forbes, the MACV Commander walked to Lieutenant Morris' platoon sector on the perimeter. Forewarned that the General was on his way, Morris had his men standing in formation. The troops had little time to prepare, but dusted each other off to look as good as possible. Their sweat-soaked jungle fatigues showed rents and tears from hard treks through the jungle, and some of the men still had bandaged shrapnel wounds. Dressed in heavily starched, perfectly creased fatigues with four stars embroidered on each collar, the general approached Morris' platoon formation and proceeded down the line of ragged grunts, speaking a few words to each man. When he reached PFC R.D. Jones, he noticed a piece of baling twine hanging below the man's tattered jungle fatigue jacket.

"What's that?" Westmoreland asked the soldier. Jones grinned and replied with pride. "That's my belt, Sir!" The General grinned and shook Jones' hand before moving on down the line.

Schroeder was impressed with the pride and esprit that these soldiers displayed. He was also impressed with the bravery of the men
who had fought the 6 December battle, and he instructed his adjutant
to get to work on award recommendations. He also sent one of his
staff officers to the in-country hospitals to obtain eyewitness statements to support the highest of these awards, Chaplain Angelo
Liteky's Medal of Honor recommendation. The officer returned with
only three statements. Most of the men who had witnessed the
Chaplain's actions during the battle had already been evacuated to
hospitals in Japan. Undeterred, Schroeder had orders cut sending the
young staff officer to Japan to comb the hospital wards for survivors.
The lieutenant returned a week later with more than enough statements to support the award of the nation's highest medal for bravery.

In addition to Chaplain Liteky's Congressional Medal of Honor,
there were two Distinguished Service Crosses and twelve Silver Stars
awarded to participants in the battle. Seven of these awards for valor
were posthumous. There were also numerous other awards, including
more than 100 Purple Hearts for those who had suffered wounds during the battle.

CHAPTER 5

THE ENEMY LIES LOW

After the battle on 6 December 1967, the II Field Force Commander, General Weyand, ordered more troops into War Zone D. A battalion of Vietnamese Marines arrived at FSB Nashua on December 7, followed by the 2/27th Infantry, the "Wolfhounds," from the 25th Infantry Division. The Wolfhounds and ARVN Marines were assigned Areas of Operation contiguous to the 4/12th's. Brigadier General Forbes, commander of the 199th Light Infantry Brigade, later wrote, "Following the insertion of the 4/12th we quickly moved a battalion of the 25th Division (Wolfhounds) into an area we felt would surely cause the VC to react violently—the military camp area near Xam Suoi Dia (later known as FSB Keene); it was astride a junction of two major roads through War Zone D which the VC had to use to resupply their units." Forbes wanted the enemy to take the bait and bring on another major engagement. The general ordered LTC Henry Meyer, the commander of the 2/40th Artillery, to move his headquarters to FSB Nashua, and also moved his own forward CP there.

With more US and ARVN boots on the ground, the enemy began to fragment into smaller-sized units that moved quickly throughout the area harassing US troops, trying to lure them away from the Communists' major supply complexes, arms caches, and hospital facilities. These facilities were critical for the support of their upcoming Tet Offensive. In addition to safeguarding their storage and base areas, the enemy hoped to wear down the Allied forces by inflicting the maximum number of casualties without bringing on a major engagement.

On 8 December, LTC Schroeder ordered Captain Jones' Charlie Company to search an area two kilometers northwest of FSB Nashua where aero scouts from the 3/17th Cav had reported signs of enemy activity. Charlie was the only Warrior company not involved in the 6 December fight. Captain Jones, the Charlie CO, had been in command for a little over two months, but he had no experience operating in jungle terrain. His lieutenants were similarly lacking in experience but were eager to prove themselves. Lieutenant Richard Solczyk led the 1st Platoon. He was enthusiastic and aggressive, but he would not live to see the new year. The 2nd Platoon was led by Lieutenant Al Lenhardt, a thoughtful officer who had ideas of making the Army a career. Lieutenant Paul Viola was in charge of 3rd Platoon. Viola was the only married lieutenant in the company, and his amicable personality made him a favorite among his superiors and subordinates. His leadership skills would be put to the test before the month was over.

LTC Schroeder was less than satisfied with some aspects of Charlie Company's performance. He thought the company moved too slowly, and observed that its CO lacked aggressiveness and had difficulty maneuvering his platoons in difficult terrain. Nevertheless, he recognized that Captain Jones possessed some solid leadership qualities, and he knew that the Captain was respected by his men. Schroeder decided that he would continue to mentor the Captain.

On 8 December, Charlie Company stood to before dawn and Captain Jones briefed his platoons on their mission. The company's three rifle platoons, along with three ACAVs from Delta, 17th Cav, would move along a road that led north from Nashua for approximately two kilometers. At a point where the road turned east and crossed the stream, Suoi Dia, the company would halt and take up defensive positions while Echo Company air assaulted into an LZ two kilometers to the west. Echo Company would then sweep east toward Charlie Company's blocking positions. It was a classic "hammer and anvil" operation employed by US forces in Vietnam. In this case, Charlie Company was the anvil.

Charlie Company departed Fire Base Nashua around 0800 hours, with 2nd Platoon in the lead followed by 3rd Platoon, while 1st Platoon brought up the rear. The three ACAVs from D/17th Cav, with the Charlie Company command group mounted aboard one of the vehi-

cles, started along the road. The column moved slowly since each platoon had flank security traipsing through dense jungle on either side
of the road. Lieutenant Paul Viola, the 3rd Platoon leader, was having
foot problems, and Captain Jones told him to ride on the lead ACAV
with his RTO. The column moved north searching for signs of the
enemy.

When the column approached the stream crossing, the 2nd and
3rd Platoons began to spread out into the dense jungle on both sides
of the road. Captain Jones' command group, along with 1st Platoon
and two of the ACAVs, halted behind a slight rise in the road waiting
for the lead platoons to move into their blocking positions. Lieutenant
Viola instructed the driver of the ACAV on which he was mounted to
move forward so that he could direct 3rd Platoon into its positions.
When the ACAV reached his platoon's location, he dismounted the
ACAV with his RTO. At that moment, the VC opened fire with small
arms and machine guns from across the stream. Two of Viola's men
were hit, one with a serious head wound. Viola later wrote, "The VC
had armor-piercing ammo as the rounds were going through both
sides of the APC [ACAV] which I had been on."

Specialist Jim Choquette of Warwick, Rhode Island was behind
the .50 caliber machine gun on the ACAV. As he returned the enemy
fire, an armor-piercing round slammed through the gun shield, slicing
off a portion of his upper lip and splattering him with blood. Another
round struck crewman Don Crueller in the mid-section.

On the west side of the road, Lindhart's 2nd Platoon also came
under fire that wounded four men. Lieutenant Viola radioed the
Charlie Company CO requesting artillery support. Jones passed the
request to his FO, but the artillery officer refused to call in a fire mission to his artillery battery. The FO thought the enemy was too close
to risk a fire mission. Lieutenant Viola was furious and told the FO to
move his ass forward to where he could adjust fire. Instead, the FO
sent his recon sergeant, Sergeant Hapgood, forward to Viola's position. Hapgood dashed forward with the FO's radio until he was close
enough to adjust fire, and radioed a fire mission to his battery.

As Sergeant Hapgood rushed forward, an enemy RPG team fired
several rounds at the ACAV, but the rounds fell short and exploded in
the dirt in front of the track. The track commander attempted to

return fire with the ACAVs .50 caliber, but the gun jammed. The ACAVs M60 machine gunner took up the slack, and suppressed the RPG fire, but the distinctive crack of AK-47s continued. Meanwhile, Sergeant Hapgood continued adjusting fire on the enemy, walking the rounds back toward the enemy positions along the stream. While Hapgood adjusted the artillery, Lieutenant Viola radioed for a dust-off for the wounded. Fortunately, a resupply ship was on the ground at FSB Nashua and responded within minutes, landing on the road near Viola's position. A pair of 3/17th Cav gunships suppressed the enemy fire during the dust-off. Three of the most seriously wounded were loaded aboard the resupply bird and flown to 93rd Evacuation Hospital at Long Binh.

Fifteen minutes later, Echo Company air assaulted into an LZ two kilometers west of Charlie Company's location, and began to move toward the scene of the firefight. Meanwhile, Captain Jones ordered his 1st Platoon to move forward to the point of contact. With another rifle platoon in the fight, Charlie Company gained fire superiority and the enemy began to withdraw from their positions. Captain Jones then ordered Lieutenant Solczyk's platoon to cross the stream and finish the fight. As Solczyk's men crossed the stream, the remaining enemy pulled out of their fortifications and withdrew northward, leaving behind seven of their dead. Thirty minutes later the Echo Company troops linked up with Charlie Company. A second medevac was called for to evacuate three additional Charlie Company grunts, and two Delta Troop cavalrymen who were wounded in the fight.

After examining the enemy fortifications, it was determined that Charlie Company had been ambushed by an enemy platoon-size force. Although the enemy had been outgunned, they'd fought stubbornly for more than two hours before they were driven from their positions. There were questions that were never answered in Lieutenant Viola's mind about the fight. Upon reflection, he never understood why his CO didn't move forward with his FO to direct the fight. He wrote that, "He [Jones] seemed reluctant to push or pursue."

Back at the Brigade Main Base Camp (BMB) at Long Binh, the Charlie Company XO, First Lieutenant Carl Frazier, was notified that the company's WIAs were at the 93rd Evacuation Hospital a few miles away. Frazier and his jeep driver, Specialist Bob Archibald, drove to the hospital to check on the wounded men and retrieve their weapons and equipment. Archibald had been pulled out of the field and sent back to base camp after only one month in-country to be the XO's driver. He had a cushy job, but he was worried. With the recent high casualty rate in the battalion, he knew his days in the rear were numbered. There weren't enough replacements coming in to fill all the vacancies in the rifle platoons. His intuition was correct. By mid-December, he was "humping the bush" again with Charlie Company's 3rd Platoon.

The fact that an enemy platoon was able to ambush one of Schroeder's rifle companies within two kilometers of FSB Nashua angered Brigadier General Forbes. General Creighton Abrams, the Deputy MACV Commander, arrived at Fire Base Nashua minutes after Charlie Company's contact. Abrams and Forbes conferred in private. Abrams told Forbes to expand the area of operations to locate the enemy's large logistic bases that were in the area and destroy the enemy main force units. Forbes knew he had to clear the areas immediately surrounding the firebase first. After General Abrams departed, Forbes summoned LTC Schroeder and told him to get the area around Nashua cleared without delay.

LTC Schroeder increased the number of patrols around the base, and from 8 December onward, every patrol that left Fire Base Nashua uncovered evidence of recent VC/NVA activity. Overland movement to and from Nashua continued to be hazardous. On 9 December, a 2/40th Artillery convoy en route to Nashua lost a 2-1/2-ton truck when it hit a mine several kilometers east of the FSB. Two artillerymen, Staff Sergeant Glenn Livingston and Specialist Four Charles Jasmine, were KIA and two men were WIA.

In the days that followed, several Warrior patrols engaged the enemy in short violent firefights, after which the enemy would melt away into the jungle, but two of these encounters resulted in company or larger-size fights. In both cases, the firefights began after LRP teams encountered enemy units and had to call for reinforcements.

The first of the company-size fights occurred on December 19th, when an air cavalry rifle platoon reinforcing a LRP team made contact with a squad-size enemy force some three kilometers northwest of Nashua. After suffering two KIAs, the cavalrymen called for reinforcements. Captain Stan McLaughlin's Echo Company conducted an airmobile assault into an LZ about one kilometer to the west of the air cav platoon. McLaughlin's company landed unopposed at 1000 hours, and began to sweep toward the beleaguered platoon's location.

After linking up with the air cav platoon, both outfits came under intense automatic weapons fire that wounded another of the air cav troopers. McLaughlin's grunts responded with a volley of rifle and M79 grenade fire, killing one enemy soldier. The remainder of the enemy force fled south with McLaughlin's grunts in hot pursuit. In a running firefight, the Echo Company grunts dropped four more of the enemy. The KIAs were all armed with new AK-47 rifles and grenades, and were clad in khaki uniforms. After searching the bodies, McLaughlin's men pushed on in pursuit of the others. The Echo Company point man soon reported finding green commo wire laid up the trail where the enemy had fled. After following the wire for a kilometer, the grunts rounded a bend in the trail and came face to face with two enemy soldiers laying the wire from a spool. The VC dropped their spools and opened fire, killing one Echo Company soldier. The grunts returned fire, killing the two VC. Captain McLaughlin moved forward to assess the situation. He didn't want to march his company into an ambush.

After eyeballing the terrain to his front, McLaughlin ordered three of his platoons to deploy on line while the fourth followed in reserve. The jungle was eerily silent as the grunts crept silently forward, their weapons off safety. Moments later they spotted several enemy bunkers. Crawling forward through the dense vegetation, the Echo Company grunts methodically tossed hand grenades into each bunker. The muffled explosions reverberated through the jungle. After the dust settled, the platoons moved forward to discover that the bunkers were all unoccupied. The company pushed on in a westerly direction. It didn't take long to find their quarry.

The jungle suddenly erupted into murderous fire from four dug-in enemy platoons in an L-shaped defensive position. At least six light machine guns and dozens of AK-47s raked the Echo Company platoons. Several of McLaughlin's men dropped, riddled with bullets.

Others hit the dirt and frantically crawled toward the nearest cover. The grunts returned fire with everything they had to try to suppress the enemy fire. Echo Company casualties began to mount. McLaughlin directed a pair of gunships as they raked the enemy platoons with rockets and machine-gun fire. As the Echo Company grunts maneuvered forward to engage the enemy bunkers, they were hit with murderous blasts from command-detonated enemy Claymores. Several men were seriously wounded by the blasts. Two men, Corporal Junior Lott from Athens, Alabama, and PFC John Barnett from Reading, Pennsylvania, died after sustaining multiple fragmentation wounds.

William McLean, a rifleman from Philadelphia, recalled seeing his CO, Captain McLaughlin, walk to a forward position where he halted with his back toward McLean. Seconds later he heard an ear shattering explosion and his Captain disappeared in a cloud of thick black smoke. McLean thought at the time that McLaughlin had tripped a booby trap and was probably dead, but he was not. However, the Captain was seriously wounded and out of the fight.

The enemy small arms and machine-gun fire continued unabated, despite the gunship and artillery support that pounded their positions. Their supply of ammunition was "seemingly inexhaustible." Corporal Winfield Spoehr, Specialist Anthony Mantouvales, and PFC Raymond Zimmerman were KIA, and ten more men were WIA. Mantouvales had joined the Army after attending college in Boston, though he had served a previous hitch in the Army before attending college and was exempt from the draft. He loved his country and wanted to serve.

With darkness coming on, Echo Company was unable to continue the attack. Colonel Fred Davison, the 199th Light Brigade's Deputy Commander, who was following the fight from the air, ordered Echo Company to break contact and move to an LZ for extraction. While Echo Company moved toward their LZ, LTC Schroeder called for a flare ship, and continued to direct artillery and gunship strikes on the enemy positions. At 2000 hours, Echo Company was extracted along with its dead and wounded. Five Warrior KIAs and ten WIAs were evacuated to the 93rd Evacuation Hospital, and the remainder of Echo Company returned to Fire Base Nashua. LTC Schroeder had lost one of his best company commanders in Captain Stan McLaughlin. The wounded captain would recover to complete his tour in Vietnam as an aide-de-camp to Brigadier General Forbes, and later as the Intelligence Officer in the 3/7th Infantry, but his disabilities from the wounds he received on 19 December disqualified him from returning to rifle company command.

Combat operations around Fire Base Nashua were put on hold during the Christmas truce period, 24–26 December 1967. The enemy took advantage of the ceasefire to continue the movement of replacements and supplies through War Zone D, and did so with impunity. There were numerous sightings of enemy trucks moving through the area. Specialist Cliff Kaylor, an RTO with Charlie Company recalled that on Christmas Eve "the hillsides around the fire base were alive with truck headlights." The buildup for the Tet Offensive was in high gear.

The Warriors went into action again as soon as the truce ended. On 27 December, F Company's LRP Team 14 reported that an enemy platoon-size unit was moving through the jungle to the west of their overnight position. The LRP team was hunkered down in a tight perimeter along the eastern bank of a stream called Suoy Tay Loi, a little more than two kilometers south of Fire Base Nashua. In a hushed whisper, the patrol leader radioed in a fire mission on the enemy force. Moments later, five 105mm howitzer rounds roared over the heads of the patrol members and exploded in the jungle beyond.

The LRPs heard screams from the enemy in the distance, an indication that the rounds had found their target. For the remainder of the night the patrol lay silently staring into the darkness, listening and waiting for the night to pass. At dawn, the LRPs retrieved their Claymores and moved silently westward. At 0735, they made contact with an unknown-size enemy force. In the ensuing firefight, four members of the patrol were wounded, two seriously. The team broke contact, called for reinforcements, and made their way to an extraction LZ.

At 0750 hours, the aero rifle platoon from 3/17 Cav was inserted into the area of the LRP contact to cover the extraction of the badly shot-up LRP team. Meanwhile, LTC Schroeder ordered Charlie Company to stand by on Nashua's LZ for an airmobile assault to reinforce the Cav's aero rifle platoon. Charlie Company was in better shape than the other Warrior companies to undertake the mission, having suffered fewer casualties in the preceding weeks. The company also had a new First Sergeant who was an experienced combat infantryman with a star on his CIB.

First Sergeant George Holmes was a 17-year veteran, on his second tour in Vietnam. As an 18-year-old private he had spent his first night in combat on "Old Baldy" during the Korean War. He was one of a handful of survivors who walked off the hill the following day. Before he left Korea, Holmes was promoted to platoon sergeant. On his first tour in Vietnam in 1963, he was assigned to an aviation unit supporting the ARVN. There were no US infantry units in-country at that time. He returned to the US where he was promoted to First Sergeant in the prestigious "Old Guard," 1/3 Infantry at Fort Meyer, Virginia.

Thus, Holmes knew how to be a "spit and polish" soldier, but he also knew how to run a combat outfit. Over the previous two weeks, Holmes had spent most of his time reorganizing the company's rear detachment. There were, in his opinion, far too many able-bodied grunts lingering in the rear doing meaningless tasks. He cleaned house, sending the men back to their platoons in the field. Then he headed for the field himself where he planned to spend most of his time. December 27th was Holmes' first combat operation with Charlie Company, and it was to be one of his most challenging.

Charlie Company went in heavy with all four platoons, a total of some 120 men. First Platoon was lead by 23-year-old First Lieutenant Richard Solczyk, a Chicagoan by birth. Solczyk had attended the University of Illinois at Urbana, joined the Army in 1966, and arrived in Vietnam in early November 1967. Second Platoon was led by Second Lieutenant Al Lenhardt, and the 3rd by newly assigned Second Lieutenant Robert Stanley. First Lieutenant Paul Viola led the 4th Platoon, normally armed with 81mm mortars, that was the company's reserve. This time the mortars were left behind at Fire Base Nashua with a minimum of crew members while the majority of the platoon deployed as reserve rifle platoon.

As the troops lined up in chalk loads on the PZ, Specialist Bob Archibald, the XO's former jeep driver, lined up with his 3rd Platoon stick. He spotted his friend PFC Guy Kistner, a machine gunner with

2nd Platoon, on the opposite side of the PZ. Kistner and Archibald had arrived in Charlie Company as replacements at the same time. They were both Californians and Kistner grew up a few miles from San Mateo, where Archibald attended high school and junior college. Archibald recalled that he had had a terrible premonition about Kistner the day before. He debated whether or not to talk with Kistner about it, but in the end decided to ignore it. He didn't want to alarm his friend.

The morning sun's incandescent rays glinted off the Hueys' windshields as the flight of ten touched down on the PZ. Troops lined up in chalk order and ran to board the helicopters. The chopper pilots brought their engines to full RPM as the troops climbed aboard and scrambled for space on the floor of the aircraft. It was less than a five-minute flight to the LZ, and grunts slid toward the open doors and stood on the Huey's skids as they touched down. Charlie Company's first lift was on the ground by 0815. There was no enemy opposition. Minutes later the second lift touched down, and the company was ready to move out. It was the beginning of a very long day for Charlie Company.

The company moved south from the LZ to link up with the Air Cav rifle platoon. At 0925 hours, the two units linked up in the vicinity of the earlier LRP contact. Two enemy bodies were found near some abandoned bunkers. After finding a fresh blood trail, the Charlie Company CO radioed the battalion TOC and requested that a combat tracker team be flown in. The team arrived some twenty minutes later, and the company moved out following the tracker team.

Shortly after 1000 hours, the tracker team located another enemy body. The man had been carrying an RPG-7 and extra rounds on his backpack. One of the extra rounds had apparently been struck with an M16 bullet. The anti-tank grenade cooked off, burning through the man's back. It was not a pretty sight, and a couple of the grunts "tossed their cookies" on the ground after viewing the body. Upon checking the area further, the tracker team picked up the trail of the dead man's companions, and Captain Jones ordered his platoon leaders to move out. The aero rifle platoon received orders that they were to move to a nearby PZ where they would be extracted.

LTC Schroeder was following Charlie Company's progress closely.

An aerial "People Sniffer" mission detected a group of enemy to the west of Charlie Company's location. Schroeder decided to insert Echo Company into an LZ southeast of Charlie Company's location. He ordered Charlie Company to hold their position until Echo Company was on the ground. Schroeder's plan was to have Echo Company follow a route behind Charlie Company close enough to exploit any enemy contact.

Echo Company's second lift was on the ground by 1115, and by 1245 Echo's point element had visual contact with Charlie Company. Schroeder, orbiting overhead in his C&C ship, gave the OK for the two companies to move out with the combat tracker team in the lead. The trackers were on a trail that led east into the jungle. Charlie Company moved in two columns with two platoons forward and two back, 1st and 2nd Platoons in the lead, followed by the 3rd and 4th Platoons.

The combat trackers moved cautiously and silently through the deep thickets, examining the ground for tracks and any disturbed foliage that would indicate an enemy presence. The sun's rays blazed through occasional openings in the triple canopy, and insects buzzed around the men's eyes. For the grunts following the trackers it was an agonizingly slow pace. The men tried to force their way through the thickets with as little noise as possible, but the swishing of saplings and rustle of bushes could be heard by an alert enemy. There was no way that a large body of men could move through such intricate landscape undetected.

Shortly before 1400 hours, the tracker team spotted three enemy soldiers setting up a huge Claymore-like mine next to a trail. The diameter of the saucer-shaped mine was at least 36 inches. The trackers cautiously backed off and passed the word back to Charlie Company's 1st Platoon that was halted about fifty meters to their rear.

PFC Gary Coufal, a member of Charlie's 1st Platoon recalled, "The scout told us that there was a Claymore mine to our front. My squad of the first platoon was up front and directed to proceed and try to make our way around it and disable it. Half of the team went around to the right and another part went to the left . . . the platoon leader was with the group that went to the left."

Approaching the area where the mine was set up, Lieutenant Rich

Solczyk, 1st Platoon leader, decided to have a look for himself. Ordering his men to stay put, he moved forward with his RTO, 20-year-old Specialist James Loudermilk. The lieutenant spotted the mine next to the trail, but the VC were gone. Inexplicably, the platoon leader with his RTO in tow then walked directly toward the device. When the lieutenant was less than ten feet away, the concealed VC detonated the mine. The powerful blast killed the lieutenant instantly and mortally wounded Loudermilk, his RTO. The concussion shook the ground and sent a shockwave through the trees and bushes all the way to the rear of the Charlie Company column. Specialist Tim Szelagowski was also wounded by a piece of shrapnel, but ignoring it he moved forward to assist the wounded RTO. Specialist Loudermilk's wounds were extensive and he died as Szelagowski held him in his arms.

Captain Jones, the Charlie Company CO, moved forward to the scene of the blast. He was visibly agitated at the sight of the mangled bodies of the dead lieutenant and his RTO. They resembled bloody bundles of discarded clothing. The Captain jerked his eyes away from the scene and mumbled to his RTO, Cliff Kaylor, to radio for a dust-off. Kaylor recalled that his CO was badly shaken.

It took more than an hour to cut a one-ship LZ for the medevac chopper to land and evacuate the two KIAs and wounded man. Captain Jones then ordered the company to move out, putting 2nd Platoon in the lead. Bob Archibald recalled seeing his friend Guy Kistner walk by him as 2nd Platoon moved out. Once again, Archibald had a premonition about him. The two friends nodded at each other, but neither man spoke. Meanwhile, the tracker team picked up the trail of the VC and followed them eastward toward a base camp six hundred meters away.

Alerted by the Claymore blast, the VC hunkered down in their bunkers and interconnecting trenches waiting for the Americans. They could hear the Charlie Company grunts pushing through the jungle toward their positions. The enemy soldiers peered through their gun sights down pre-cut firing lanes in the brush. The lanes were cut low, about knee high, and were difficult to detect. Camouflaged command-detonated Claymore mines were positioned at ten-meter intervals in front of the trench line. Some of the mines were hanging from trees to shower thousands of bits of razor sharp shrapnel downward on the attackers. By 1600 hours, Charlie Company's lead platoons were less than 100 meters from the enemy bunkers. The Vietnamese held their fire.

Charlie Company was moving in two columns, 2nd Platoon leading on the left and 1st Platoon at the head of the right column. A distance of about 75 meters separated the two columns. Specialist Larry Norris was walking point for the left column, and his buddy Frank Mascitelli was his cover man. Walking point was tedious and nerve-wracking work. Norris moved slowly, stopping every few paces to scan the area ahead and to his flanks, and to listen for any telltale noises. Visibility in the dense brush was limited to about ten meters in any direction; therefore he could not see the column moving to his right. In Norris' words, "Moving through the brush became easier and I slowed down, . . . I noticed a couple of bushes cut off at ground level. . . . I got down on one knee behind a bush . . . the rest of my squad was about ten yards back."

Charlie Company's 1st Platoon kept moving when Norris stopped the forward movement of 2nd Platoon. When the 1st Platoon was about 10 to 15 meters from the enemy fortifications all hell broke loose. Chicom and Russian-made AK-47 and AK-50 assault rifles and RPD machine guns fired short and long bursts at the attackers, and several Claymores were detonated on the exposed Americans. Several men near the front of the column went down immediately from the volley, including 20-year-old Guy Kistner, who was almost on top of an enemy bunker. Kistner was hit in the chest but managed to crawl forward and drop a hand grenade into the bunker's firing aperture. The grenade went off, killing the enemy soldiers inside the bunker. Staff Sergeant Skelton, who took over 1st Platoon when his lieutenant was killed, crawled forward trying to reach Kistner, but the fire from the adjacent bunkers was too intense. He pulled back far enough to engage one of these bunkers with a M72 LAW, destroying it, but the backblast from the weapon pinpointed his location for the enemy and they concentrated their fire on him. Skelton managed to get another LAW round off at a third bunker before shouting to his men to pull back and find cover.

Staff Sergeant Billy Walker, a squad leader with 1st Platoon, reorganized the men as they withdrew for another attack to recover the platoon's wounded. Having arrived in Vietnam as a PFC, Walker was promoted to the rank of Staff Sergeant in less than a year. The tall, serious-minded Texan and former schoolteacher-turned-soldier was a natural born leader. Walker personally led the next assault to recover the platoon's wounded and dead. Crawling close to the enemy emplacements, he personally extracted many wounded soldiers while under heavy enemy fire. For his actions, Walker was awarded the Silver Star.

Second Platoon was 50 to 75 meters from the enemy bunkers when the fight started. Larry Norris was still on point when the enemy opened fire. He wrote, "Suddenly there was a loud explosion and all hell broke loose everywhere. I was taking lots of fire. . . . I was as close to the ground as I could get and I could hear the knocking sound just inches from my ear. . . . Every time I moved I would get more directed at me. I was yelling for the M79 and finally the platoon opened up to cover me." Norris' cover man hit the dirt when the VC opened up. He too was pinned down and unable to move forward or backward. Although the 2nd Platoon suffered several casualties when the enemy opened up, the platoon was not taking the same volume of fire as 1st Platoon.

David Taylor, who was moving about midway in the 2nd Platoon formation, wrote that "Bullets were flying in our direction, but we did not receive a great deal of small arms fire to our position." He wondered, "Why we were not readjusting our positions for better cover and assisting the fighting ahead of us." The situation became further confused when Taylor's platoon got the order to don their gas masks. Apparently, someone had passed the word that CS gas was going to be used to dislodge the enemy from their fortifications. The grunts donned their masks and desperately tried to get protective masks on the wounded, but some had head facial wounds. After several minutes the order was cancelled.

When a Light Fire Team from the 3/17th Cav arrived over the scene of the fight, Taylor's platoon leader, Lieutenant Lenhardt, received instructions to pop smoke to mark his platoon's positions. The smoke grenades hissed and popped, sending plumes of yellow smoke skyward. Unfortunately, the smoke identified the platoon's position to the enemy as well. Taylor recalled that shortly after the smoke grenades were thrown, "The enemy mortars were dropped in the tubes and launched. . . . I was hearing the 'thumps.'. . . I was making counts of 22 before each mortar round hit the ground . . . and the rounds were marching to our position—to the smoke." He further recalled that, "The round landing closest tore apart a tree at my position, and the branches were landing on me. I was hugging closely to the ground at that moment."

Second Platoon's point man, Larry Norris, was finally able to pull back with the rest of his platoon after vowing to himself to "re-up" for a new MOS that would take him out of the field. He forgot all about it by the next day. Frank Mascitelli was not as lucky as Norris. He was still pinned down, and more than a little pissed off that his platoon had left him, assuming he was dead. Eventually he was able to link up with members of the 1st Platoon. Norris's squad leader, Sergeant Stan Clark, wanted to attempt a flanking movement on the enemy bunker line, but was overruled by his platoon leader.

Lieutenant Robert Stanley's 3rd Platoon was also under fire, but moving behind the lead platoons, Stanley's men were not drawing the same volume of fire as the others. Bob Archibald and Al Lewis were positioned by their platoon leader to protect the platoon's flanks and rear. Archibald wrote, "Neither myself nor Al ever fired a round or saw anything." Armed with an M79 grenade launcher, Archibald was concerned with his position in the dense jungle. He knew that the 40mm round fired by his grenade launcher had to travel about 30 feet to arm. He figured if he had to use the M79, "it would be like throwing rocks." Archibald's platoon leader, Lieutenant Stanley, waited for orders from his CO, Captain Jones. He never received any orders so his platoon took cover and stayed put.

LTC Schroeder flew over the scene, trying to determine the layout of the enemy's fortifications. It was not an easy task. The jungle base camp was situated under a thick green canopy, and the enemy bunkers were well camouflaged to prevent detection from the air or the ground. He radioed the Charlie Company commander:

"Bishop 41, this is Knight 52, over."

"This is Bishop 41, we're taking fire, we're pinned down, over!"

"This is Knight 52, pop smoke; mark your position over."

"This is Bishop 41, popping smoke, over."

Moments later, little wisps of yellow smoke began to drift through openings in the canopy, but the origin of the smoke was difficult to determine. Schroeder radioed his TOC at FSB Nashua and directed the duty officer to put Alpha Company and a platoon of Delta Troop ACAVs on alert for possible commitment to the scene of Charlie Company's contact. Then he radioed his Echo Company commander and instructed him to circle in behind the enemy base camp. His radio transmission was interrupted by a call from a very distraught Captain Jones.

"Knight 52, Knight 52, this is Bishop 41, we're taking heavy fire, mortar fire, I think we're surrounded, heavy casualties, over!"

"This is Knight 52, I want you to get your platoons in assault formation and assault that bunker line, over."

"This is Bishop 41, can't move over, pinned down!"

Charlie Company's situation on the ground was one of utter chaos. Panic-stricken grunts, some dragging their wounded comrades, sifted back through the dense foliage seeking cover from the heavy fire. Most found their way to Charlie Company's CP group's location, about fifty meters from the bunker line. First Sergeant Holmes grabbed several of the panicked troopers and set up a small perimeter to protect the command group. Ignoring the hostile fire striking around him, he walked around trying to restore order. Specialist Kaylor, the Captain's RTO, tried to look cool, but his hands trembled as he worked his radio. He noticed a medic working on a seriously wounded soldier. The medic tried to inject the man, who was writhing in pain, with morphine. The medic fumbled with the syrette, dropping it twice before jabbing the needle through the man's skin and then moving on to the next man. There were more than a dozen wounded in the CP area.

Enemy mortar rounds began to explode near the CP. After each CRRRRUMMP, the grunts tried to scrape out shallow shelters in the dirt. Kaylor's radio suddenly cackled to life. The RTO recognized LTC Schroeder's call sign.

"Bishop 41, this is Knight 52, over!"

Kaylor answered the call, "This is Bishop 41 Alpha standby, over."

"This is Knight 52, put 41 on, over," Schroeder replied impatiently. He wanted to talk directly to Captain Jones, not the RTO.

Kaylor started to crawl toward Captain Jones, who was sitting with his back against a nearby tree. When he got closer he saw tears in the Captain's eyes. He refused to take the radio handset from Kaylor. The radio cackled again.

"Bishop 41, this is Knight 52, get your company moving, over."

Moving in a low crouch and panting, Kaylor dragged his radio toward First Sergeant Holmes, who was moving around the tiny perimeter distributing ammunition.

"You've got to take this call Top, it's the battalion commander. The Captain is in bad shape."

The First Sergeant grabbed the radio's handset from Kaylor and depressed the "push to talk" button.

"Knight 52, this is Bishop 41 Charlie, over," Holmes said in his resonant bass voice.

"This is Knight 52, what's your situation, over," Schroeder replied.

"This is Bishop 41 Charlie. Things are pretty fucked up. We're under heavy small arms and mortar fire. We need some help down here. We need gunships and a medevac. Where the hell is Echo Company?" Holmes replied.

"This is Knight 52, who's in charge down there?" the battalion commander queried.

Glancing at his CO, who sat nearby staring at the ground between his feet, Holmes replied, "This is Bishop 41 Charlie. I guess I am, over."

"This is Knight 52, Roger, gunships are on the way; mark your positions and direct them in."

"Roger, out," First Sergeant Holmes replied, passing the handset back to Kaylor.

Holmes knew that one of the company's officers was KIA, but there were still three lieutenants leading platoons. His CO, however, was no longer capable of commanding the company. Each platoon was fighting on its own without any direction. Specialist Kaylor, the company's senior RTO, summed up the situation, describing the company as "an amoeba without any supporting structure." Kaylor prepared himself for the worst, and thought about being captured by the VC. He silently vowed to take his own life rather than be taken prisoner.

Lacking any orders or direction from their CO, Charlie Company's platoon leaders were attempting to get the situation under control as best they could. Unlike their CO, the platoon leaders knew that they weren't surrounded, but they were receiving incoming fire from their flanks. The lead platoons were also taking sniper fire from VC hidden in trees forward of their bunker line. The battle continued as each platoon conducted its own fight.

Fourth Platoon moved at the rear of Charlie Company's three rifle platoons. The 4th Platoon, led by Lieutenant Paul Viola, had deployed with only fourteen men that day, the rest of its men left back at the fire base with the platoon's 81mm mortars. When the lead platoons made contact with the enemy's perimeter, Viola's platoon was ordered by Lieutenant Colonel Schroeder to move forward to evacuate the casualties. Viola had just monitored a disturbing radio transmission between Schroeder and Captain Jones. According to Viola, Jones sounded shaken and had asked his battalion commander, "What am I going to do?" Schroeder told Jones to "turn the company over to the next senior man at his location."

Viola wrote, "We had to fight our way in. Because of our strength and lack of stretchers, the casualties had to be moved using ponchos and poncho liners using all the platoon's men." Under Lieutenant Viola's and Platoon Sergeant Cliff Jaynes' direction, 4th Platoon managed to evacuate most of the seriously wounded men down a trail that led to the rear. Viola recalled that his men were under small arms fire as they were carrying the casualties, but since they were moving down a slight hill, the fire was overhead. Lieutenant Colonel Schroeder, orbiting overhead in his C&C ship, directed Viola to move the casualties toward an LZ to the south. The medevac ship arrived overhead before Viola's men reached the LZ. Viola made a quick decision. His men had reached a "fairly open spot on the trail," and he instructed his platoon sergeant to make an LZ at that location, using C4 to blow down several trees to expand the open area.

As soon as the LZ was large enough, the dust-off pilot eased his UH-1 into the small clearing, clipping the branches off several trees still standing around the perimeter. Platoon Sergeant Jaynes directed the loading of the wounded men on the chopper as Lieutenant Viola received more instructions from Schroeder. Viola wanted to return to the fight, but Schroeder had other plans. He instructed Viola to continue moving south to secure a larger LZ. Schroeder had already made up his mind to pull Charlie Company out of the fight.

While the Charlie Company platoons continued the fight, Echo Company maneuvered around Charlie Company to the eastern side of the enemy base camp and launched an assault, surprising the defenders. PFC Lou Alexander was point man for Echo Company's lead platoon. Alexander skillfully guided his platoon into an assault position, and then armed only with a pistol and several hand grenades, he stood up and charged an enemy bunker. After tossing a grenade into the bunker's firing port, he waited until the grenade exploded and then crawled into the bunker and recovered the weapons from the dead VC. Following Alexander's lead, Specialist Don Slagle led his squad forward, using fire and movement, and was able to gain a foothold in part of the enemy trench system. Slagle consolidated his position and, after treating his wounded, proceeded to attack the enemy fighting bunkers along the trench, destroying them one by one.

Lieutenant Bill Danforth led his platoon on Echo's left flank, skillfully maneuvering his platoon to assault the enemy trench system. Once his men gained the trench line, they turned their attention to the enemy bunkers. After several of their bunkers were destroyed with hand grenades, the VC defending the eastern perimeter withdrew toward secondary positions within the camp. They left behind 15 dead. Echo Company lost two KIAs in the assault, PFC Gordon Dalton and Specialist Thomas Malloy, and 15 men were WIA.

The enemy resistance began to crumble when two platoons of Alpha Company supported by 3rd Platoon, Delta Troop, 17th Cav arrived in the vicinity of the northern edge of the enemy base camp, and directed a heavy volume of fire against the defenders. As darkness began to fall, the VC started to withdraw from their fortifications. Orbiting overhead in his C&C ship, LTC Schroeder spotted several small groups of enemy soldiers fleeing the area.

At 1755 hours, Charlie Company reported that the enemy had broken contact on the western side of the perimeter. Schroeder decided to extract Charlie Company. He knew Jones had lost control of his company, and he wanted to find out what had happened. He ordered the company to move to a PZ for a night extraction. Echo Company and two platoons from Alpha Company dug in around the perimeter of the enemy base camp under a black night sky.

It was not until Charlie Company returned to Nashua that anyone noticed that the body of one of their KIAs had not been recovered. When he found out about the missing KIA, LTC Schroeder informed the company that they'd be going in at first light to recover their dead. He decided that Captain Jones would have to be removed as soon as he could find a replacement.

Bob Archibald was stunned when he learned his friend Guy Kistner had been killed that day, and he told his foxhole buddy, Al Lewis, about his premonition. Lewis then asked Archibald if he thought he'd make it out of Vietnam alive. Archibald stared at Lewis, and then said that he had no premonitions about him. In his own words, Bob Archibald later said, "I lied."

The 27 December fight was the last contact between the Warrior battalion and units of the Dong Nai Regiment that month. On 5 January 1968, the 4/12th Infantry moved to an area south of the Dong Nai River to the east of Bien Hoa. This redeployment was part of a plan by the II Field Force Commander, Lieutenant General Weyand, to pull a number of US battalions out of the remote jungle and border areas, and reposition them around the Saigon-Bien Hoa-Long Binh areas. Weyand was concerned about the possibility of an enemy offensive directed against South Vietnam's population centers, and his analysis of the situation was right on target.

The 199th Light Infantry Brigade's foray into War Zone D inflicted considerable damage on the Viet Cong's Dong Nai Regiment. The regiment did launch attacks on the District Capital of Tan Uyen during the Tet Offensive, but was not able to hold the town for any length of time. A document found on the body of the Regimental XO indicated that the Regiment started the Tet Offensive with only 1,100 men. Normal strength of the Dong Nai Regiment was around 2,200 men. If the captured document was accurate, the enemy regiment had only 50 percent of its strength during the Tet Offensive, and was not combat effective. The 199th LIB's operations in War Zone D during

December 1967 also disrupted the Communists' lines of supply and communication. In some cases, major VC units such as the 5th VC Division had to alter their planned invasion routes to reach the Long Binh and Bien Hoa areas. That Division's attacking regiments were forced to take long circuitous routes to reach their objectives.

The 199th LIB's infantry battalions, particularly Schroeder's 4/12th, inflicted heavy losses on the enemy during December of 1967, but their victories came at a high price. Forty-two men were killed during that month, and the wounded numbered in the hundreds. No one anticipated that the heaviest fighting was yet to come. At the end of January, the 199th LIB was destined to face an enemy onslaught that was to go down as the most famous battle of the Vietnam War: the Tet Offensive of 1968.

CHAPTER 6

THE GATHERING STORM

While the 199th LIB's December incursion into War Zone D partially disrupted the Communist buildup, it was far too limited to disrupt the enemy's timetable for the Tet Offensive. As the new year began, the VC and NVA preparations for the general offensive went into high gear. Enemy tactical commanders reconnoitered their assigned objectives, while their quartermasters continued to push forward massive amounts of weapons, ammunition, and other war fighting supplies. Special emphasis was placed on equipping VC assault battalions with AK-47 and AK-50 assault rifles, and RPG-2 and RPG-7 anti-tank rockets. At the same time, NVA replacements from the north began to arrive in increasing numbers to bring the main force VC units up to their authorized strength levels. By mid-January, attack regiments and battalions were on the move toward their assembly areas. Weapons, ammunition, and other equipment were pre-positioned in forward areas. US intelligence units detected some of the preparations, but analysts were slow in putting the pieces of the puzzle together. Most senior analysts discounted the likelihood of major ground attacks on Saigon, Bien Hoa, and Long Binh.

Despite the movement of men and supplies toward the built-up areas around Saigon, there were few contacts between US forces and Communist units in those areas during most of January 1968. The Communists went to great lengths to insure that operational security was maintained. Enemy infiltrators and reconnaissance teams traveled unarmed in civilian clothing as they moved about their target areas. Contact with US and ARVN forces was avoided, and every possible effort was made to blend in with the civilian population. Some of the insurgents were recognized and even welcomed by family members and former acquaintances, but no alarms were raised. The South Vietnamese, including their armed forces, continued preparations for the upcoming holiday, ignoring the warning signs.

There was, however, one senior US commander who closely monitored the intelligence and had the foresight to take action. Lieutenant General Weyand, the II Field Force Commander, suspected that the Communists' objectives in III Corps were the population centers and the nearby US installations. At a meeting held on 10 January 1968, Weyand convinced his boss, General Westmoreland, that a "strategic reversal" or shift in gravity of US forces was needed to prepare for a major enemy offensive in the III Corps area. With General Westmoreland's approval, Weyand ordered the movement of a number of US maneuver battalions from the remote jungle and border areas to locations closer to Saigon, Bien Hoa, and Long Binh. By 29 January 1968, 27 battalions were deployed around the periphery of the Saigon metropolitan area, up from the 14 battalions that had been in the area during early January.

As part of this redeployment of forces, the 199th Light Infantry Brigade was released from its mission in War Zone D. Three new areas of operation were assigned to the brigade: AO UNIONTOWN, AO COLUMBUS, and AO HAVERFORD.

AO Uniontown encompassed some 130 square kilometers, and included the main avenues of approach leading from War Zone D into the Long Binh and Bien Hoa areas. For control purposes, the AO was broken down into three sectors. AO NORTH UNIONTOWN was the area north of the Dong Nai River in the southernmost portion of War Zone D, and was commonly referred to as the "rocket belt." The 199th LIB was charged with disrupting enemy rocket attacks directed on Long Binh and Bien Hoa from this area. CENTRAL UNIONTOWN included the area south of the Dong Nai River, stretching south to Highway 1 that ran from Bien Hoa to Xuan Loc. SOUTH UNIONTOWN extended eight kilometers south of Highway 1, and was bordered on the west by Highway 13. The 199th LIB's main base camp, II Field Force Headquarters, USARV Headquarters, the Long Binh ammunition dump, and a number of aviation units and medical support facilities were located in South Uniontown. The 199th LIB's mission was to protect these installations from rocket, mortar, and ground attack. The 4/12th Infantry was assigned responsibility for AO Uniontown.

AO Columbus was an area bordering the northeast corner of Central Uniontown. This area was hilly and sparsely populated with dense jungle growth covering most of the terrain. Columbus was located south of the confluence of the Song Be and Dong Nai Rivers, and was a perfect staging area for the enemy's combat formations preparing to attack Long Binh and Bien Hoa. The 199th LIB's 2/3d Infantry was given responsibility for conducting operations throughout this area.

The brigade's third infantry battalion, the 3/7th Infantry, was forward deployed to AO Haverford southwest of Saigon, and operated under the direction of the Capital Military District (CMD). AO Haverford, which included a large portion of Gia Dinh Province, stretched from the outskirts of Cholon southwest toward the Mekong Delta. Highway 4, the primary artery connecting the main population centers in IV Corps with Saigon, ran through the center of the AO. Numerous waterways and canals flowed throughout the flat terrain, most of which consisted of rice paddy areas and swamplands.

The men of Lieutenant Colonel Schroeder's battle-scarred Warrior battalion experienced mixed emotions when they learned that they were to be redeployed out of War Zone D to more familiar terrain around Bien Hoa and Long Binh. They had learned many lessons from the battles around Fire Base Nashua, and were reluctant to relinquish the terrain to enemy control. On the other hand, they knew life would be easier after the redeployment. There would be more opportunities for visits to the brigade's rear base camp at Long Binh, more hot chow and the occasional shower, and perhaps even some visits to the bars and whorehouses in Bien Hoa. Above all, they expected a respite from the heavy fighting they had experienced in War Zone D during the bloody month of December. A ceasefire was scheduled during the Vietnamese Tet Holiday, promising a respite from the high tempo of operations.

Redeployment of the Warrior battalion to its new AO was completed on 13 January 1968. The battalion headquarters was established at FSB Concord. After the move south, LTC Schroeder relinquished his command to a new Warrior battalion commander, LTC William Mastoris. Schroeder's six-month command tour was complete, and he was reassigned to the G3 section of II Field Force Headquarters. After the change of command ceremony, Schroeder and his company commanders lined up for a final photo. Several of the commanders had tears in their eyes as they bid goodbye to their outgoing commander who had led them through such tough close-quarter battles.

Lieutenant Colonel Bill Mastoris, the incoming commander, was a USMA graduate of the class of 1950. The 39-year-old native of Sharon, Pennsylavania was a soft-spoken, even-tempered man who had great confidence in his subordinates. With a strong infantry and airborne background, Mastoris made no immediate changes in the battalion, and relied heavily on his experienced S-3, Major Ed King. Mastoris was about to face the greatest challenge of his life. He would lead the Warrior battalion through six months of the heaviest fighting of the Vietnam War.

FSB Concord sat atop a ridgeline overlooking the Dong Nai River, about eight kilometers northeast of Bien Hoa in AO Central Uniontown. The sprawling US base complex at Long Binh lay ten kilometers to the southeast. North of FSB Concord across the Dong Nai was "the rocket belt." It was from this area just north of the Dong Nai River that the enemy launched 122mm rocket attacks on the strategic Bien Hoa Airbase, and the US Army facilities at Long Binh.

With a maximum range of about 15,000 meters (even greater ranges could be achieved with a booster rocket), the 122mm rocket was used to attack area targets such as ammo dumps, aircraft parking areas, fuel dumps, and troop cantonments. The 122mm rockets and their launchers were relatively lightweight, and were usually transported by foot through the jungle to pre-selected firing sites. The rocket launch crews typically arrived at the firing sites after dark, and were able prepare the weapons for launch in about twenty minutes. After launching their rockets, the crews would recover their launchers and quickly depart the firing area. By mid-January, enemy rocket survey teams were busy selecting and surveying launch sites for the upcoming Tet Offensive. Precise firing azimuths, elevations, and ranges were calculated for each target.

Situated on high ground just two kilometers south of the Dong Nai River, FSB Concord was an excellent firing location for the 105mm howitzers of Charlie Battery, 2/40th Artillery. With a maximum range of 11,000 meters, Charlie Battery's howitzers could plaster enemy firing sites anywhere in the "rocket belt" within a matter of a few minutes. Target acquisition support was provided by the TPSI/25 Radar operated by the 101st Division Artillery. When the TPSI/25 acquired a target, the 101st Division Artillery notified the 4/12th TOC at FSB Concord. The artillery liaison officer (LNO) would then send a fire mission to the bases's howitzers and adjust the fires using the 2/40th Artillery's Q4 Radar. Secondary explosions from direct hits were often observed from the fire support base.

To the west of FSB Concord, the terrain sloped gently downward toward a square kilometer of rubber trees. The rubber trees were pushed back by Rome Plows, huge bulldozers with angular tree-cutting blades, to make room for a ten-ship LZ. On the east side of FSB Concord, the ground dropped sharply into a narrow valley. A stream flowed lazily northward through the narrow valley toward the Dong Nai River. The headwaters of the stream were just east of the Bien Hoa airbase. The valley was a natural infiltration route for enemy ground troops entering the Bien Hoa area. The Warrior battalion's 81mm mortars fired nightly into the valley to interdict enemy movement.

FSB Concord was a much smaller base than FSB Nashua, and its perimeter was secured by a single rifle company reinforced with a platoon of ACAVs from D/17th Cav. The Warrior battalion's Charlie Company was assigned the mission of securing FSB Concord. The present author took command of Charlie Company at FSB Nashua on January 1st, replacing the commander who was reassigned after the December 27 firefight. For the remainder of this narrative, the author will be referred to in the third person as Captain Bob Tonsetic.

Captain Tonsetic reported to the 199th Light Infantry Brigade's headquarters at Long Binh during October 1967, and was assigned to the Brigade's S-3, Operations section. In December 1967, he was selected by Brigadier General Forbes to take command of Charlie

Company 4/12th, after the near disastrous fight on 27 December. On January 1, 1968, Tonsetic packed his rucksack, drew a CAR-15 from the company arms room, and hopped aboard a UH1 helicopter for a flight to Fire Base Nashua, where he took command of Charlie Company the same day. The company was still in recovery mode from its less than satisfactory performance on December 27th, and Lieutenant Colonel Schroeder informed his newest commander that he planned to keep Charlie Company at FSB Nashua for a few days to allow the Captain "to get his feet on the ground and size up the company."

When the Warrior battalion received the order to depart FSB Nashua for it's new AO, Tonsetic's Charlie Company was assigned the mission of securing FSB Concord. The company was also assigned as the Brigade Ready Reaction Force. That meant that the company was on-call to respond within 30 minutes to any emergency situation in the Brigade's area of operation. Deployment of the company could be by helicopter lift, vehicle, or dismounted, depending on the location of the action and the availability of transportation assets. The remainder of the battalion's rifle companies were deployed throughout AO Uniontown.

The civilian population density was heavy in most areas of CENTRAL and South Uniontown, but AOs NORTH Uniontown and Columbus were sparsely populated. A total population of some 19,000 civilians lived mainly in the 14 villages and hamlets scattered throughout the region. The villages and hamlets were connected by road networks that were easily trafficable by wheeled vehicles. During the day, road traffic was heavy with an assortment of trucks and smaller vehicles transporting vegetables, cabbages, eggplants, melons, and all types of other fruits into the towns and cities. Firewood was another major commodity. Woodcutters moved into the forested areas on a daily basis using ox drawn carts, and returned before sundown, their carts loaded down with firewood. The enemy took advantage of the trade being carried on to camouflage and conceal the weapons and ammunition being brought into the cities. The rivers, streams, and canals were also major transportation arteries in and out of the populated areas, and were used extensively by the enemy to move men and supplies into the cities of Saigon and Bien Hoa. On any given day, thousands of sampans and other craft plied these waterways, bringing an assortment of legitimate goods into the cities, but along with these goods flowed a steady stream of military equipment for the upcoming offensive. Despite this increase in enemy activity in the countryside surrounding the capital and the US base areas to the north at Bien Hoa and Long Binh, few contacts were made with enemy forces in those areas during early and mid-January of 1968.

The mission of attacking targets in the Long Binh area was assigned to the 5th VC Division. This Division was also assigned the mission of attacking the Bien Hoa Airbase. The main attack units of the Division were the 274th and 275th VC Regiments, supported by combined Artillery Group U-1. A Local Force Battalion, and other local force VC units were also assigned to support the 5th VC Division's attacks.

During early and mid-January, the 5th VC Division and its subordinate units were steadily moving into AOs NORTH Uniontown, and Columbus. To the southwest of Saigon, no less than six VC battalions planned to infiltrate through the 3/7th's AO Haverford toward Saigon. As the month of January passed, the enemy's attack regiments and battalions continued to slip closer to their objectives for the offensive.

The enemy plan was to seize and hold the US installations until Saigon fell and a general uprising of the population occurred, resulting in the capitulation of the South Vietnamese government. At that point, the leaders in Hanoi believed that the US would have no choice other than to withdraw its forces from Vietnam. No one on the US or ARVN side anticipated the scale or the ferocity of the planned attacks.

Since 199th LIB units experienced few contacts with enemy forces in their new AOs during the first two weeks of January, Brigadier General Forbes, decided that it was an opportune time to take his stateside leave. It was a leave well earned, for Forbes had been in Vietnam for a year and needed a rest. On 14 January 1968, Forbes departed for the States, leaving the 199th Deputy Commander, Colonel Fred Davison, in temporary command of the brigade. Forbes later wrote that he "left the brigade for home leave believing the enemy threat for the period of my absence to be minimal and in the complete confidence in the ability of the REDCATCHERS under

Colonel Davison to do a bangup job." His assessment of the enemy threat was dead wrong, but his confidence in Colonel Davison and the men of the brigade proved to be more than justified.

Colonel Fred Davison was well qualified to command an infantry brigade in combat. It was a leadership position that he spent his entire career preparing for. Frederick Davison was born in Washington DC in 1917, and graduated from Howard University in 1938, receiving an ROTC commission. Davison was called to active duty during World War II in 1941, and was assigned to the all-black 366th Infantry Regiment. The regiment deployed to Italy where it was attached to the 92d Infantry Division, the WWII "Buffalo Soldiers." Proving his mettle in the heavy fighting in the mountainous terrain of Italy, Davison was promoted to captain and took command of a rifle company of the 371st Infantry regiment, a position that he held until the end of the war. Afterward, Davison returned to civilian life for two years before receiving a regular Army commission in 1947. Although President Truman officially desegregated the Army in 1948, African-American officers of that era had to constantly struggle to overcome racial prejudice and bias. This did not deter Fred Davison. He continued to earn promotion and was selected to attend the Army's Command and General Staff College, and was later promoted to full colonel before attending the Army War College. It was no small accomplishment for an African-American officer to reach the rank of colonel in the Army of the 1960s.

When Davison arrived in Vietnam as a full Colonel in 1967, he hoped to command a brigade in one of the Army's combat divisions. Brigade command positions in the Army's divisions were full colonel billets. However, the bar was set high for these positions, and a black officer had never been assigned to command a brigade in combat. Instead, Davison was told that the 199th LIB needed a Deputy Commander, a position that was filled by a full colonel.

There was one hitch. The brigadier general commanding the 199th would have to accept him for the job. Brigadier General Forbes reviewed Davison's qualifications for the job and eagerly accepted him for the position. He later said it was one of the smartest personnel decisions he ever made. Though Davison would have to wait for his chance to command a combat brigade,. his chance would come.

Colonel Davison had a sixth sense that something was afoot in the 199th's AO during January 1968. It wasn't all based on a gut instinct. He was particularly attuned to the information gathered by the Brigade's reconnaissance and intelligence assets. Aerial reconnaissance was one source of battlefield intelligence. A Troop, 3rd Squadron, 17th Air Cavalry supported the 199th LIB with aerial sightings. This versatile outfit provided continuous aerial patrols of the brigade area of operations including the rocket belt. In addition to locating the enemy, the troop could engage the enemy with its light fire teams, and an aero-rifle platoon reaction force.

Davison also relied on Company F, 51st LRP, the II Field Force's long-range reconnaissance company, and the 199th's own 71st Infantry Detachment (LRRP) to monitor and report enemy activity. Each day and night, the LRPs, dubbed "the men with painted faces" by the Vietnamese, prowled jungles of AO s Uniontown and Columbus, shadowing the enemy units.

Along with the human intelligence gathering assets, the brigade also received information gathered by technical means. Helicopters equipped with electronic devices known as "people sniffers" flew daily missions of the brigade's AOs. The "people sniffer" was a 24-pound device that was mounted in the nose of UH-1 helicopters and other aircraft, and could locate enemy forces by picking-up the carbon dioxide and ammonia gases produced by human perspiration. Some 264 "hotspots" of probable enemy locations were detected by "people sniffer" missions during late January and early February 1968. Another source of operational intelligence was the 856th Radio Research Detachment. Only a few members of the brigade knew of the existence of this highly secretive unit.

The 856th was a 50-man unit working to support the 199th LIB and other US units through the collection, analysis, and dissemination of signal intelligence. This organization intercepted radio traffic of the North Vietnamese Army and Viet Cong. Part of the collection effort was Radio Direction Finding (DF). The DF effort was conducted by three PRD-1 teams. These two-man teams were forward deployed with US forces with their PRD-1 Direction Finding equipment. The PRD-1 was World War II vintage equipment with limited range. Typically, the DF teams would set up on a fire support base where they would set up their equipment and go about the business of scanning the airwaves for enemy transmitter sites and determining bearings to these sites. Once a site was identified, the team would report their results to other DF teams that would attempt to identify the same site. The information was also passed back to the 856th headquarters where the bearings from the field teams were plotted on a map. The idea was to gain a "tight fix" on the site using triangulation, or by identifying a small triangle encompassing a small area where the enemy transmitter was located. The information was then passed to the 199th Brigade's commander. The brigade commander could pursue several courses of action. He could order artillery or mortar fire on the target to attempt to destroy it, or he could employ his aviation fire support elements to neutralize the site. He could also direct that his ground forces attempt to locate the enemy site and destroy it, or attempt to capture it intact. In all cases time was of the essence since the enemy typically moved their transmitters on a routine basis after going on the air, and they rarely used the same site twice. Since the enemy knew that US forces were capable of locating their transmitters, they often remoted their radios and antennas to distances of a mile or more from their headquarters.

Specialist-five Dave Parks led one of the PRD-1 teams that supported the 199th LIB. Son of an Army command sergeant major, Parks joined the Army in 1965, opting for an enlistment in the Army Security Agency (ASA). After a tour with an ASA outfit in Okinawa, Parks volunteered for Vietnam where he was trained as a Direction Finding (DF) operator. Under the best of circumstances it was a tough and demanding job. With only two men on each team, the men worked continuous twelve-hour shifts under austere conditions on the firebases. On occasion, they also operated out of remote Special Forces camps and Vietnamese Popular Force (PF) compounds to get closer to the enemy units. The PRD teams were responsible for their own security when deployed and received little in the way of support from their host units.

When the 199th deployed into AO s Uniontown and Columbus, Dave Parks' team set up operations at Bien Hoa Airbase. The airbase was a high value strategic target for the enemy. It was the first and last stop for US troops entering and leaving Vietnam, and was one of the major fighter support bases in Vietnam. It was also located just a few kilometers from the southern portion of War Zone D and the "rocket belt."

Parks selected a site just off the end of one of the bases's main runways. The team lugged their PRD-1 to the top of a large sandpile. The site afforded good coverage of the surrounding area with line of sight all the way to the Song Be River and across it. Parks wrote, "We lugged that damned heavy PURD up the sand hill and installed it—leveled it, shot an azimuth and oriented it north-south, plotted our position on the map . . . and radioed that information to the detachment. We lugged up some water and c-rats, ammo and grenades and remote unit for our Jeep radio and went to work." Parks and his partner were surprised at the amount of enemy radio traffic around the base. Parks recalled, "We were supposed to work 12 (hours) on and 12 off, but in practice, 12 hours in the heat and dust was too much for anyone, so we set up our own schedule and worked two on and two off during the day and four on four off during the night." The VC/NVA usually used the early evening and night to communicate. Parks recalled that the enemy radio traffic continued to increase throughout the month of January, a strong indicator that the enemy was up to something.

While the 856th Radio Detachment provided signal intelligence to the 199th LIB, the 179th Military Intelligence (MI) Detachment provided all other intelligence. The MI Detachment had 38 men assigned. The detachment was broken down into five sections: Headquarters, Order of Battle, Prisoner of War Interrogation, Image Interpretation, and Counterintelligence. Colonel Davison relied heavily on the MI Detachment to pull together all the enemy information that was gathered from the field assets. He later credited the 199th LIB's success in countering the Tet attacks to the 179th MI Detachment. The 179th MI had many experienced personnel, some of whom had more than a year in-country. One such individual was Chief Warrant Officer Ken Welch.

Welch was the chief of the 179th MI Detachment's analysis section, and was well qualified for the job. Arriving in Vietnam in 1963 as a Specialist Fifth Class, Welch worked his way up through the intelligence ranks to Chief Warrant Officer by the time he was assigned to the 199th LIB in 1967. He knew the intelligence business, and had personal contacts in all the major US and Vietnamese military and civilian intelligence outfits in Vietnam. He later received a direct commission to second lieutenant and made captain before leaving country. Welch attributed his success to the many great people he had working for him, such as 26 year old John Durby. Durby held a PhD, and was a college professor before joining the Army and volunteering for duty in Vietnam. Welch and the brigade's personnel officer worked closely together to screen incoming replacements, selecting the "best and brightest" for Welch's analysis section.

Chief Warrant Officer Ken Welch and his section started to put the pieces of the puzzle together in mid-January. He noted that small groups of VC were detected moving with increasing frequency between War Zone D and the Bien Hoa and Long Binh areas. Welch thought that these were supply parties charged with the movement and positioning of weapons and ammunition in preparation for an attack. Additionally, Welch and other members of the 179th, including Warrant Officer James Creamer, were well aware that VC agents dressed as civilians were operating in the villages surrounding Long Binh. The Communist agents gathered information from Vietnamese civilians who worked on the US bases concerning their layout and defenses. Welch and Creamer were particularly concerned about enemy activity in Ho Nai village.

Ho Nai village sat astride Highway 1 just north of the main base camp of the 199th LIB. The village was eight kilometers east of Bien Hoa and six kilometers south of the Dong Nai River. Houses on the south side of the village were within pistol shot range of the base camp's outer perimeter. Many of the residents of the village were Catholic refugees who had fled North Vietnam when the country was divided. The Than Tam Refugee Hospital, and Da Minh Orphanage were located in Ho Nai Village, along with a thriving Catholic Church. The hospital was sponsored by the Order of St John of God in Montreal, Canada. This Roman Catholic order of nursing brothers had organized and partially staffed the hospital since its founding in 1952. A distinctive architectural feature of the hospital was a 50-foot tower that overlooked the village and the surrounding area. Medical personnel assigned to the 199th LIB provided technical assistance, supplies, and drugs to the hospital as part of the civic action program.

Many of the residents of Ho Nai were employed at the U.S. installations in and around Long Binh. Welch recruited Vietnamese agents who lived in the village to track VC activity in the area. One such agent was a young girl who worked as kitchen help in one of the brigade's mess halls. The girl was well connected, a niece of the mayor of Ho Nai, and a cousin of the commander of a VC reconnaissance unit. The cousin visited the village prior to Tet to warn family members to move out of the village before the end of the month. He even identified the 275th VC Regiment as the unit that would attack through the village to reach the 199th LIB base camp and other targets in the area. The girl reported this cousin's visit to Welch, who took the information seriously.

In addition to his agents, WO Welch relied on intelligence gathered by a Combined Reconnaissance Intelligence Platoon (CRIP). The platoon consisted of Vietnamese and US military personnel, and it conducted nightly roving patrols and ambushes to prevent VC infiltration of the village. The platoon, which rarely exceeded two dozen men, lived in the village and had numerous contacts among the villagers. The CRIP reported directly to WO Welch. Along with his agents, the CRIP was his eyes and ears in Ho Nai village.

Along with the collection of intelligence from its own assets, the MI detachment received intelligence from other in-country assets. From 15 through 25 January 1968, numerous reports were received that indicated units of the 5th VC Division as they moved out of War Zone D toward their Tet targets. By 27 January, the 5th VC Headquarters was located in eastern Uniontown, while the division artillery and supporting divisional units were confirmed to be in the central portion of AO Columbus. The division's assault regiments, the 274th and 275th VC Regiments, were also located in AO Columbus and Uniontown. The movement of these two regiments, numbering almost 3,000 men, gave a clear indication of an impending attack. Assisting the 274th and 275th Regiments was the U-1 Local Force Battalion. This battalion provided reconnaissance support, communication liaison, and guides to for the main force regiments as they infiltrated into the Bien Hoa and Long Binh areas. The 179th Order of Battle specialists were also trying to locate the 88th NVA Regiment, which was known to operate with the 5th VC Division. US intelligence units were not able to locate the 88th. An unaccounted for NVA Regiment of 1,500 hard-core regulars, weighed heavily on Colonel Davison's mind. He realized that his own brigade was opposed by a division-size force of three regiments.

Despite the large number of VC/NVA forces pouring into the 199th's AO s, enemy contacts with brigade forces were few and far between during early January 1968. In part, this was due to the size of the brigade's AO s. The Warrior battalion's area alone encompassed more than 130 square kilometers, a large area for a single infantry battalion to cover. To the east the 2/3d Infantry was responsible for AO Columbus, an area almost the size of Uniontown.   Some intelligence analysts thought that the 5th VC Division was located in the rugged jungle terrain in the northern portion of Columbus. US operations in this AO were limited because of a lack of artillery coverage. Much of the area was beyond the maximum range of the artillery located at FSB Concord. To remedy this situation, Colonel Davison ordered the establishment of a new fire support base, FSB Hotel. The location of the new FSB was eight kilometers to the northeast of FSB Concord, just east of Highway 24 that paralleled the Dong Nai River. Three 105mm howitzers from A Battery 2/40th Artillery, and two 8-inch self-propelled howitzers from II Field Force Artillery were moved to FSB Hotel. Security was provided by two platoons from Bravo Company, 4/12th, along with four ACAV from Delta Troop, 17th Cav. While the additional artillery coverage was needed, the establishment of another fire support base with the requisite security requirements, stretched the brigade's resources even further.

The 3/7th Infantry's AO Haverford, southwest of Saigon, was slightly smaller than AO Uniontown, but the terrain presented different challenges. Streams and canals flowed throughout the AO, slowing cross-country movement by ground troops. The enemy took full advantage of the waterways to move supplies and men toward Saigon. At night, sampans and other watercraft plied the waterways moving men and equipment from numerous small base camps and way stations toward the city.

During January 1968, there were six VC Local Force, District, and Provincial Force battalions operating in and around the 3/7th's AO

Haverford. From 15 January through 29 January, however, there were only three company-size contacts in the AO. Most contacts with VC elements were platoon-size or smaller. Attempts to bring on a major engagement with the enemy were unsuccessful. The VC commanders limited their operations to occasional mortar attacks on US and ARVN positions, and harassing attacks designed to draw attention away from the stealthy movement of Communist units infiltrating into Saigon.

The 4/12th Infantry was a battalion in transition during January of 1968. Three of four rifle company commanders were new. Captain Pete Albers took command of Alpha Company in mid-December. Captain Bob Tonsetic was even newer, having assumed command of Charlie Company at the beginning of January. The Warrior battalion's newest company commander was Captain Jim Dabney who assumed command of Delta Company in mid-January. Echo Company was redesignated as Delta Company shortly after Dabney assumed command, and a new Echo Company was formed as a heavy weapons company equipped with 4.2-inch mortars and 106mm recoilless rifles. A reconnaissance platoon was also formed as a part of Echo Company. In addition to the new line company commanders, there was a huge turnover in other officers and enlisted men in the battalion during the period December 1967 through January 1968.

Beginning in December 1967, many of the seasoned combat veterans of the brigade began to leave for home. These men were part of the original cohort that had arrived with the brigade in December 1966. Their 12-month tours were over. To offset the loss of combat experience, USARV directed the infusion (in-country reassignment) of soldiers from other units in Vietnam into the 199th LIB, but there was still a shortage of seasoned combat veterans in almost every rifle company. This personnel problem could not have come at a worse time. LTC Mastoris, the Warrior battalion commander, knew full well that his battalion, including himself, had a lot to learn. What he didn't know was the limited amount of time the battalion had to do it.

From mid to late January 1968, Lieutenant Colonel Mastoris deployed two companies, Alpha and Echo, in the "rocket belt" to disrupt 122mm rocket attacks on Bien Hoa and Long Binh. Contacts with enemy forces were few and far between. On 15 January, an Echo Company patrol encountered an enemy squad and killed three of the VC. Two US soldiers were wounded in the firefight. Then on 25 January, Alpha Company engaged two VC protecting a rest station. The two enemy soldiers fled the area with the Alpha Company grunts in pursuit. They followed the pair to a fortified position on a jungle covered hill mass just two kilometers north of the Dong Nai River. When the Alpha Company grunts assaulted the position they were met with a hail of small arms and RPG fire.

Fighting continued throughout the afternoon and early evening. The Charlie Battery howitzer crews firing from FSB Concord could clearly see their 105mm rounds slamming into the hilltop across the river. Fighting continued until nightfall when Mastoris ordered Alpha Company to withdraw to a more secure position. Alpha Company sustained four casualties, three men wounded and one KIA. The body of the US KIA was not recovered until the following day. It was found inside the labyrinth of tunnels that honeycombed the hilltop. It was difficult to identify the body after it arrived at the morgue, and Mastoris was shown the grim photographs. The corpse had been mutilated by the enemy before they withdrew.

Alpha and Echo Company continued to patrol the "rocket belt," reinforced on daylight operations by Charlie Company. Charlie Company was still charged with guarding FSB Concord, and was on 30-minute standby as the brigade ready reaction force, but Mastoris got permission for the company to conduct daylight sweeps of the "rocket belt." The company would airmobile assault into the area, search an assigned area, and then return to FSB Concord before nightfall. This was an excellent opportunity for the new commander to get a feel for the company.

The Warrior battalion was spread thin during the latter part of January. On 23 January, it was spread even thinner when the battalion was assigned the mission of securing the large Prisoner of War (POW) compound that was located between just off Highway 1 between Bien Hoa and Ho Nai village. Over 2,000 VC and NVA POWs were held at this facility. It was normally secured by ARVN troops, but the ARVN had a liberal leave period for the Tet national holiday, and asked for US troops to secure the facility. During daylight hours, defense forces consisted of five ACAVs from Delta Troop, 17th Cavalry, and the brigade security platoon. At night, however, the security was beefed up with a rifle platoon from the Warrior battalion's Charlie Company. Charlie was also tasked to send a rifle squad to secure an engineer dredge site on the Dong Nai River south of Bien Hoa, further dissipating the unit's combat power.

Despite the warning signs, the Army of the Republic of Vietnam continued to send its officers and men to their homes throughout the country on holiday leave, oblivious to the looming threat. Approximately fifty percent of the soldiers assigned to the 46 ARVN battalions in the III Corps area were on leave status by 29 January 1968. Regional and Popular Force units were similarly undermanned by the end of the month.

On 24 January, Colonel Davison ordered the commander of the Old Guard, 2/3d Infantry to terminate operations in AO Columbus and commence operations in AO Uniontown. LTC Carper, the Old Guard Commander, deployed two of his rifle companies on the border of Central Uniontown, and two companies south of Highway 1 in South Uniontown. Colonel Davision ordered this realignment of brigade forces to facilitate the defense of Long Binh. He was convinced that a major attack was only days away.

By late January, there were strong indications that attacks on the Bien Hoa and Long Binh areas were imminent. Ground surveillance radars at FSB Concord began to detect enemy movement through the valley to the east of the fire base. Each night, Charlie Company's 81mm mortar platoon located at FSB Concord fired dozens of rounds into the valley in attempts to interdict the enemy as they attempted to slip into the Bien Hoa area. Additionally, the number of sightings reported by the brigade's and II Field Force's LRPs were on the rise. When the sightings were plotted on operational maps, a disturbing pattern began to emerge. The sightings were steadily moving toward Long Binh. Consequently, Colonel Davison made the decision to deploy the LRPs closer to the city. The LRPs normally operated in remote areas forward of the areas patrolled by the brigade's infantry battalions, but with Davision's new order they patrolled the areas immediately surrounding the Long Binh base area. It was a gamble that paid off.

On 27 January, a LRP team ambushed an enemy reconnaissance team in a graveyard just north of Ho Nai village. Davison quickly ordered his ready reaction force, Charlie Company 4/12th, located at FSB Concord to reinforce the LRP team. The reaction force, consisting of two Charlie Company platoons mounted on ACAV from Delta, 17th Cav, and commanded by Captain Tonsetic, sped to the scene. A sweep of the area turned up a single enemy body. The dead VC was a lieutenant who had been leading a VC reconnaissance unit. He was armed with a US caliber .45 pistol, and carried a US lensatic compass and a pair of East German Zeiss binoculars. The incident took place less than two kilometers from the brigade's main base. After radioing in a report to brigade headquarters, Tonsetic's force was ordered to return to FSB Concord.

The following day, a patrol from Bravo Company of the Warrior battalion killed another enemy soldier armed with a pistol in AO Central Uniontown, and on 29 January, two members of a Local Force VC unit were captured in the same AO. Under interrogation, the POWs revealed that they were serving as guides for main force VC units that were moving toward their attack positions. LRPs and local agents continued to report numerous enemy units moving into AO CENTAL Uniontown over the next two days. Intelligence analysts continued to put the pieces of the puzzle together. The question was not "if" the enemy was going to attack, but "when and where."

On the afternoon of 29 January, The 199th LIB communication center received a "flash" II Field Force message warning of "positive intelligence indicators that the enemy will deliberately violate the truce by attacking friendly installations during the night of 29 Jan. or the early morning hours of 30 Jan." The addressees were instructed to take action to insure maximum alert posture through the Tet period.

When the alert went out, the 199th LIB was in a defensive posture, but the infantrymen were spread thin across its assigned AOs. Colonel Davison knew he had to have early warning of any attack in order to concentrate his forces to counter the threat. The LRPs were key to an early warning. After the II Field Force message was received, Colonel Davison met with Major Maus, commander of F/71st LRPs. Davison was concerned that the area to the north of Ho Nai village was not under surveillance by the LRPs. Maus had five LRP teams deployed in

AO Uniontown and Columbus. Deployment of a sixth team would limit his ability to reinforce any team that got into trouble. Davison was adamant to the point of ordering the Major to do it. The LRP Commander was not happy, but knew he had to comply. He was a good soldier. The two looked at the map, and Davison pointed to a road that ran directly north out of the center of Ho Nai village toward the Dong Nai River. The unpaved road had a gravel base, and had been constructed by US Army engineers some months earlier. Colonel Davison recognized that the road was seldom used after the hours of darkness, and had the potential to be a high-speed avenue of approach for enemy infantry right into the heart of Ho Nai village. Davison wanted a LRP team deployed north of the village in a position where they could observe the road. It was a prescient decision.

During the early morning hours of 30 January, a second II Field Force "flash" message announced that the Tet Truce was terminated, and instructed all units to resume normal operations. Word of the Tet Truce cancellation was passed down the chain from brigade to battalion to the rifle companies. Warnings of imminent attacks and possible attacks were not unusual and were taken in stride by the line units. Combat battalions resumed their operations, unaware of all the intelligence behind this warning. Meanwhile, every intelligence unit in Vietnam was humming with the knowledge that the level of enemy activity had reached unprecedented proportions.

The morning and afternoon of 30 January were quiet in the Warrior battalion's AO. Alpha and Echo Companies resumed their patrolling operations in the "rocket belt," while Bravo Company patrolled around FSB Hotel in AO Central Uniontown. Charlie Company worked to improve the bunkers on the FSB Concord perimeter.

Charlie Company's 1st Platoon, led by newcomer 2nd Lieutenant Howard Tuber, departed around midday for their security mission at the POW compound. Charlie Company's 2nd Platoon, under 2nd Lieutenant Al Lenhardt, prepared for their night ambush patrol. The ambush site selected by the Warrior battalion commander, LTC Mastoris, was in the valley just east of the firebase. Neither Captain Tonsetic nor his First Sergeant, George Holmes, were particularly concerned that the truce had been cancelled, but the two decided not to authorize any of the troops to leave the firebase to visit Bien Hoa that afternoon. For the past few days, Holmes had appointed an NCO to take a 2-1/2-ton truck load of troops into Bien Hoa for a few hours relaxation at the local bars

Captain Tonsetic and his 81mm mortar platoon leader, Lieutenant Paul Viola, conferred on the defensive fires concentrations (DEFCONS) around the fire base perimeter, and pre-planned 81mm mortar fires for the 2nd Platoon ambush site. The two also conferred on the Company's Ready Reaction Force mission. Options were limited on which platoons would deploy on such a mission, since 1st Platoon was at the POW compound, and 2nd Platoon had an ambush mission. If brigade called for Charlie Company to deploy, it would be the company headquarters, 3rd Platoon, and part of the 4th (mortar) Platoon. Tonsetic instructed Viola to leave a minimum of two crewmen on each of the platoon's three 81mm mortars, and to man the fire direction center with two men only. The remainder of the platoon would deploy as a rifle platoon with the Ready Reaction Force, leaving the 81mm mortars behind at FSB Concord.

After conferring with Viola, Tonsetic visited his 3rd Platoon. The platoon's leader, Lieutenant Bob Stanley, was on R&R, so Captain Tonsetic spoke with the platoon sergeant, Orville Wyers. Wyers asked who would take over the 3rd Platoon's portion of the fire base perimeter if the company was called out on the Ready Reaction Force Mission. "That's battalion's problem, probably the clerks, cooks, drivers and other headquarters personnel," Tonsetic replied.

While the Warrior battalion resumed normal daylight operations, Specialist Dave Parks and his partner worked atop their sandpile off the Bien Hoa runway. They tried to rig a poncho to shade themselves from the brutally hot sun as they manned their DF equipment, trying to intercept enemy radio transmissions and identify DF targets. The wind took the poncho and blew it toward the bunker line. According to Parks, "The eve of Tet was . . . nothing special beyond working on the PRD-1, flash reports to the 856th, other DF sites for bearings, drinking gallons of water and sweating it out, munching Cs, while sweat ran out from under the hot headsets attached to the DF unit."

But he remembered that throughout the afternoon the enemy radio traffic was "perhaps a little less than normal." Not enough to alarm the operators, however. The PRD team anticipated another quiet night.

At dusk on 30 January, all remained quiet at FSB Concord. Captain Tonsetic walked the firebase checking light discipline. He'd had his "ass chewed" several times by the battalion S3, Major Ed King, who had spotted lanterns and generator-powered light sets illuminating bunkers and tents on the base. Most of the violators were battalion headquarters troops, or the artillerymen. Concord sat on a bare hilltop, and even a lit cigarette could be spotted from miles away. The enemy knew the precise coordinates of the firebase, but the lights made nice aiming points for rockets, mortars, and RPGs.

As he walked the perimeter, Tonsetic stopped to observe Charlie Company's 2nd Platoon ambush patrol slipping silently through the coils of razor sharp concertina and barbed wire that ringed the base, headed for their ambush site. He observed that the men wore blackened face camouflage and soft jungle hats as opposed to their steel helmets. All loose equipment was tied down on their bodies to prevent it being snagged on bushes and other vegetation. These were precautions that he'd stressed with his platoon leaders. After, the last man in the patrol was out of sight entering the surrounding jungle, Tonsetic returned to his CP, where he stretched out for a nap. He hoped to get a couple of hours sleep in case the company was called out on a reaction force mission. He didn't have long to wait.

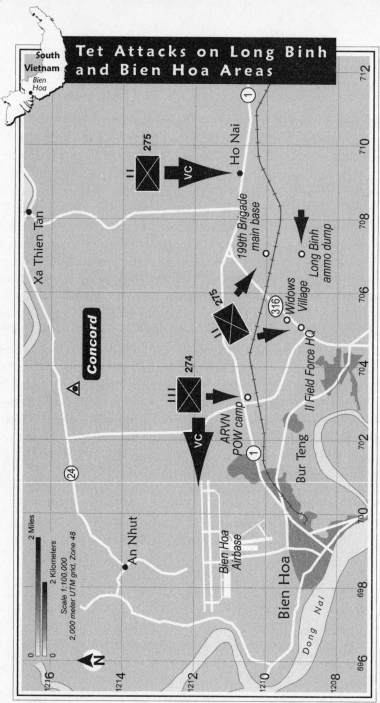

Tet Attacks on Long Binh and Bien Hoa Areas

South Vietnam

Bien Hoa

275 VC

Ho Nai

1

Xa Thien Tan

199th Brigade main base

Long Binh ammo dump

275

Widows Village

316

Concord

II Field Force HQ

274

ARVN POW camp

Bur Teng

VC

1

An Nhut

Bien Hoa Airbase

Bien Hoa

Dong Nai

24

2 Miles

2 Kilometers

Scale 1:100,000
2,000 meter UTM grid, Zone 48

N

712
710
708
706
704
702
700
698
696

1216
1214
1212
1210
1208

Cartography by Michael Podolny

CHAPTER 7

A BATTLE JOINED

The Vietnamese national holiday called Tet, celebrating the lunar new year, was to have been a brief period of truce. Just as Christmas 1967 saw a cessation of hostilities on behalf of the Christians, primarily American, 1968's Tet was to have been a brief interlude in the war on behalf of the Vietnamese. Instead the Communists scheduled their greatest offensive of the war on the holiday, correctly assuming that many opposing units, particularly ARVN, would be caught off guard. The Tet Offensive of 1968 became one of the greatest battles in history. The 199th Light Infantry Brigade was engaged with all units and at all points in the immediate environs of Saigon.

Bien Hoa Airbase—2300 Hours, 30 January 1968

Specialist Dave Parks was puzzled when around 2300 hours on 30 January, enemy radio traffic "petered out to nothing, nothing at all." Parks further recalled that "This was surprising, very unusual, I'd never heard nothing before. . . .We switched off, taking turns on the knobs, that is, turning the frequency knob while straining to hear an enemy radio. Neither of us were able to bring one up—the whole NVA-VC radio world had gone silent." Parks got on his radio and contacted his teammates at other sites who reported the same anomaly. Then he radioed the 856th Detachment's duty officer at Long Binh. The duty officer confirmed what Parks was thinking. The enemy had gone to radio silence everywhere. To signal intelligence analysts this meant one thing: a major attack was about to begin.

111

AO North Uniontown, "The Rocket Belt"—2300 to 0300 Hours

At 2310 hours, Charlie Battery, 2/40th Artillery fired on a suspected enemy rocket site three kilometers north of the Dong Nai River. A platoon-size patrol from the Warrior battalion's Delta Company patrolling in the same area observed the artillery fire and reported a large secondary explosion. After requesting a C-47 Spooky flareship for illumination and fire support, Captain Dabney, the new Delta CO, ordered the patrol to search the area.

Captain Jim Dabney was still getting a feel for his company. He was a career officer who first joined the Army at age 17 as an enlisted man. He made Sergeant on his first hitch, and was leading a squad in the 101st Airborne Division before his 20th birthday. Shortly thereafter, he was selected to attend Officer Candidate School. Upon graduation, Second Lieutenant Dabney was assigned to Panama, where he honed his jungle warfare skills. After his tour in Panama, Dabney was promoted to Captain and reassigned to Vietnam. He was assigned to the 9th Infantry Division where he commanded a company until he took an AK round through his lower leg. Brigadier General Forbes was assistant commander of the 9th Infantry Division at that time. When Forbes took command of the 199th LIB, he had Dabney, who had recovered from his wound, reassigned to the 199th. Captain Dabney was subsequently assigned to command Delta Company of the Warrior battalion. Forbes knew a good company commander when he saw one.

Delta's patrol moved cautiously, stopping every few meters to listen and observe. Spooky orbited overhead and began to drop flares. The flares suspended from tiny parachutes floated slowly downward, casting long shadows on the ground below. As the patrol moved closer to the scene of the explosion, the patrol leader, Lieutenant Wayne Smith, reported hearing voices chattering excitedly in Vietnamese. Smith radioed his company commander and reported that the enemy force probably numbered in the hundreds. He then called in an artillery fire mission, and Captain Dabney ordered his 3rd and 4th platoons to reinforce the patrol. The Captain decided to accompany the reinforcing platoons with his CP group. Dabney considered Smith, a lanky Texan, his best platoon leader , who would not exaggerate the size of an enemy force. As the reinforcements moved to link up with the 2nd Platoon patrol, the flare ship was diverted to another mission. Dabney requested a helicopter gunship team to for aerial fire support.

After linking up with the 2nd Platoon patrol, Dabney ordered his platoons to form a defensive perimeter in an area that close enough to observe the artillery strikes. At 0250 hours, all artillery fire ceased. A "checkfire" was called on all artillery firing north of the Bien Hoa air corridor. The checkfire could not have been called at a worse time. The enemy rocket artillery crews rushed to load their launchers with 122mm warheads. Unaware that Delta Company was less than a kilometer away, the enemy rocket artillerymen made no effort at noise control. Delta Company estimated that a force of about 200 to 300 enemy including a security force were preparing multiple firing sites and fighting positions. Captain Dabney later recalled that he considered launching a ground attack, but after weighing the odds he decided to wait for some heavy fire support.

Ho Nai Village—2300 Hours, 30 January

Twelve members of the brigade's Combined Reconnaissance/ Intelligence Platoon (CRIP) were on stake-out in the village's Catholic orphanage. Earlier in the day, the team had heard rumors circulating among the villagers that there were small numbers of VC hiding in the village. Warrant Officer Ken Welch of the 179th MI Detachment drove into Ho Nai village around 2300 hours to get the latest information from members of the CRIP. Welch recalled that the village was eerily silent when he drove up to the orphanage. Too quiet for a national holiday, he thought. After getting the latest information from the CRIP leader, Welch hopped in his jeep and instructed his driver to "haul ass" back to the base. He was convinced that an attack on the 199th LIB's base camp, Camp Frenzell-Jones was just hours away. As the two Americans drove the village's darkened streets, they heard the familiar sound of the bolts of AK-47 rifles jacking rounds into the firing chambers. After returning to the base camp, Welch went straight to the Brigade TOC to brief Colonel Davison on the latest information. He told Davison that the attacks would be launched before dawn. He wasn't wrong.

North of Ho Nai Village—0100 Hours, 31 January

Two kilometers north of Ho Nai village, Specialist Vincent's six-man LRP team lay hidden in the brush as a long column of enemy troops moved quickly through the darkness past their position. The enemy troops were moving along the engineer road that led south from the Dong Nai River straight towards Ho Nai village. The LRPs stopped counting after 80 VC passed their hiding place. There were just too many more to count. The VC were armed with assault rifles, heavy and light machine guns, shoulder -fired rocket launchers, and 61mm mortars. Shaken by the numbers of enemy troops in their immediate vicinity, the LRPs hunkered down lower in the grass. Vincent whispered into his radio handset to report the sighting to the 71st LRP TOC. LTC Maus, the F Company CO, listened carefully to the report and ordered his team leader to sit tight. Realizing that the team might be discovered at any moment, Maus grabbed his S3, Captain Randall, and the pair ran to the helipad and climbed aboard the Huey that was on strip alert. It was around 0130 hours, when the UH-1 lifted off the pad. Maus knew his team was in imminent danger, and he wanted to extract them from the area.

Fire Support Base Concord—0115–0145 Hours, 31 January

Captain Tonsetic dozed on his air mattress in the Charlie Company CP. He'd grown used to the nightly H&I fires of Charlie Battery's 105mm howitzers, and the rushing sound of the CP's radios. Specialist Cliff Kaylor, the company's senior RTO, was on radio watch. First Sergeant George Holmes, the commo chief, Larry Abel, and Bob Archibald, who carried the company's second PRC-25 radio, were also asleep in the CP. At 0115 hours, a runner from the battalion's TOC arrived at the Charlie Company CP to inform Captain Tonsetic that his unit was on alert for deployment as the brigade's ready reaction force. Colonel Davison, the brigade commander, wanted Captain Tonsetic's men to move to intercept the VC unit that was moving toward Ho Nai village.

Tonsetic's Ready Reaction Force consisted of two platoons from Charlie Company and seven ACAV from 1st Platoon, Delta Troop

17th Cavalry, reinforced with one 106mm recoilless rifle track. Captain Tonsetic was skeptical of the LRPs' report of 80 VC. The number seemed too large. He was unaware of the latest intelligence that was pouring into the brigade headquarters.

Checking the LRPs' position on his map, the Charlie Company CO recognized the area. It was close to where his unit had deployed on 27 January after the LRPs had ambushed a VC reconnaissance unit. Captain Tonsetic began to take the LRPs' latest sighting more seriously. There was no doubt in his mind that there was a connection between the two sightings.

FSB Concord was a beehive of activity. Bleary-eyed battalion headquarters troops, rousted from their bunkers on the inner perimeter, grabbed their M16s and bandoliers of ammunition, and rushed toward fighting positions along the base's outer perimeter. Meanwhile, Charlie Company soldiers assembled in full combat gear near the ACAVs that were lining up in column formation. As the grunts grabbed extra hand grenades, Claymore mines, and bandoliers of ammunition from open boxes strewn on the ground near the tracks, First Sergeant Holmes got a quick head-count from Platoon Sergeants Wyers and Jaynes. Holmes had to shout over the noise of the ACAVs' engines to make himself heard. Captain Tonsetic arrived with his two radio operators after conferring with the Warrior battalion commander, LTC Mastoris. Holmes informed his CO that the combined strength of the two Charlie Company platoons was 38 men. Half of the 4th Platoon had to remain on the firebase to man the platoon's 81mm mortars.

The Charlie Company CO gave the word for his men to board the ACAVs. The infantrymen scrambled on the crowded ACAV decks, trying to find a few inches of space. With the extra men, rucksacks, and weapons aboard, space was at a premium. The ACAV crew members who manned each vehicle's two M60 machineguns and the track commander's cupola-mounted .50 caliber machine gun advised the grunts not to block their fields of fire. Once his men were loaded, Captain Tonsetic climbed aboard the lead ACAV, and the track commander tossed him a headset so the two could communicate over the vehicle's intercom system. Donning the headset, the Captain ordered the column to move out. The column of eight ACAVs moved south from FSB

Concord leaving a cloud of dust along the trail. Tonsetic looked at the luminous dial on his wristwatch. It was 0145 hours, 31 January.

Camp Frenzell-Jones (199th LIB Main Base Camp)—0200 Hours

While the brigade's ready reaction force sped toward their first checkpoint, the 199th TOC at the brigade's main base was at full alert status. Senior staff officers, including Lieutenant Colonel Ken Hall, the Brigade S3, along with the other primary staff officers began to arrive. Duty officers and NCOs were monitoring the radios and plotting friendly and enemy locations with black and red grease pencils on acetate covered maps mounted on the walls of the TOC. A US Air Force liaison officer hovered over his radio talking to a Forward Air Controller (FAC) who sat in his OV-10, on "strip alert" at Bien Hoa Airbase. Colonel Davison was huddled with his S3, LTC Hall, at a small desk in the corner of the TOC, when WO Ken Welch of the 179th MI Detachment approached. He had some alarming new intelligence. He told Davison that a reliable source had reported there were 17 enemy battalions moving on Saigon. According to Welch, Davison calmly responded. "Good! For the first time in the entire war, I know right where the enemy is!"

The scene outside the large bunker that housed the brigade's TOC resembled a large anthill that had been poked with a stick. Rear echelon soldiers were rushing from their barracks toward their company arms rooms to draw weapons and ammunition. Most of the troops were members of the 7th Support Battalion, who in accordance with the base defense plan were to man the perimeter bunkers in the event of an attack. The men were a mixture of cooks, mechanics, clerks, drivers, and a host of other military specialists. Few of the support troops had fired their weapons since they zeroed them after they arrived in-country. Those support troops not assigned to the perimeter bunkers were organized into a provisional rifle company. This company was to act as a reaction force to reinforce the more than two-mile long perimeter and counterattack any enemy that managed to penetrate the wire barriers around the camp.

Backing up the support troops were three 105mm howitzers from 2/40th Artillery. Contingency firing positions for the howitzers were located at various points around the base perimeter. The defense plan called for the howitzers to displace to those positions during attacks to place direct fire on assaulting enemy troops. The artillerymen were prepared to fire high explosive rounds or "bee hive" rounds to break up the enemy's ground attacks.

Although Camp Frenzell-Jones had come under mortar and rocket attack on several occasions, a full-scale ground attack had never been launched against the brigade's main base camp. Its defense plan looked good on paper, but it had never before been put to the test.

Bien Hoa Airbase, Long Binh—0300 Hours, 31 January

Precisely at 0300 hours, a battalion of the 5th VC Division's 84th Rocket Artillery launched a salvo of 122mm rockets from several firing sites north of the Dong Nai River and from AO Manchester. As each rocket blasted from its launcher, it left a fiery vapor trail as it arched upward to its apogee in the pitch-black sky, then plunged downward like a burning comet as it shrieked toward its target.

This first salvo, an estimated forty-five rockets, were aimed at targets on Bien Hoa Air Base. These targets included the base control tower, barracks, warehouses, parking ramps, and POL storage tanks. At least one of the high explosive warheads struck a POL storage tank, setting off huge explosions that sent shock waves throughout the base and surrounding area. Flames and thick black smoke from the burning fuel could be seen from miles away. The base control tower, several barracks and warehouses, and a number of vehicles were also damaged or destroyed. Additionally, there was significant damage to aircraft on the parking ramps. An F-100 SuperSaber and a Vietnamese Air Force Skyraider were set ablaze. Three airmen were killed and sixteen more were wounded in the rocket attack on Bien Hoa Airbase.

Specialist Dave Parks and his teammate, Specialist Anderson, returned to their sleeping quarters shortly after midnight after the enemy went to radio silence. Parks recalled that he was awakened at 0300 hours by the exploding 122mm rockets. He wrote, "122mm rockets were walking toward our area. I leaped out of my top bunk and grabbed my M79, as I began running for a bunker. . . . The rockets walked over us and then came back. One impacted a barracks nearby—blew it down to matchsticks, all I saw was the flash and roar of it."

After the rocket attack, Parks and Anderson jumped in their jeep and drove to their PURD site. They were stopped by an Air Police patrol and warned that sappers had entered the base under cover of the rocket attack. The pair made it back to their DF monitoring site at the end of the runway, brought their equipment up, and began to scan the airways. From atop their sandpile, they could see a firefight at the other end of the runway. Parks noted that the enemy had switched from using Morse Code on their radios to voice transmissions—a sure sign that they were on the move and launching a ground attack.

Minutes after the rocket attack on Bien Hoa airbase, another indirect fire attack was launched against the US base complex at Long Binh. Camp Frenzell-Jones (199th LIB) and the Plantation (Headquarters II Field Force) received an estimated 90–100 rounds of mixed 82mm mortar rounds and 122mm rocket fire. The barrage resulted in few US casualties since most of the defenders were already in their assigned bunkers. Material damage to the US base complex was also minimal.

AO Uniontown, "The Rocket Belt"—0300 Hours

Captain Dabney's Delta Company was located less than 300 meters away from one of the 122mm rocket launch sites when seven rockets aimed at Bien Hoa airbase were fired. Dabney recalled that the rocket launches reminded him of "the grand finale of a 4th of July fireworks display." The Captain's FO immediately called for artillery counter-battery fires. It was a race against time, as the enemy artillerymen rushed to reload their launchers for a second salvo. Charlie Battery's howitzer crews at FSB Concord responded quickly, putting five HE rounds in the air. Then they reloaded and fired again. The enemy artillerymen who were still reloading and aiming their launchers were torn to pieces as Charlie Battery's rounds found their target.

A USAF Forward Air Controller at Bien Hoa airbase took off seconds after the first 122mm rockets impacted on the base. The FAC flew north over the Dong Nai River searching for the rocket launch sites. It didn't take long for him to find his targets. Two fully armed strike aircraft, F-100s on strip alert at Bien Hoa, roared down the runway past the burning VNAF and US aircraft . Both pilots banked to the right on a northerly heading as the burning fuel tanks on the base illuminated the night sky. At 0350 hours, the FAC marked his target with rockets, and the jets swooped down on the enemy firing sites, dropping napalm and finishing up with 20mm cannon fire. The air strikes continued throughout the night as more launch sites were located. The enemy's 84th Artillery Battalion was all but destroyed during the ensuing air and artillery strikes. Consequently, the 5th VC Division's ground attacks on the US bases at Long Binh and Bien Hoa were conducted without additional rocket artillery support.

Highway 1 between Bien Hoa & Long Binh—0300–0325 Hours

Captain Tonsetic's force halted at a road junction on Highway 1, three kilometers east of Bien Hoa. LTC Mastoris ordered the halt, anticipating a possible change of mission from brigade. The ARVN POW Compound was located one kilometer to the east. Tonsetic ordered his two infantry platoons to dismount the tracks and set up a perimeter around the vehicles. Except for the idling engines of the tracked vehicles, the night was eerily silent. A stand of rubber trees stretched toward the east on the northern side of the highway. Shortly after the Charlie Company grunts took up their positions, the first salvo of 122mm rockets streaked across the night sky toward Bien Hoa Airbase just three kilometers to the west. The explosions and fiery flames from the burning fuel storage tanks then illuminated the night sky in that direction. Captain Tonsetic radioed the Warrior TOC and requested instructions. LTC Mastoris informed him that the original mission to link up with the LRPs had been put on temporary hold by brigade. Mastoris then told Tonsetic to move east on Highway 1 to the ARVN POW Compound, where he was to await further instructions.

Captain Tonsetic ordered his men to mount up and the column of ACAVs rolled eastward toward the POW Compound, arriving at 0320 hours. The Captain radioed for his 1st Platoon leader, 2nd Lieutenant Howard Tuber, to meet him at the front gate of the compound. The lieutenant, who had only been in Vietnam for two weeks and had never been under fire, assumed that he was being reinforced. His small force was stretched thin. More than 2,000 enemy POWS were confined within the compound, and all but a few members of the ARVN MP guard force were on Tet holiday leave. The barbed wire fences and guard towers that surrounded the facility were meant to keep the POWs from escaping, not to withstand a ground attack.

One of the Vietnamese MP sergeants who remained on duty informed Lieutenant Tuber that there were explosives buried beneath the POW Quonset hut barracks, and that he was under orders to "blow the whole damn place up" rather than let the prisoners escape. The ARVN sergeant refused to tell Tuber where he had hidden the electronic firing devices. The lieutenant was worried that his men might be blown up as well.

Captain Tonsetic informed Lieutenant Tuber that the ready reaction force was, as far as he knew, on its way to link up with a LRP team north of Ho Nai village. The stop at the POW compound was only temporary. Lieutenant Tuber's platoon and the attached Cav platoon would have to defend the POW Compound on their own. While the two were conferring, the Captain's RTO took a message for the Ready Reaction Force to move out immediately for Ho Nai village. Tonsetic bid the lieutenant farewell, warning him to stay alert. "If you get hit, it will probably come from the rubber across the road." The rubber trees on the south side of the highway had been cleared by giant Rome plows, but the trees still grew north of the road. Tonsetic gave the word, and the Charlie Company reaction force sped away into the darkness en route to Ho Nai village.

Camp Frenzell-Jones—0330 Hours

As the Charlie Company reaction force rolled eastward on Highway 1 headed for Ho Nai village, several mortar rounds impacted along the road that paralleled the northwest side of the base camp perimeter. The enemy mortar rounds fell short of their target, the brigade helipad. Simultaneously, helicopter crews, aviation mechanics, and a "People Sniffer" team from the 503d Chemical Detachment were pinned down in their bunkers by incoming small-arms fire. Colonel Davison ordered the 7th Support Battalion's reaction force to reinforce the helipad. The brigade's four UH-1Ds sitting on the helipad were the brigade's only organic aviation assets. Davison wanted to go airborne to direct the battle as soon as possible, and did not want his helicopters destroyed on the ground.

Moments later, the northern perimeter of the base began receiving small arms fire from houses on the northern edge of Ho Nai village. The brigade troops manning the perimeter bunkers opened fire with small arms and machine guns, temporarily silencing the enemy fire. The enemy fire had been premature. The VC battalion tasked to assault the base's northern perimeter was still moving toward its attack positions.

A sketch map removed from the body of a VC after the battle, plus information received from prisoners, revealed the enemy plan of attack. One battalion of the 275th Regiment was to launch a frontal assault against the base, attacking through Ho Nai village to overrun the base's northern perimeter. While that assault was underway, a second battalion of the 275th VC Regiment would attack Camp Frenzell-Jones from the southeast. During this attack, a sapper unit was to infiltrate and destroy the large Long Binh Ammunition Depot with explosives and rocket fire. Simultaneously, a third battalion of the 275th would attack the PLANTATION (II Field Force Headquarters and 12th Aviation Group), just down the road from Camp Frenzell-Jones. That battalion was in an attack position in Widows Village located directly west of Highway 316 from the PLANTATION complex. The 275th Regimental machine gun company was to support the attacks against the aviation unit helipads to destroy the helicopters on the ground before they could take off to provide crucial fire support to US ground forces. Heavy enemy rocket and mortar fires were planned to support the ground attacks. It was a bold plan that was heavily dependent on surprise, timing, and coordination. The plan was a good one, but in war things seldom go as planned.

North of Ho Nai Village—0230–0300 Hours

The VC battalion assigned the mission of attacking Camp Frenzell-Jones from the north moved into its final attack positions near Ho Nai Village. The lead elements of the battalion began to close on the area around 0230 hours after completing a 12-kilometer forced night march. The march had not gone well. Subordinate units had become separated. Some got lost, while others continued to arrive piecemeal throughout the early morning hours. Upon arrival, the enemy troops began to prepare for their upcoming assault. The attack was scheduled to begin after the heavy rocket attack on Camp Frenzell-Jones scheduled for 0300 hours. While they waited for the rocket attack to begin, scouts were sent into Ho Nai village to make contact with infiltrators already in place in the village. Meanwhile, the enemy assault troops began to dig positions for their heavy weapons. A 12.75mm machine gun was sighted on the road that led south into the village, while two additional heavy machine-gun teams were sent into the village to establish an anti-aircraft position in the 50 foot tower that was part of the village hospital. The battalion's 61mm mortars were set up in a cemetery just north of the village to support the ground attack.

The 122mm rocket attack on Camp Frenzell-Jones began on schedule at 0300 hours. The VC battalion commander heard the explosions, but did not at once launch the ground attack. He was waiting for more of his troops to arrive, and a second barrage of rockets. The battalion waited in positions just north of a small creek bed that ran perpendicular to the road that led south to the village. A trickle of a stream ran through a culvert on the west side of the road emerging on the other side. South of the culvert the road sloped upward as it ran into the edge of the village. A few houses were situated along the road. The houses were unoccupied. The residents had fled to the sanctuary of the village's Catholic Church when they heard the VC battalion had arrived.

Ho Nai Village—0345–0415 Hours

The Charlie Company ready reaction force rumbled east on Highway 1, through the center of Ho Nai village. Captain Tonsetic ordered the ACAVs to a halt at the intersection of Highway 1 and an engineer road that led north toward the Dong Nai River. The infantrymen dismounted the tracks and set up a security screen around the ACAVs. The night was eerily silent in the village as Tonsetic conferred with his platoon sergeants and the Armored Cav platoon leader.

The Charlie Company CO outlined his plan to move north to link up with LRP team 37. Platoon Sergeant Wyer's 3rd Platoon was to move north on the west side of the road, while Platoon Sergeant Jaynes, leading the fourth platoon, would advance on the east side of the road. The eight ACAVs from Delta Troop would move north along the road staying slightly behind the advancing infantry on their flanks. Tonsetic and his CP group would follow Wyer's 3rd Platoon on the west side of the road.

The Captain was preparing to give the order to his men to move out when he noticed that one of his two radio operators was walking with a bad limp. Specialist Bob Archibald had injured his ankle when he jumped off the side of the ACAV with his rucksack and PRC-25 radio strapped to his back. The Captain told his commo sergeant, Larry Abel, to find another soldier to carry the radio. Archibald was surprised that he only received a scowl from his boss rather than an "ass chewing." Of his former CO, Bob Archibald later wrote, "He was incredibly serious virtually all the time. Heaven help the subordinate, who appeared to make a mistake." Relieved of the extra weight on his back, Archibald picked up his M16 rifle and limped along behind the CP group as the company cautiously headed north out of the village.

As the 3rd and 4th platoons moved slowly on the flanks, the ACAV's inched forward down the road about 50 meters behind the ground troops. The ACAVs were using blackout drive, but the noise of their 209 horsepower Chrysler engines alerted the enemy troops a few hundred meters up the road. The commander of the VC battalion ordered two RPG teams to move forward across the culvert to take up positions in a house on the east side of the road. He also ordered a 12.75 machine-gun team supported by a platoon-size force of infantry forward to a position on the west side of the road. It was a last-ditch effort to ambush the advancing US force.

The PLANTATION (II Field Force HQ)—0300–0330 Hours

An estimated nine rockets slammed into or near the compound that housed Lieutenant General Weyand's II Field Force Headquarters. The barrage lasted about ten minutes and resulted in minimal damage. Counter-battery artillery fires and gunships located most of the firing sites in AOs North Uniontown and Columbus after the first volley, and destroyed the rocket firing batteries before they could launch another salvo. Fortunately, Weyand's above-ground TOC was not hit. The TOC was located in a steel World War II-type Quonset hut that offered only minimal protection from shrapnel and small-arms fire. A direct hit would have destroyed it along with the General and most of his staff.

About twenty minutes later, the II Field Force came under machine-gun and small-arms fire from Widows Village directly across Highway 316 from the headquarters. The village housed a number of widows and children of ARVN soldiers who had found employment on the nearby US bases, and provided laundry services for the US soldiers stationed at those bases. The VC had slipped into the sleeping village several hours earlier, digging positions among the rows of shanties that faced the highway.

MPs guarding II Field Force Headquarters returned fire from their M60 machine-gun jeeps. Concerned about a ground attack, the II Field Force Commander ordered Lieutenant Colonel John Tower's 2/47th mechanized infantry battalion of the US 9th Infantry Division to move to the Long Binh area. The battalion was in a night laager position off Highway 15 southeast of Long Binh. The mechanized infantrymen quicky rolled up their defensive wire, mounted their M113 personnel carriers, and rumbled down Highway 15 toward Long Binh, ready for a fight.

Long Binh Ammunition Depot—0300–0330 Hours

The huge Long Binh Ammunition Depot was located 1,500 meters south of Ho Nai village, and 1,000 meters southeast of the II Field Force Headquarters. The depot had one hundred ammo bunkers containing all types of Army and Air Force munitions. The 12-kilometer perimeter of the facility was protected by barbed wire fences and a series of observation towers The depot was run by the Army's 3d Ordnance Battalion. From 0300 to 0330 hours, the enemy fired an undetermined number of mortar and RPG rounds into the northeast sector of the perimeter in the vicinity of Tower 13. When the fires were lifted, the U1 Local Forces Battalion launched a ground attack. Using bangalore torpedoes to blast their way through the defensive barbed wire, the VC penetrated the outer defenses of the facility. While the enemy ground troops battled the Ordnance troops and MPs, enemy sapper teams headed for the ammunition bunkers and pads to rig them with explosives. Three MP s were killed and several more were wounded in the fighting. The Ordnance battalion radioed II Field Force Headquarters requesting reinforcements. Bravo Company, 2/47th Infantry, minus one platoon, was ordered to move to the ammo depot at all possible speed and secure it.

ARVN POW Compound—0410–0430 Hours

At 0410 hours, Lieutenant Tuber's reinforced platoon at the ARVN POW compound received 30 to 40 rounds of small-arms fire. Tuber's grunts fired handheld flares to illuminate the area across the road from the compound. As the parachute flares drifted over the rows of rubber trees, Tuber's men spotted a number of figures running through the shadows carrying individual and crew-served weapons. Lieutenant Tuber radioed the Warrior TOC and requested a helicopter gunship team to provide suppressive fires.

The gunship team arrived ten minutes later and saturated the area with its machine guns, temporarily suppressing the enemy fire. The ACAV platoon at the compound shifted their firing positions to defend against a frontal assault on the main gate. Two ACAVs were positioned to cover the gate. A company-size unit of the VC 275th Regiment continued to arrive in the vicinity of the POW compound. Their mission was to seize the compound and liberate the 2,000-some prisoners held at the facility.

Ho Nai Village—0420–0530 Hours

Nick Schneider's squad was in the lead of 3rd Platoon as the Charlie Company grunts moved north from Ho Nai Village. Suddenly, Schneider signaled his men to halt. Schneider spotted three figures crossing the road from east to west in the darkness about fifty meters to his front. Unable to make out whether the men were members of the LRP team or villagers, Schneider and his men held their fire. The lead ACAV, Track 12, moving north along the road spotted the figures at the same time. Suddenly, someone popped a handheld flare, illuminating the area. Schneider's point man, Specialist Ken Barber, sized up the situation immediately. He saw three VC running toward a 12.75 machine gun positioned on the west side of the road. The men were carrying a belts of 12.75 ammunition. Schneider yelled for Barber to take cover just as the alert 20-year-old Virginian blasted the trio with his 12-gauge pump-action shotgun, killing all three before they reached the gun. Dozens of AK-47 assault rifles and light machine guns opened fire on the Americans. The battle for Ho Nai village began in earnest.

Platoon Sergeant Wyers saw that Schneider's men were pinned down, and shouted to his other squad leaders to bring their men on line and lay down a base of fire. The lead ACAV also rolled forward to support Schneider's embattled squad. Platoon Sergeant Jayne's 4th Platoon pressed forward on the east side of the road, trying to stay on line with the column of ACAVs.

From the cupola of the lead ACAV, Sergeant Payne, the track commander, spotted a group of some 30 to 40 VC crossing the stream on the west side of the road, trying to flank Wyer's 3rd Platoon. He turned his .50 caliber machine gun on the group, mowing down a number of the enemy soldiers. The survivors rushed forward until they ran into an unexpected obstacle. Months earlier, Army engineers had dug a large gravel pit while constructing the road. The VC ran right into it until they reached a steep embankment about ten feet high. The lead ACAV turned all of its firepower on the trapped VC. Schneider and a couple of his men took advantage of the covering fire and rushed to the ACAVs to retrieve their rucksacks that contained more ammunition and grenades.

An enemy RPG team moved to a firing position next to a house on the east side of the road. The VC took aim at the lead ACAV as Sergeant Payne fired the vehicle's .50 caliber machine at their comrades trapped in the gravel pit. Nick Schneider had just retrieved his rucksack from the ACAV and was rushing back to his squad when the RPG struck the vehicle's right front side. The shaped charge burned into the engine compartment, setting the engine on fire and blowing the engine access panel into the side of the driver. Jim Choquette, the

ACAV's M79 gunner, was standing in the rear of the troop compartment when the RPG struck the vehicle. Miraculously, shrapnel from the blast blew over Choquette's upper torso and head, missing him completely. He knew immediately, however, that the track was immobilized and that the fire in the engine compartment would soon reach the fuel lines and eventually the gas tank. He moved forward to assist the injured driver and other crewmembers off the vehicle.

Hobbling along on his sprained ankle, Specialist Bob Archibald took cover in a ditch that paralleled the road once the firing began. He and two other grunts who were in the ditch made their way to the burning ACAV to assist the cavalrymen off the vehicle. George Hauer, a medic attached to Charlie Company, patched up the injured men and sent them to the rear. John Payne, Jim Coquette, and PFC Jerry Byers, crewmembers on the disabled ACAV, elected to stay in the fight. Under heavy fire, they ran to the second ACAV in the column and climbed aboard. Seconds later, two more RPGs slammed into the road, slightly damaging two ACAVs behind the lead track. The near misses caused only minor damage to the vehicles. A piece of the shrapnel from the blasts nicked Nick Schneider as he ran back to his squad's position. The Cav platoon leader, Lieutenant Ehler, gave the order for the ACAVs to withdraw. Since the road was too narrow for the vehicles to turn around, and it had ditches on both sides, the ACAVs began to move in reverse.

Platoon Sergeant Cliff Jaynes and most of 4th Platoon took cover in the drainage ditch on the east side of the road. Jaynes spotted the hideout of the RPG team in the abandoned house and yelled to his M79 gunners to fire their 40mm grenades at it. Two of the grenades dropped on the thatched roof of the house, setting it ablaze, while the riflemen took aim and poured a heavy fire into the windows and doors.

Captain Tonsetic and his CP group were moving a few meters behind Wyer's 3rd Platoon when the fight broke out. His immediate concern was that his men were about to be flanked on the west side of the road. After spotting a group of VC dart behind a house to his left, Tonsetic and his senior RTO, Cliff Kaylor, fired a couple of shots at the men. Then the Captain pulled two grenades from his web gear and lobbed them over the roof of the house. The grenades landed behind the house and exploded. The Captain then turned his attention to the house across the road. Tonsetic saw members of his 4th Platoon firing at the house that was now ablaze, and he shouted to the gunner on the recoilless rifle track to finish the job with a 106mm round. The ACAV was in the process of backing up the road, and Tonsetic couldn't get the track commander's attention over the noise of the battle. It didn't matter. Seconds later, the burning house , containing a cache of enemy ammunition, including a stockpile of B40 rockets, exploded in a fiery blast that sent shock waves in all directions.

LRP Team 37 was still concealed in their position about a kilometer to the north of the battle. Lieutenant Colonel Maus was unable to land in the area to extract his team. Enemy soldiers were still arriving in the area. At 0445, the LRP team leader, Specialist Vincent, radioed to his CO to report a huge explosion to his south. The team saw smoke rising 200 to 300 feet in the air. He reported that several houses in the village had blown up. In fact, it was the house that Tonsetic's men had just destroyed. The patrol also spotted the flames and thick black smoke that engulfed the burning ACAV. Ammunition stored on the ACAV was cooking off, showering the surrounding area with sparks and shrapnel. It was like an awesome fireworks display. Orbiting overhead in his C&C ship, LTC Maus radioed his patrol leader, Specialist Vincent, and told him to sit tight, telling him, "We will pull you out when you link up with the infantry." There was one problem. Vincent knew that the better part of a VC battalion was between his team and the embattled Charlie Company.

South of the LRP team's position, the battle continued to rage. Captain Tonsetic radioed for gunship support and was told a gunship team was en route. The heavy volume of enemy small arms, machine gun, and 61mm mortar fire was taking its toll. The enemy held the high ground to his north, and continued to place accurate fire on Tonsetic's two platoons. Lieutenant Ehler's ACAVs had backed up the road out of RPG range, and were no longer able to provide covering fire for the infantrymen.

Platoon Sergeant Wyers' 3rd Platoon held the most exposed position. Wyers' had been wounded and knew he could not hold his position for long. Sizing up the situation, he ordered Specialists Nick Schneider, Alonzo Shelton, Ken Barber, and PFC Dale Reidenga to lay down a base of fire to cover the platoon's withdrawal. The remainder of the platoon began to pull back with their wounded. In addition to Platoon Sergeant Wyers, Specialists Lester Brown, James Hayward, Terrance Miller, and Jerold Partch were all wounded, as were PFCs Ronald Bills and Mattlaw.

Fourth Platoon was in better shape than 3rd Platoon, but Jayne's unit had casualties as well. Sergeant Ronny Simons was wounded, and so were Specialists Frank Tesler and Michael Tuszl. Jaynes told his wounded sergeant to take the platoon's casualties back to the rear, while the remainder of 4th Platoon continued to protect the company's right flank with rifle and grenade fire. Most of Jaynes' men were firing from the drainage ditch that paralleled the road.

Captain Tonsetic and his CP group took cover in one of the houses, along with an M60 machine gunner from 3rd Platoon. He directed the machine gunner to cover the rear of the house from a window, while Bob Archibald covered a side window with his M16. Archibald recalled that after squeezing off a few rounds, "My M16 jammed up tighter than a sealed drum . . . if my CO hadn't been there, I might have just smashed it." Specialist Cliff Kaylor and the Captain worked the radios as enemy fire was directed at the house.

Sergeant Wyers radioed that his platoon was falling back, and Tonsetic told Kaylor to call for artillery fire to cover the withdrawal. He had no idea of the whereabouts of his FO. While Kaylor radioed for artillery support, Tonsetic radioed the Warrior battalion TOC requesting gunship support and reenforcements. LTC Mastoris informed Tonsetic that a gunship team was en route, and that a company from 2/3d Infantry was conducting a forced night march to reinforce Charlie Company. The Old Guard company was reportedly five kilometers to the north and moving south to link up. Charlie Company's request for artillery support was denied. According to the arty FDC, the impact area was too close to the village, and the rules of engagement did not allow for collateral damage.

CHAPTER 8

FIGHTING ON ALL SIDES

Camp Frenzell-Jones—0500 Hours, 31 January 1968

As dawn broke on the first full day of the Tet Offensive, both the west and east perimeters of Camp Frenzell-Jones (the LIB's main base) were under heavy fire. UH-1C gunships from A Troop, 3/17th Air Cavalry, nicknamed the "Silver Spurs," engaged the VC positions. Streams of green tracer rounds arched skyward as the VC anti-aircraft gunners tried to bring down the gunships. The gunships took multiple hits but managed to stay airborne, pounding the VC positions with rockets and machine-gun fire. Under murderous fire from the Silver Spur gunships, the VC were unable to mass their troops for a ground attack.

A 12.75mm machine gun firing from the hospital tower in Ho Nai village was scoring most of the hits on the gunships. The pilots radioed for assistance to silence the anti-aircraft gun. Two howitzers from A Battery, 2/40th Artillery were moved to firing positions on the northeast side of the perimeter where they could engage the tower with direct fire. LTC Myer, the 2/40th commander, shouted directions to the gun crews manning the guns. The crews lowered the tubes to the direct-fire level, and began slamming 105mm rounds into the tower. The gun section scored six direct hits on the tower, silencing the enemy antiaircraft fire.

After knocking out the anti-aircraft position, LTC Myer was informed that the 195th Assault Helicopter Company pad and the II Field Force Headquarters area were taking heavy fire from a densely overgrown area east of their perimeter. The artillery commander responded, displacing a howitzer section to that threatened area. The howitzer was towed by truck to a firing position near the 12th Aviation Group helipad, where it was soon in action. The howitzer crew zeroed in on the target area with three white phosphorus rounds. The gunners then followed-up with 20 HE rounds, and a beehive round for good measure. The enemy fire ceased. Days later, an engineer unit that was clearing away the brush from the area found 18 mangled enemy bodies.

While LTC Meyer's howitzers blasted away at the VC, Colonel Davison contacted the II Field Force Commander requesting reinforcements for his embattled brigade. At 0500 hours, the 199th LIB was given operational control of a task force consisting of a portion of the battalion headquarters and Companies A and C of the 2/47th Infantry. Colonel Davison directed the force to link up with the brigade's embattled Ready Reaction Force north of Ho Nai village. A 2/47th mechanized task force under the command of Major Bill Jones was more than 12 kilometers away when it received the order to reinforce the 4/12th company. The enemy, not the distance, was the problem. In order to link up with Captain Tonsetic's force at Ho Nai village, Major Jones' task force had to move west of Highway 15 to an intersection with Highway 316, and then turn northeast and fight its way to the intersection with Highway 1. The mech infantry column then had to move east through Ho Nai village until it reached Charlie Company's position on the north-south engineer road. There were enemy snipers and likely ambush sites all along the route.

Ho Nai Village—0530–0630 Hours

First Sergeant George Holmes began moving Charlie Company's wounded back toward the center of Ho Nai village. When he reached a schoolyard that was large enough to land a medevac chopper, he set up a perimeter using the walking wounded, and called Long Binh dust-off control. Holmes had two things on his mind. First, he wanted to medevac the most serious of the wounded. He was also concerned that his CO, Captain Tonsetic, his RTOs, and a few grunts were cut off from the remainder of the company. Holmes knew from the radio traffic that the "Old Man" was in a forward position directing gunship strikes on the enemy battalion. When the gunships had to leave station to rearm and refuel, Holmes knew that the Captain's position would likely be overrun.

Dust-off 19 arrived on station over Ho Nai village at 0538 hours. A VC anti-aircraft machine gun opened up on the helicopter with 12.75mm fire. Braving the heavy machine-gun fire, the pilot tried to land at the LZ in the schoolyard, but was driven off on its first two attempts after sustaining several hits. Undaunted, the WO pilot landed on the small LZ on his third attempt. Amid a whirlwind of dust and smoke kicked up by the chopper's rotor blades, three wounded Charlie Company grunts and four Cav troopers were loaded onto the UH-1H. At 0605, the dust-off ship lifted off and flew toward the 93d Evacuation Hospital at Long Binh. Four wounded grunts from Charlie Company opted to stay and fight it out with the company.

From his forward position, Captain Tonsetic continued to direct the gunships on the enemy battalion less than 100 meters to his north. The burning ACAV illuminated the area, and Tonsetic could clearly see the VC as they were cut down by machine-gun and rocket fire from the gunships. A few 3rd Platoon grunts dashed by the door of the house where the Captain stood directing the strikes. Figuring that none of his men were forward of his position, Tonsetic began to direct the strikes closer to his own position. He told the gunship team leader to plaster the area around the burning ACAV that was about thirty meters away from the house where his CP group had taken cover. The Captain was not aware that Platoon Sergeant Jaynes and a few men from 4th Platoon were still providing covering fire for the command group from a drainage ditch across the road. Jaynes' men spotted several VC rushing toward the house where Tonsetic and his RTOs were holed up, and cut them down with M16 fire.

When First Sergeant Holmes saw the dust-off ship lift off, he grabbed a squad from 3rd Platoon and headed north through the village to find his CO. Holmes and his squad crept forward to a position about twenty meters from the house where the CP group was set up. He shouted to his CO to withdraw toward his position: "You've got to fall back. The rest of the Company is back up the road. We'll provide covering fire."

Since the gunships were running low on ammunition, Tonsetic

decided his CP group had better make a break for it. One by one, the
RTOs, machine gunner, and the Captain sprinted out the doorway
toward Holmes' position, while the rifle squad accompanying the First
Sergeant laid down a base of covering fire. Once Jaynes saw that
Captain Tonsetic and his men had made it out of the house, he began
pulling back toward the company position at the juncture of the engineer road and Highway 1 in the village. Dawn began to break over the
smoke-covered battlefield.

When Captain Tonsetic and his RTOs arrived at the road junction
where his men had set up a perimeter, he assessed the situation. Of the
original eight ACAV, one was destroyed and two were damaged. The
106mm ACAV was positioned to cover the engineer road leading
north out of the village, while the undamaged tracks were positioned
in a herringbone pattern along Highway 1. The Captain asked his
First Sergeant how many men were still able to fight. Holmes replied
that there were 30 men in the two platoons, including four who were
slightly wounded. The Captain knew that there was a Company from
the 2/3d Infantry somewhere to his north, and that a 9th Division
mech outfit was on the road headed for his location, but he didn't
know how long it would take for either of the reinforcing units to
arrive. He knew that the VC battalion to his north was not going to
sit and wait. He had to keep the pressure on, or the enemy would
regain the initiative.

Captain Tonsetic decided to attack the enemy dug in on the high
ground to his north. With gunship support, he hoped to gain a
foothold on the high ground. Then he would hopefully be reinforced.
The Captain ordered the Cav platoon leader to secure the road junction with his ACAVs. The 106mm recoilless rifle track was positioned
facing north on the engineer road to support the attack. The signal for
Charlie Company's infantrymen to move out was a blast from the
106mm Recoilless rifle aimed straight down the road. Third Platoon
again took the west side of the road while 4th Platoon moved out on
the east side. Resistance was light until the grunts arrived in the vicinity of the destroyed ACAV.

As the Charlie Company grunts approached the burned out
ACAV, enemy 61mm mortars opened fire from the high ground to the
north. Some rounds fell short into the stream bed, but one detonated

in the branches of a tall tree that grew next to the road, showering the area with shrapnel. Scanning the ridgeline, Captain Tonsetic spotted the enemy mortar crews dropping rounds into their tubes, and shouted to Platoon Sergeant Jaynes to take them out with M79 fire. Jaynes' grenadiers, all experts with high-trajectory fire, lobbed round after round of 40mm grenades at the enemy mortars, destroying the position.

Platoon Sergeant Wyers' 3rd Platoon made good progress on the west side of the road until an enemy squad concealed in a patch of brush south of the streambed opened fire with a light machine gun and AK-47s. Wyers' men hit the dirt and returned fire. PFC Alfred Lewis, a 21-year-old from Detroit, and 20-year-old Mike Raugh, a native New Yorker and new replacement, jumped into the ditch that paralleled the road. Standing upright in the ditch, Lewis fired several 40mm grenades from his M79 toward the enemy position. From the ditch, Lewis couldn't tell if his grenades hit their target. After telling Mike Raugh to stay put, Lewis crawled forward for several feet, then crept out of the ditch. He made his way up a gentle slope until he was silhouetted against the skyline. The VC machine gun opened up with a long burst that was answered by a volley of M16 fire from a group of 3rd Platoon riflemen. Lewis, who was caught in the crossfire between his own men and the VC, was shot.

Several members of 3rd Platoon crawled forward to pull Lewis to safety, but he died before they reached him. Continuing on, the 3rd Platoon grunts engaged the enemy squad with hand grenades and M16 fire, killing eight and capturing a light machine gun and several AK-47 rifles. The 3rd Platoon was then taken under fire from the enemy-held ridgeline north of the stream. Specialist Byrd took a round through the cheek that shattered his jaw and knocked out several teeth. Bleeding profusely, he stumbled to the rear, assisted by the platoon medic, George Hauer. The 3rd Platoon's advance was stalled by the heavy volume of enemy fire.

Captain Tonsetic was standing beside the burned-out ACAV hulk directing a gunship team when an enemy soldier armed with a machine pistol jumped out of the brush fifteen meters away, and fired a burst at the Captain and his RTOs. Sharp pings of bullets against the armored hull of the ACAV sent Tonsetic, his commo sergeant Larry

Abel, and his RTO Cliff Kaylor diving for cover. The intrepid VC then dashed for the cover of a culvert that ran beneath the road. Several Charlie Company grunts fired at the fleeing VC, but missed as he dove into the culvert opening. The artillery FO, Lieutenant Tillotson, and his recon sergeant were closest to the culvert. The pair moved forward and the FO pulled the pin from a hand grenade and tossed it toward the culvert opening before hitting the dirt. The grenade bounced off the rim of the culvert into some weeds. The artillery lieutenant thought that the grenade was a dud. As he moved his body to the push-up position to have a look, the grenade exploded. A small piece of shrapnel tore into his right shoulder.

Moments later, the trapped VC emerged from the culvert on the west side of the road and sprinted for a vine-covered embankment, firing his machine pistol as he ran. Two men from 3rd Platoon blasted the VC's hiding place with their M16s and followed up with hand grenades. The first grenade detonated and blew the upper half of the man's torso out of the brush. Then a second grenade exploded and the remainder of the body was blown out of the brush.

The close combat continued as the Charlie Company grunts tried to cross the streambed. Their advance was stalled by the heavy fire coming from the high ground to their north. As his gunship support departed to rearm and refuel, Captain Tonsetic realized that his outnumbered and outgunned platoons could not seize the high ground by themselves. He decided to pull back toward the village and await the arrival of reinforcements.

POW Compound—0600–0730 Hours

PFC Gary Coufal, an M79 gunner from Syracuse, New York, and another grunt from 1st Platoon were in the observation tower scanning the area across the highway from the main gate of the compound. It was just after dawn, and the morning mists still hugged the ground. The compound had received about twenty minutes of small-arms fire shortly after 0400 hours, but the VC were silenced by helicopter gunship strikes. Lt. Tuber had kept his men on 100 percent alert. It had been a long night, and the men welcomed the first light of dawn.

PFC Coufal thought he spotted movement in the rubber trees

across the road, but he didn't have time to process what he saw. Coufal later wrote, "As I looked in that direction rounds struck the sandbags in front of me. The type of fire we had coming in was small arms fire. But I was worried that we were going to be RPG'd. I told my buddy to get out fast, which he did, and I was getting all the equipment together as fast as I could."

After tossing their rucksacks to the ground below, the two men climbed down the ladder in a hail of VC gunfire, and ran for cover in one of the ground bunkers. Then, according to Coufal, "All Hell broke loose. . . .We were being hit by automatic weapons and small arms fire and I don't recall any RPG fire, but the fighting was very intense. D Troop and our unit were putting out a lot of rounds. I was an M79 gunner and ran out of ammo and had to get to one of the tracks for more." A company from the 275th VC Regiment began to assault the compound, bent on freeing the 2,000 POWs held there.

Twenty-two-year-old Lieutenant Howard Tuber and his RTOs were in a ground bunker directing the defense of the compound. As soon as the fighting started, Tuber radioed his CO, Captain Tonsetic, requesting gunships and reinforcements. Tonsetic, who had his own fight going on north of Ho Nai village, told Tuber to switch radio frequencies and pass his request directly to the battalion TOC at FSB Concord. When the lieutenant radioed the TOC, LTC Mastoris told him that a relief force from the 11th Armored Cavalry Regiment was on the way. The 11th ACR's 2d Squadron was given the mission of reinforcing the POW Compound, but the unit was north of the Michelin Rubber Plantation in War Zone C when they received the order. It would take a nine-hour road march through hostile territory for the troopers of the "Black Horse" regiment to reach the beleaguered compound. Tuber and his platoon were on their own.

At 0635 hours, Tuber's men spotted an enemy assault force, including six enemy soldiers armed with rocket launchers, moving to firing positions across the road from the main gate. A gunship team, that had so far held the VC company at bay, had expended all its ordnance and departed the area ten minutes earlier. The enemy intended to breach the gate of the compound before the gunships returned.

When Tuber's men spotted the enemy assault force, they opened up with everything they had, hoping to break up the attack before it got started. ACAV gunners manning their .50 caliber and M60 machine guns fired burst after burst at the enemy assault force, while Tuber's infantrymen zeroed in on the enemy with their M16s and M79s. The M79 grenadiers concentrated their fires on the enemy RPG teams, setting off two secondary explosions. The massed US firepower halted the enemy before they could cross the highway and rush the main gate. Lieutenant Tuber then sent two ACAVs and a reinforced rifle squad across the road to sweep the area north of the compound. The patrol killed 12 VC, and found several more enemy bodies. They also recovered a number of B-40 rocket launchers, 12 rockets, a number of AK-47 rifles, and 300 blocks of TNT. The VC had planned to blow up the compound once they liberated their comrades. Most of the survivors from the VC company withdrew, although the POW compound continued to receive sporadic sniper fire throughout the morning, resulting in a number of US wounded.

Long Binh Ammo Dump—0630–0800 Hours

Bravo Company, 2/47th Mechanized Infantry, minus one platoon, arrived at the ammunition dump at 0630, and after coordinating with the MPs, began to clear the dump. The company took fire immediately and several infantrymen were wounded. After an hour of tough fighting, Bravo Company succeeded in driving the remaining enemy from the ammo dump. Then they began to help the EOD teams locate, remove, and disarm timed explosive devices left behind by the enemy sappers on eighteen separate ammo pads. By 0730 hours, the EOD teams had disarmed enemy satchel charges left on seven of the eighteen pads. It was a race against time, and the clock was ticking.

At 0739 hours, timed explosive devices began to explode on the uncleared ammo pads. One of the first explosive charges detonated on a pad of 175mm artillery shell charges, followed in rapid succession by three more pads of various types of ammunition. A huge fireball erupted over the pads, followed by a blast that sent shockwaves, shrapnel, and debris in all directions. The ground shook like an 8.0 earthquake, and a huge mushroom cloud rose above the ammo dump. Sandbagged bunkers along the facility's perimeter were blown apart from the blasts. Four US soldiers were killed and 24 others were wounded. The mech infantrymen from Bravo Company, 2/47th, who were better protected in their APCs, had four men wounded. Enemy explosive devices detonated on eight more pads, but the ammo stored on the pads did not explode.

Shock waves from the ammo dump explosions shook the Quonset huts and wooden buildings throughout the Plantation area. The blast was seen and felt by troops fighting for their lives miles away from the ammo dump, and it remains indelibly etched in their memories. Despite the fact that the VC managed to destroy several ammo pads, the attack on the ammo dump did not significantly reduce the stocks of ammunition on hand, or alter the final outcome of the enemy offensive in the III Corps area.

Fire Base Zinderneuf, 3/7th Infantry CP, Binh Chanh—0800 Hours

Lieutenant Colonel John Gibler, commander of the 3/7th Infantry, the "Cottonbalers," spent a restless night at his CP. Gibler's battalion had moved south to the Binh Chanh area three weeks earlier. It was familiar territory to Gibler and his men. The Cottonbalers had conducted operations in the same locale for several months, prior to moving north to the Bien Hoa area in December. Since mid-January, the 3/7th had made several contacts with local force VC units, but the enemy seemed intent on avoiding decisive engagements. On 30 January, LTC Gibler called his company commanders in for a conference and told them that he intended to pull all companies back to the vicinity of FSB Zinderneuf, where the Cottonbaler CP was set up. Days earlier, Gibler had advised his commanders to start thinking about urban warfare tactics. The Cottonbaler commander's sixth sense was right on target.

FSB Zinderneuf was located about one kilometer west of the Binh Chanh District Headquarters, and about fifteen kilometers from the center of Saigon. On the morning of 31 January, Gibler's Cottonbalers saw columns of thick black smoke rising over the city. The 3/7th commander was informed by radio that six major targets—the Presidential Palace, the US Embassy, the Vietnamese Joint General Staff Headquarters, Tan Son Nhut Airport, the Vietnamese Navy Headquarters, and the National Broadcasting Station—were all under attack. He was also informed that the Phu Tho Racetrack, located in the Cholon section of the city, had been seized by Communist forces. The battle for Saigon was underway.

Built during Vietnam's colonial period, the Phu Tho Racetrack was situated in the heart of Cholon about six kilometers south of Tan Son Nhut airbase. Located at the hub of several city avenues, it was a well known landmark. Highway 4, the main highway connecting Saigon to the Mekong Delta, was just four blocks south, and Highway 1 was two kilometers to the north. Because of its location, the racetrack was a convenient rally point and assembly area for VC and NVA troops entering the city. The 3,000 seat bleachers towered above the surrounding buildings and provided excellent observation of most of Cholon. Mortars firing from the infield could reach targets located throughout the city including, Tan Son Nhut. The racetrack's infield was also the only area in Cholon that could be used as a helicopter landing zone. To insert U.S. troops into the city by air, the racetrack would first have to be retaken.

At 0808 hours on 31 January, the Cottonbalers received their first mission of the Tet Offensive. The 3/7th was ordered by the Capital Military District (CMD) to send a force into Cholon to seize the Phu Tho Racetrack. Since the VC had set up anti-aircraft weapons at the racetrack, Gibler's men would have to move by ground convoy into Cholon. Once the enemy troops were driven from the racetrack, Gibler planned to move the remainder of the battalion in by helicopter. Gibler selected Alpha Company to lead the attack to recapture the racetrack.

Ho Nai Village—0800–1400 Hours

After fighting their way up Highway 316 past the main gate of Camp Frenzell-Jones, Major Jones' 2/47th task force turned east on Highway 1 and rumbled through Ho Nai village. The improvised unit, dubbed Task Force (TF) Panther, included Alpha Company and elements of battalion headquarters company.

As TF Panther sped through the village, enemy snipers took aim at the M113A1s and their crews. Specialist Russ Vibberts from the 2/47th Scout Platoon was driving the lead vehicle, taking his orders from Major Jones, who rode in the commander's cupola. Eleven M113A1s carrying Alpha Company's infantrymen followed behind the command track in column formation. When Major Jones learned that the rear of his column was taking heavy sniper fire, he ordered Vibberts to pick up speed. As Vibberts pressed the accelerator to the floor, he saw a tall first sergeant on the road waving for him to stop. A platoon of ACAVs were parked along the road in a herringbone pattern.

Major Jones' command track sped past First Sergeant Holmes, who had to jump out of its path to avoid being run over. The column rolled on for another kilometer before the commander realized that the First Sergeant had been trying to direct him to Charlie Company's location.

The 2/47th column then rolled to a halt and reversed direction, speeding back to Holmes' position at the road junction. First Sergeant Holmes told the Major that Charlie Company was in heavy contact some three hundred meters north on the engineer road. Major Jones ordered his infantrymen to dismount and follow First Sergeant Holmes up the road, followed by the M113s. The odds were now turning in the Americans' favor.

The battalion of the VC 275th Regiment had been stopped in its tracks by Captain Tonsetic's Charlie Company. The enemy battalion had been badly battered by almost constant gunship strikes and small-arms fire. Its lead elements that engaged Charlie Company during the night were for the most part destroyed or taken prisoner. The bodies of more than 50 VC were strewn around the gravel pit and streambed. The ridgeline to the north was also strewn with enemy dead and wounded. Some VC took advantage of the opportunity to flee into the surrounding jungle when the gunship teams departed to rearm and refuel, but the diehards remained.

A number of the fleeing enemy soldiers ran right into Specialist Vincent's LRP team. The LRPs killed eleven, but three members of Vincent's team were wounded in the clashes. LTC Maus decided to extract the team. He knew their situation was precarious; they were running low on ammo. In full view of the enemy, he ordered his C&C ship to land and pick up the team. Amid a hail of gunfire, the LRPs rushed toward the helicopter with their wounded. Seconds later the pilot pulled pitch and took off as the door gunners opened up on the VC below. LTC Maus was awarded the Distinguished Service Cross for his role in the battle, and Specialist Vincent was awarded the Silver Star. The LRP team had provided critical early warning of the 275th Regimental attack on Long Binh, and triggered the US response.

The remainder of the enemy battalion, many of whom were wounded, still held the ridge line that ran northwest to northeast some 1,500 meters north of the village. A US rifle company from 2/3d Infantry had established a blocking position 1,200 meters to the north astride the engineer road, closing that escape route. The enemy were left with two choices: fight to the death or surrender. The majority chose the former option.

Major Jones, the TF Panther commander, briefed Captain Tonsetic and his Alpha Company commander on a plan of attack. He instructed Captain Tonsetic to attack northward with his two platoons of light infantry on the west side of the road while Alpha Company's mechanized infantrymen would attack on the east side. During the first phase of the attack, infantrymen from both units had to cross the streambed and seize the high ground to the north. They would then continue the attack up a gentler slope to rout the dug-in enemy from their positions. Major Jones would then lead the M113A1s across the culvert and up onto the high ground to assist in final phase of the attack.

The attack jumped off around 0830 hours. Alpha Company drew the tougher assignment. The enemy strongpoint on the ridgeline was in a small cemetery east of the road. It was not well maintained. Knee high bushes and weeds grew between the graves and positions dug by the enemy during the night. West of the road, the enemy positions were spread farther apart, and several had sustained direct hits during the gunship strikes. However, the diehard defenders were still capable of putting out a heavy volume of automatic weapons fire.

The Charlie Company grunts maintained a steady pace as they crossed the stream, climbed its bank, and began to move uphill. Enemy positions were taken out using fire and movement, usually ending with a hand grenade tossed into the enemy foxhole. Alpha Company also crossed the stream quickly and began to sweep northward into the cemetery, killing 13 VC and capturing a number of others. However, the mech infantrymen missed several well-concealed enemy positions. As the attack continued, the VC who were bypassed began to pop up from their holes and fire into Alpha Company's ranks from the rear. Three Alpha soldiers were killed before a lone infantryman from Charlie Company saw what was happening.

Specialist Bob Archibald, still limping badly on a sprained ankle, hobbled across the road to the Alpha Company sector where he engaged the enemy positions with hand grenades and blasts from his 12-gauge shotgun. Archibald was credited with killing 12 diehard VC. It wasn't until after the battle that Archibald realized he'd sustained a minor flesh wound to his leg. Commenting on his role in the battle, Archibald wrote, "I was really pumped then. Later, I thought I might just get a Bronze Star . . . then I forgot about it." The 21-year-old Californian knew his friend Al Lewis had been killed an hour earlier, but he had no thoughts about retribution when he attacked the enemy positions. He said, "I did what I thought I was supposed to do."

As mopping up actions continued, Major Jones led his tracked vehicles forward. After the tracks crossed the culvert they left the road and assisted the dismounted infantrymen in eliminating additional enemy positions. It was slow and dangerous work. As the light infantry and mech infantry companies swept northward for another 1,500 meters, they continued to flush the VC from their hiding places. Gunships from A Troop, 3/17th Cav cut the fleeing VC down in their tracks before they could reach the surrounding jungle. Thirteen prisoners were taken during the attack. Battlefield interrogation of these prisoners revealed that they were NVA fillers assigned to the 275th VC Regiment. North Vietnamese documents and currency found on their persons substantiated their identities. The POWs also told their interrogators that there were two additional VC battalions of the 275th Regiment in and around the Long Binh area.

As the 4/12th and 2/47th soldiers pushed closer toward the blocking position held by Bravo Company, 2/3d Infantry, the few remaining enemy soldiers were caught in a deadly crossfire. As the attackers neared the blocking position, a Bravo Company soldier was shot and killed by a fleeing VC. At approximately 1400 hours, the troops from Charlie Company 4/12th and Alpha Company 2/47th Infantry reached the 2/3d Infantry blocking positions.

The enemy battalion was all but destroyed as a fighting force with its men either killed, captured or fleeing into the surrounding jungle. A captured sketch map found on a dead VC officer indicated that the main objective of their attack had been Camp Frenzell-Jones. The enemy battalion never got to launch its attack due to the early warning given by Specialist Vincent's LRP team, and the subsequent deployment of the 199th LIB's Ready Reaction Force.

Charlie Company had fought the VC battalion to a standstill, and the timely arrival of the 2/47th Infantry's TF Panther insured its total defeat.

Widows Village—0600–1200 Hours

While the VC attack on Camp Frenzell-Jones was stalled by the deployment of the 199th LIB's ready reaction force, another battalion-size attack on the PLANTATION (II Field Force Headquarters Compound), was also stalled. A second enemy battalion of the 275th VC Regiment occupied Widows Village across Highway 316 across from II Field Force Headquarters, but the VC commander never ordered his men to begin the ground assault. Prisoners taken later in the day said that the VC battalion commander had waited for a heavy barrage of several hundred 122mm rockets to soften up their target before the ground attack. When only ninety rockets landed on the entire Plantation complex, the battalion commander delayed the ground assault to wait for a second round of rocket attacks. It was a fatal error. Ground forces from the 199th LIB, and air cavalrymen from A Troop, 3/17th Cav spotted the 122mm rocket launch sites after the initial salvos and called in artillery counter-battery fires, gunship strikes and tactical air strikes to destroy the sites. There would be no more 122mm rocket barrages that day.

Nonetheless, as dawn approached, the II Field Force Plantation Compound continued to receive fire from the enemy battalion holed up in Widows Village. The MP and headquarters personnel defenders returned fire from the bunker line, but couldn't suppress the enemy fire. The incoming fire was aimed at the helicopter gunships and their crews as they took off from and landed at the refueling pads located within the compound. Something had to be done.

Combat medic and Silver Star winner, George Hauer.
(Photo courtesy of George Hauer.)

Rifleman and Silver Star winner, Jim Pittman (center) with Charlie
Company 4/12 Infantry buddies. (Photo courtesy of George Hauer.)

Medal of Honor winner, 199th Infantry Brigade Catholic Chaplain Angelo Liteky (left), and Major Ed Kelley, 4/12 Infantry, talk with a Warrior infantryman. (Photo by 40th Public Information Detachment [P.I.D.], 199th Infantry Brigade.)

4/12 Infantry Warrior commanders, January 1968. From left to right: Captain Pete Albers, Captain Bob Reynolds, Captain Bob Eaton, LTC Bill Schroeder, Captain Stan McLaughlin, Captain Bob Tyson, Captain Bob Tonsetic. (Author's photo.)

Specialist Cliff Kaylor, Charlie Company, 4/12 Infantry RTO, January 1968. (Photo courtesy of Cliff Kaylor.)

Army helicopter gunships blast 275th VC Battalion positions north of Ho Nai village in support of Charlie Company 4/12 Infantry attack on 31 January 1968. (Photo by Specialist Depuis, 40th P.I.D., 199th Infantry Brigade.)

Warriors of 4/12 Infantry await helicopters to land on pick-up zone near Fire Support Base Stephanie, June 1968. (Photo by 40th P.I.D., 199th Infantry Brigade.)

Destroyed ACAV from 3d Platoon, Delta Troop, 17th Armored Cavalry at Ho Nai village on 31 January 1968. (Photo by 1LT Mike Swearingen, 40th P.I.D., 199th Infantry Brigade.)

Weapons and VC dead left in the aftermath of battle on the first full day of the Tet Offensive, 31 January 1968. (Photo by Capt. R.K. Anderson, 40th P.I.D., 199th Infantry Brigade.)

Above: Charlie Co. Warriors with .51 caliber machine gun captured near Ho Nai village on 31 January 1968. From left to right: Specialists Ken Barber, Jerold Partch, and Nick Schneider. (Photo by 40th P.I.D., 199th LIB.)

Charlie Company, 4/12 Infantry command group prepares for lift-off during airmobile assault. Captain Tonsetic seated next to door. (Author's photo.)

Specialist Dave Parks, 856th Radio Research Detachment. (Photo courtesy of Dave Parks.)

Below: Colonel Frederic Davison (left), Deputy Commander of the 199th Infantry Brigade, conferring with LTC Herbert Ray, 5/12 Infantry, and LTC Bill Mastoris, 4/12 Infantry. At right is 199th Brigade S3 Don Bolduc. (Photo by Capt. Anderson, 40th P.I.D., 199th Infantry Brigade.)

Above: Lieutenant Bill Trotter, 3/7 Infantry, confers with LTC Roy Herts and Major Jim MacGill. (Photo courtesy of Bill Trotter.)

Specialist Jerry Partch of Charlie Company, 4/12 Infantry, during Operation Valley Forge, March 1968. (Photo by PFC Hansell, 40th P.I.D., 199th Infantry Brigade.)

Grandstands at Phu Tho Racetrack, Tet 1968. (Photo by 40th Public Information Detachment, 199th Infantry Brigade.)

Brig. Gen. Robert Forbes (center), 199th Infantry Brigade, looks over the base camp of the 4/12 Infantry with LTC Bill Mastoris (right), 13 April 1968. 1Lt Douglas Lee (left), the General's aide, accompanies. (Photo by Specialist Whinnery, 40th P.I.D., 199th Infantry B.rigade.)

LTC Ken Hall, Commander 3/7 Infantry, confers with Cottonbaler NCOs. Major Jim MacGill, 3/7 Infantry S3, is at far right. (Photo courtesy of Bill Trotter.)

Captain Robert Tonsetic, Charlie Company, 4/12 Infantry, receives congratulations from First Sergeant George Holmes upon receiving the Distinguished Service Cross for actions on 31 January 1968. (US Army photo printed by 221st Signal Company.)

Brigadier General Robert Forbes, commander 199th LIB, presents awards to soldiers of the 4/12 Infantry for heroic actions during the Tet Offensive. Lt. Colonel William Mastoris, commander 4/12 Infantry, accompanies. (Photo by 40th P.I.D., 199th Infantry Brigade.)

Duster in action on northern perimeter of Fire Support Base Stephanie on 7 May 1968. (Author's photo.)

ACAVs of D Troop, 17th Cavalry, 199th Infantry Brigade, provide covering fire for advancing Warriors of 4/12 Infantry west of Saigon on 8 May 1968. (Photo by Specialist J. Van Wyngarden, P.I.D., 199th LIB.)

PFC James McKensie of Delta Company, 4/12 Infantry, inspects captured NVA weapons and gear after contact five miles west of Saigon, 6 May 1968. (Photo by Specialist Whinnery, 40th P.I.D., 199th Infantry Brigade.)

An NVA Hoi Chanh points out enemy positions in the village of Binh Tri Dong, two miles west of Saigon on 8 May 1968. (Photo by Specialist J. Van Wyngarden, 40th P.I.D., 199th Infantry Brigade.)

Warriors from 412 Infantry advance under fire from NVA west of Saigon on 8 May 1968. (Photo by Specialist J. Van Wyngarden, 40th P.I.D., 199th Infantry Brigade.)

A 90mm recoilless rifle team from Bravo Company, 4/12 Infantry, moves into position to fire on enemy bunkers southwest of Saigon. SFC Johnny Velasquez is seen carrying ammo. (Photo courtesy of Bill Hill.)

Two Warriors of 4/12 Infantry hit the dirt while assaulting NVA positions west of Saigon on 8 May 1968. (Photo by Specialist J. Van Wyngarden, 40th P.I.D., 199th LIB.)

Charlie Company, 2/3 Infantry, mortar squad at Fire Base Hun, left to right: Robin Hickenlooper, George Schuetzle, Tim Moore, Allen Newland. (Photo courtesy of Tim Moore.)

The II Field Force Provost Marshal was in charge of the defense of the II Field Force Compound. Not realizing the size of the VC force in Widows Village, he ordered the II Field Force Ready Reaction Force to leave the compound and clear the village. The reaction force was one mech infantry platoon from Bravo Company, 2/47th Infantry led by Lieutenant Henry Jezek. When the rocket attack began, Jesek's platoon was inside the compound buttoned up in their parked M113A1s. Shortly after daybreak, the lieutenant was called to the II Field Force TOC and told by the Provost Marshal move out of the compound, cross Highway 316, and clear Widows Village.

Entering the village from the southwest, Lieutenant Jezek deployed his platoon on a 200-meter front. His dismounted infantry-men moved on-line between the advancing M113A1s.

The platoon's right flank was anchored on a boundary road that paralleled Highway 316. Jesek's platoon advanced slowly and cau-tiously up the village streets, expecting to encounter enemy snipers.

When the mechanized force was about a third of the way through the village, a group of VC concealed in a drainage ditch that paralleled Highway 13 opened fire with RPGs and small arms. They also deto-nated several Claymore-like mines on the platoon's right flank. The M113A1 on the right took a direct hit from an RPG that disabled the vehicle and killed Corporal Robert Huie, who was firing the APCs .50 caliber machine gun. The driver and another crewman were seriously wounded. Seconds later, Lieutenant Jesek, who was moving on foot near the track, was also seriously wounded. Realizing that his platoon leader was out of the fight, Platoon Sergeant William Butler quickly took command. Butler knew his platoon was in trouble, and ordered the remaining tracks to direct their fire on the VC in the ditch. Under covering fire from the tracks, the dismounted infantrymen scrambled for cover and returned fire, while the wounded were carried toward the rear. The platoon was outnumbered and outgunned, but the 2/47th infantrymen fought off two assaults on their positions while waiting for reinforcements.

The closest unit to the hard-pressed Bravo Company platoon was the 2/47th Infantry recon platoon led by First Lieutenant Brice Barnes. When Barnes, a hard-charging Texan, got his marching orders from his battalion CO, LTC Towers, he lined up his eight ACAVs, and raced up Highway 316 toward Widows Village. After linking up with the Bravo Company platoon, Barnes put his ACAVs on line with two M113A1s from Bravo, and began to sweep through the narrow village streets. Barnes' scouts and a dozen men from the Bravo platoon moved dismounted in front of the armored vehicles. Firing from small bunkers and tunnels beneath the houses and from a series of drainage ditches and culverts, the enemy refused to yield ground. Barnes' troopers cut through barbed wire strung between some of the houses, slowing the advance. Enemy bodies soon littered the streets and ditches, but the enemy fought for every inch of ground.

At 0800 hours, Barnes' scouts saw a flight of UH-1 lift ships descending in trail formation toward an open field adjacent to Highway 316. Captain Jim Lawson's Bravo Company, 4/39th Infantry had been picked up in the Binh Son Rubber Plantation, and flown 17 miles to Long Binh to join the fight for Widows Village. The lift ships were under a hail of small-arms and machine-gun fire as they touched down. The Bravo Company grunts leapt from the helicopters , rushed for the nearest cover, and returned the VC fire as the aircraft lifted off. The II Field Force Headquarters troops manning the bunkers across the highway had ringside seats for the combat assault, and cheered as Lawson's men secured the LZ.

Captain Lawson radioed LTC Tower, the 2/47th commander, for further orders. Tower gave Lawson's company the mission of entering the village from the south and linking up with the recon platoon. Barnes' ACAVs and scouts had advanced to positions in the center of the village near the eastern side. After linking up with Barnes force, the two units began a final attack to clear the village

The .50 caliber machine guns of Barnes' ACAVs fired burst after burst into suspected enemy positions as the infantrymen closed on each enemy strongpoint in the village. The fires of the ground troops were supported by helicopter gunships that made run after run on the village, concentrating their rocket and mini-gun fires on the fleeing VC. When a number of VC took cover in a drainage ditch that paralleled the village's main street, the gunships flushed the VC from their hiding place. Lawson's infantrymen and Barnes' scouts killed the fleeing enemy with well-aimed M16 and M79 fire. By 1200 hours, the village was nominally under US control; however, sporadic fire from bypassed enemy positions continued into the early afternoon. More than fifty enemy bodies were pulled from the network of ditches and fighting positions in the village, and some 30 prisoners, many of them wounded, were taken. The 9th Division troops that fought the battle for Widows Village then moved out to join the fighting around Bien Hoa Airbase.

The battle for Widows Village ended any immediate threat of an enemy ground assault on the Long Binh PLANTATION complex. However, mopping up operations around the base area would continue for several days as small groups of VC tried to evade and escape capture as they attempted to move back to their jungle sanctuaries in War Zone D. Meanwhile, II Field Force intelligence officers remained concerned about a second wave of attacks.

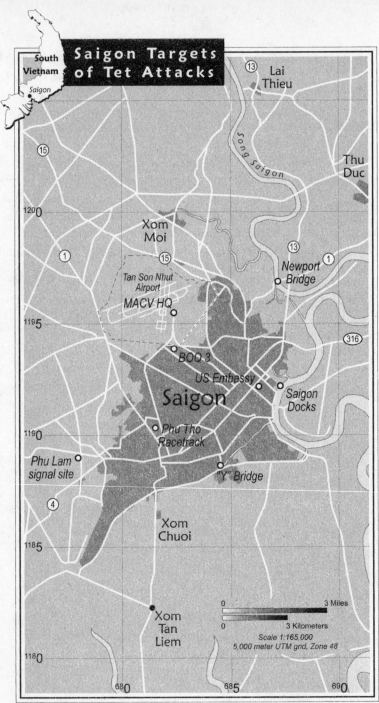

Saigon Targets of Tet Attacks

South Vietnam

Saigon

Lai Thieu

Song Saigon

Thu Duc

Xom Moi

Tan Son Nhut Airport

MACV HQ

Newport Bridge

BOQ 3

US Embassy

Saigon

Saigon Docks

Phu Tho Racetrack

Phu Lam signal site

"Y" Bridge

Xom Chuoi

Xom Tan Liem

0   3 Miles

0   3 Kilometers

Scale 1:165,000
5,000 meter UTM grid, Zone 48

Cartography by Michael Podolny

CHAPTER 9

ASSAULT ON SAIGON

Low clouds and smoke hung over the city as dawn broke on Wednesday, 31 January 1968. Reeling from Communist surprise attacks on military and political targets throughout the Saigon area, US and Vietnamese security forces struggled to maintain control of the city. No less than eleven enemy battalions were within the city limits. The Communists hoped to incite a general uprising among the civilian population that would topple the South Vietnamese government. Despite a full day's warning, US and Vietnamese security forces were not prepared for large scale attacks within the Capital Military District.

By daybreak, Army MPs, reinforced by a platoon from the 101st Airborne Division, were mopping up diehard VC at the US Embassy. The VC had blasted their way into the complex four hours earlier, killing four MPs. The attack resulted in minimal damage to the Embassy, but it had huge political consequences. For many back in the United States, the attack on the Embassy became the defining moment of the Tet Offensive, if not the entire war. However, it was just the beginning of US and ARVN operations to defeat Communist forces and reestablish security in the Capital.

While the firefight at the Embassy reached a climax, fighting also raged near the Presidential Palace, the South Vietnamese government radio station, the Vietnamese Navy Headquarters, the South Vietnamese Armored Command Headquarters, and a host of smaller installations and facilities within the city. A larger battle was also in progress around Tan Son Nhut airbase, where the enemy had attacked

the western perimeter. The main attack by three battalions was directed at Gate # 51. Attacking on a narrow front, the three battalions
were in a column formation, one behind the other. Each battalion had
a specific mission. The lead battalion's mission was to penetrate into
the base, the second battalion was to exploit and widen the penetration, and the third battalion was to destroy the facilities and equipment at Tan Son Nhut. In addition to the civilian aviation terminal,
the US MACV headquarters and US Seventh Air Force headquarters
were located at the airbase. Secondary attacks were also launched
from the north at Gate # 58, and from the east at Gate #10.

Airmen of the 377th Security Police Squadron, reinforced by three
platoons of USARV troops and a mix of RVNAF units, blocked the
penetration at Gate # 51. Helicopter gunships and USAF aircraft
pounded the attackers before they could exploit their penetration. The
timely arrival of Lieutenant Colonel Glenn Otis's 3d Squadron, 4th
Cavalry, from the 25th Infantry Division, completely disrupted the
attack, and after a long day's battle the enemy battalions were totally
decimated.

The 716th Military Police Battalion was the only US unit in the
city capable of responding immediately to the attacks. The battalion
was responsible for the security of some 130 US installations and facilities in the greater Saigon area. It was not an accident that no US combat troops were stationed in Saigon. The South Vietnamese government was always sensitive to the presence of US troops within the city
itself, preferring to rely on their own police and security forces. During
Operation Fairfax, the 199th Light Infantry Brigade had operated in
the peripheral area around the Capital, but when the operation concluded on 15 December 1967, MACV turned over full responsibility
for the close-in defense of Saigon to the Vietnamese. Neither the
Americans nor the South Vietnamese had anticipated a full-scale
attack on the city during the Tet holiday period. Most of the
Vietnamese troops assigned to security missions in Saigon were not on
duty because of the leaves that were granted for the holiday.

The 716th MPs responded to the swarm of attacks, but they were
heavily outgunned and outnumbered. As a result, the MPs sustained
heavy casualties during the first few hours of the fighting. In addition
to the casualties at the US Embassy, two MPs were killed near the

National Palace, and 16 more fell in a bloody ambush while responding to an attack on BOQ Number 3 near Tan Son Nhut airport. An additional 21 MPs were wounded in the same fight. The MPs also sustained casualties near the Phu Tho Racetrack in Cholon, when a jeep patrol was ambushed by a force from the 6th VC Local Force Battalion. The 716th MP Battalion suffered more deaths on 31 January than any other unit fighting in and around Saigon.

In recognition for their heroic efforts against overwhelming odds, twenty Silver Stars for valor were awarded to men assigned to the battalion, and PFC Paul Healey received the nation's second highest award for heroism, the Army's Distinguished Service Cross.

While the attacks in most sections of Saigon were contained and subsequently defeated in the first full day of fighting, mopping up operations continued for the next two weeks.

The most troublesome area within the Capital Military District was Cholon, and in particular the area surrounding the Phu Tho Racetrack.

CHAPTER 10

A DAY AT THE RACES

Cholon—0445–0630 Hours, 31 January 1968

At 0445 hours, the 716th MP Battalion headquartered in Saigon received an urgent radio transmission from one of its patrols. "My driver just caught a slug in the gut and I'm under heavy automatic weapons fire. Can you send some help?" Before the MP duty NCO could reply, he heard a burst of fire and the radio went dead. Both MPs were later found dead in their shot-up jeep near the Phu Tho Racetrack.

About one hour later, two soldiers from the Phu Lam Signal Site, Specialists Lacy and Behrens, were driving from Phu Lam to the Regional Communications Group Headquarters in Cholon. They never made it. They, too, were gunned down in their jeep near the racetrack.

At 0630 hours, an alert force from the 716th MP Battalion reported that it was pinned down by heavy fire near the racetrack, and the MPs ordered a reaction force from Charlie Company, 52nd Infantry to head there as reinforcements. Lieutenant Stephen Braddock, 21 years old, from Abilene, Texas, led the reaction force. As Braddock's men sped down Plantation Road toward the racetrack, they came under heavy machine-gun fire and Lt. Braddock was killed. The VC then threw a satchel charge into the lieutenant's jeep, completely destroying the vehicle. Another officer and NCO were wounded as they tried to recover Braddock's body. Despite the ambush, the reaction force linked up with the besieged MP element near the racetrack.

The enemy troops responsible for the attacks and ambushes at and near the racetrack were from the 5th and 6th Local Force VC Battalions, numbering close to 700 men. In addition to seizing the racetrack, the local force units were responsible for attacks on the dock area, the Chi Hoa Prison, and the Tran Nham and Tran Hoang and Quan areas of Cholon.

The Cholon section of Saigon was home to the majority of its ethnic Chinese population. The district is situated in the southwest quadrant of the city west of the twisting Saigon River. A number of major avenues crossed the through the district, and a grid of narrow streets and unpaved alleyways ran between the main streets and avenues. In 1968, Cholon was easily distinguishable from the rest of the city. Its teeming narrow streets were lined with numerous shops and businesses, each identified by a sign in Chinese characters. Dingy two- and three-story masonry apartment buildings and ramshackle houses were interspersed among the many shops and businesses. Many of the structures had columnades built out over the pavements providing shaded areas where foodstuffs, hardware, silk and other commodities were sold. There were also numerous restaurants, bars, gambling parlors, whorehouses, and opium dens scattered throughout the district. It was a crowded, vibrant area during both day and night. In early 1968, there were an estimated 100,000 draft-age Chinese living in Cholon, who avoided military service through payments of bribes to local police officials. The presence of a couple of thousand young strangers in the district prior to the Tet holiday went unnoticed and unreported.

The Phu Tho Racetrack was located in the heart of Cholon. It was built by the French colonialists during the early 1930s and continued in operation for the next four decades. In fact, horse races were held at the track a few days prior to the Tet Holiday. It was rumored that the horses were often drugged on race day, but this did not deter the fans or the betting. The Vietnamese, particularly the ethnic Chinese living in Cholon, enjoyed betting on the horses. Some of the owners stabled their horses at the racetrack, and there was always some activity on the grounds. Most residents of Saigon and Cholon had attended races at the Phu Tho track, or had at least passed by the facility, since it sat between two major boulevards. It was a well known landmark in the otherwise crowded urban landscape of Cholon.

Thus the Phu Tho racetrack was a convenient rallying point and staging area for enemy troops who had infiltrated into the Cholon area over a period of several weeks. After the offensive, cached weapons, ammunition, and medical supplies were found hidden on the racetrack grounds and in a nearby cemetery. VC commanders also realized that the infield of the racetrack was the only area in Cholon where US forces could land troops by helicopter. The Communists were determined to hold the Phu Tho Racetrack at all costs. It was their key strongpoint in Cholon.

Fire Base Zinderneuf, 3/7th Infantry CP, Binh Chanh—0830 Hours

Alpha Company of the Cottonbaler battalion prepared to move out. Their destination was the Phu Tho Racetrack. Lieutenant Richard Harper's 2nd Platoon, D/17th Cav was attached to Alpha Company for the operation. Captain Tony Smaldone, the Alpha Company CO, gave his men a crash course on urban warfare over the preceding two days. The Captain was a hard taskmaster, and an exceptional infantry officer. Alpha Company's officers and NCOs had to crack the Army Field Manuals (FM) to refresh themselves and their men on combat in cities. The Cottonbalers were about to enter a completely different environment from the jungles, rice paddies, and swamps where the battalion had operated for months. Cholon, with its narrow streets and alleyways, multi-story buildings, and crowded slums, was just as dangerous.

Although, the 3/7th Infantry had never before engaged in urban combat in Vietnam, the 7th Infantry Regiment had a long and storied history that included its share of city street fighting. In fact, the 7th US Infantry Regiment has served in more campaigns than any other infantry regiment in the United States Army. Its history pre-dates the War of 1812, and includes service in every major war fought by the United States to the present day. The Cottonbalers earned their nickname during the Battle of New Orleans in 1815, when they defended that city from breastworks made of cotton bales. During the Mexican War, the Cottonbalers fought at the battles of Monterrey, Cerro Gordo, and Vera Cruz, and during the Civil War a battalion of the 7th Infantry fought their way through the streets of Fredericksburg, and assaulted the stone wall at the base of Marye's Heights. During the Spanish American War the Cottonbalers fought to capture the town of El Caney, and during World Wars II, they fought their way through the rubble strewn cities in Italy, France, and Germany. Urban combat in Cholon was no less challenging and bloody.

At 0905 hours, Smaldone's column began to roll toward Cholon. The moist heat was stifling even at that hour. Two ACAVs from Lieutenant Harper's platoon led the way, followed by several 2-1/2-ton trucks carrying Smaldone's sweat-drenched infantrymen. The remaining ACAV were interspersed in the column with four tracks in the middle and two bringing up the rear of the column. Smaldone's column barreled northeast on Highway 4 through Binh Chanh headed toward Cholon. As the convoy proceeded up the highway crossing some small bridges, the grunts noticed that the PF outposts guarding the bridges were deserted. It was an ominous sign.

Major Jim MacGill, the Cottonbaler Operations Officer, and the battalion's artillery liaison officer, Captain Tom White, flew overhead of the column in an OH-23 Light Observation Helicopter. MacGill, a graduate of the USMA Class of 1957, had served a previous Vietnam tour in MACV, and he knew the Cholon area well. In addition to guiding Smalldone's convoy, MacGill was coordinating the movement of the battalion's Bravo and Charlie Companies. LTC Gibler, the Cottonbaler CO, wanted both companies to march to an LZ where they could be airlifted into the racetrack after it was secured by Captain Smaldone's Alpha Company. Captain Pietsch's Bravo Company was directed to move by RAG boats to the Binh Dien Bridge, where they would disembark and march overland to an LZ, while Captain Wald's Charlie Company was instructed to march directly to Fire Base Zinderneuf where the company would standby for the airmobile assault.

Cholon—Mid-Morning, 31 January

The mid-morning sun flooded the streets with a dazzling yellow light as the lead ACAV in Captain Smaldone's convoy reached the outskirts of Cholon. It was shortly after 1000 hours. The grunts and cavalry-men began to notice the evidence of the previous night's fighting.

There were Vietnamese bodies lying beside smashed vehicles and motorcycles along the road. Dogs were gnawing on some of the dead bodies. The scene became even grimmer when the convoy reached an overturned US jeep. The bullet riddled bodies of two US soldiers lay beside the jeep. The Captain radioed in the location of the bodies, and the convoy pressed on for the racetrack.

The convoy passed a few anguished civilians rushing to flee the area, but most of Cholon's residents had vanished from sight. They sat behind shuttered windows and in basements listening to their radios, eating their rice and Tet sweets, while hoping that the war would pass them by. Unsure which side would prevail, the badly frightened but stoic Chinese prepared themselves for the worst.

About six blocks from the racetrack, the Cottonbalers and cavalrymen began to draw automatic weapons fire from the rooftops and houses along the street on which they were moving. Reacting immediately, Captain Smaldone ordered his infantry off the trucks. The grunts ran through the hail of incoming fire to take up firing positions in the surrounding buildings and doorways. Firefights raged from one side of the street to the other. The cavalrymen returned the fire with bursts from their .50 caliber machine guns, and the 106mm recoilless rifle track blasted one of the buildings, temporarily silencing the enemy fire. Smaldone's men moved out on foot, clearing buildings as they went.

Specialist Four Doug McCabe was with one of Alpha Company's lead squads moving up the street. Born in Scotland, McCabe had emigrated to the US from Canada, and served a four-year hitch in the US Air Force before becoming a naturalized citizen in 1964. While attending California Polytechnical University, McCabe, in his own words, "got so angry with the draft dodger professors that I just couldn't take it anymore . . . so I enlisted."

McCabe described what happened as Alpha Company pushed further into Cholon. "My squad took the left side with another squad on the right side. Within a block or so we came under heavy automatic weapons fire with rounds smacking off the walls and ricochets everywhere. We took cover by getting into the buildings and started to clear them one by one as we moved up the street."

McCabe's squad made better progress than the other Alpha

Company elements. From their advanced position at the end of the street, they could look across a wider street at the outer wall of the racetrack. They were ordered to pull back as Smaldone realigned his platoons for a final push to seize the racetrack.

From his C&C ship, Major MacGill saw a disturbing sight. Hovering over a street near the racetrack, he saw a pair of wrecked US jeeps. Sprawled beside the disabled vehicles were the bodies of several US officers in khaki uniforms. MacGill thought that the officers had been ambushed as they attempted to drive from their BOQ in Cholon to their duty station, probably MACV headquarters at Tan Son Nhut. It was a grisly sight not easily forgotten.

Captain Smaldone reassembled his platoons, and issued orders for the final push to seize the racetrack. Lieutenant Harper's Cav platoon was to support the attack with its .50 caliber machine guns moving slightly behind the infantry. The attack began moments later.

Jim MacGill recalled that Lieutenant Harper's platoon of ACAVs "got in front of Smaldone's company, and reached an intersection on the southeast corner of the racetrack before the dismounted infantry arrived." When the lead ACAV reached the intersection, it was hit with a hail of small arms, machine-gun, and rocket fire. Lieutenant Harper was riding in the lead track as the driver attempted to cross the intersection. A well-aimed RPG slammed into Harper's vehicle. The damaged ACAV continued to rumble forward before it was hit with a second B40 round. The second blast killed the 27-year-old officer and immobilized the track. The remainder of the platoon's ACAVs stopped short of the intersection and provided covering fire for the disabled vehicle.

Sergeant Mike Holiday, the track commander, ordered his men off the disabled vehicle, removing the lieutenant's body along with the wounded. Specialist Denny Jackson continued to fire one of the ACAV's M60 machine guns to cover the evacuation. Spotting a ditch beside the road, Sergeant Holiday led his wounded men toward it. Before reaching its relative safety Holiday was hit, but he managed to get all the casualties into the ditch.

Just as the party reached the ditch, the badly damaged ACAV was hit a third time, forcing Specialist Jackson to abandon the vehicle. Grabbing his M16 rifle, he leapt off the track and sprinted toward the ditch. He never made it. The 20-year-old native of Santa Paula, California was mortally wounded after courageously providing covering fire that allowed five of his wounded buddies to reach cover. Sergeant Holiday continued to place suppressive fire on the enemy from the ditch until he too was mortally wounded. The remaining tracks began to pull back to better firing positions. Enemy fire seemed to come from everywhere.

Orbiting overhead, Major MacGill observed the fighting and tried to find an alternate route for Smaldone's men to reach the racetrack. MacGill expected the ground force to link up with a platoon of MPs, but he had no radio frequencies for the MP force. In fact, the MP platoon was scattered all around the streets and buildings near the racetrack.

When MacGill spotted two MPs on a rooftop four blocks south of the track, he ordered his pilot to land on the rooftop. After instructing his pilot to find a refueling pad, MacGill and his artillery LNO jumped off the helicopter to coordinate with the MPs on the rooftop. Before the OH-23 lifted off, the officers grabbed a belt of ammo for the MPs' M60 machine gun. When the MPs were ambushed, they had removed the M60 from their gun jeep before taking up a position on the rooftop. Along with the MPs there were two Saigon policemen, "white mice," defending the building. The policemen guarded the stairwell leading to the lower floors, while the MPs fired their M60 at VC positions in the surrounding buildings. Major MacGill was shocked to learn that the VC also held the lower floors of the building on which he had landed. The Major and Captain joined the MPs in firing at the surrounding VC.

As Captain Smaldone's grunts fought their way up the street, Major MacGill radioed the Alpha Company CO, pinpointing the enemy strongpoints. The major also radioed for gunship support, but was told by the US advisors at the Capital Military District (CMD) headquarters that none were available. At that time, Major MacGill was unclear about who the Cottonbalers were working for. It was very unusual for a US infantry battalion to be under the operational control (OPCON) of a Vietnamese Headquarters. Fortunately, that situation was about to change for the better.

CMD Headquarters, Saigon—1000–1100 Hours

General Fred Weyand, the II Field Force Commander, had already made the decision to send his Deputy, Major General Keith Lincoln Ware, and a select group of officers to Saigon to form a US Task Force to assume operational control of all US forces fighting in the city. He could not have chosen better men.

General Ware, a WWII Medal of Honor recipient, was a calm and unassuming general officer who knew just what to do in a crisis. Ware had hand-picked a lieutenant colonel from the II Field Force G3 section to be his Task Force operations officer. That choice was LTC Bill Schroeder. Schroeder was reassigned to II Field Force Headquarters after completing his command tour with the Warrior battalion. General Ware and LTC Schroeder helicoptered in to the CMD compound in Saigon, on the morning of 31 January, and "Task Force Ware" became operational at 1055 hours.

Bill Schroeder recalled that he and Major General Ware were met at the CMD helipad by a jeep driven by a US Air Force sergeant. The helipad, which was adjacent to the CMD compound, was under sniper fire from the surrounding buildings when Ware's C&C ship landed. It was obvious that the USAF sergeant driving the jeep was anxious to make the pick-up and get back to the relative safety of the compound. Schroeder recalled that the General stepped out of the Huey and walked calmly to the jeep, unperturbed by the rounds striking the ground around him. As soon as the General, his aide, and LTC Schroeder were in the jeep, the sergeant popped the clutch and drove at breakneck speed to get himself and the three officers out of harm's way. The jeep swerved around the dirt-filled 55-gallon drums that were positioned in front of the compound's gate and nearly rolled over. From that point on, the US forces battling for control of Saigon had a two-star general on the ground to direct their efforts.

Cholon, Near the Phu Tho Racetrack—1000 Hours

While Task Force Ware was setting up shop at the CMD compound, Captain Smaldone's grunts continued to fight their way through the throbbing late-morning heat of Cholon toward the racetrack. The

Alpha Company platoons moved out filing down both sides of the street, checking out each building for enemy snipers.

Twenty-five-year-old Specialist Fletcher Lewis from Danville, Virginia led his squad up the street searching for VC. Suddenly, his squad was taken under fire by three enemy snipers. Lewis spotted the trio and killed two. The third ran into a building. Noticing that one of his own men was wounded and lying in the street, Lewis rushed to his side, applied first aid, and then carried the injured soldier to safety. As he returned to his squad to search for the third sniper, Specialist Lewis was shot in the head.

Moving a few feet behind Lewis, Specialist McCabe saw him go down. McCabe later wrote, "When we tried to reach him we came under fire from down the alley somewhere." McCabe's squad then took cover behind the corner of a building. McCabe continued: "We just put our rifles around the corner without looking and blazed away to keep their heads down so we could pull Lewis back under cover." A grunt crawled forward and dragged Lewis back around the corner of the building, but the head wound was fatal.

Specialist Dennis Cave spotted one of the snipers and moved forward into an exposed position where he was repeatedly fired on by the VC. Trading shots with the sniper, Cave finally found his mark and killed the enemy sharpshooter. The fighting continued doorway to doorway, and block to block.

Specialist McCabe's platoon sergeant ordered him to take another man and work down an alley to flush out another sniper nest. McCabe wrote, "These guys were well trained and damn good shots because after three steps they fired at us and one round grazed the top of my helmet and another hit the machine-gun ammo I was carrying on my back." McCabe and his buddy worked their way down the alley, busting through houses until they reached one with walls too thick to break through. Peering around the corner of a porch on the front of the house, the grunts spotted an enemy position within hand grenade range. McCabe's partner hurled a grenade, but it bounced off a wall and landed a few feet in front of the grunts. McCabe recalled, "I never knew we could move so fast but the walls saved us anyway."

The distinctive chattering sound of AK-47 assault rifles continued to echo off the bullet-pocked buildings that lined the streets, and spent rounds ricocheted off the pavement around the grunts. Instinctively the Cottonbalers ran in a low crouch, making the short rushes between buildings while their buddies provided covering fire from doorways along the street. Smoke grenades were popped to screen their moves. Broken glass from shattered shop windows along with bricks and masonry from B40 rocket explosions littered the streets and sidewalks.

When the grunts were pinned down by enemy fire in the street, they remembered the urban warfare refresher training they had had and blasted their way through walls from one building to the next using C4 explosives. One Cottonbaler recalled, "We used our 90mm recoilless rifles a lot during fighting in the city. We would use them on windows when we received fire from a building." Progress was slow, measured by buildings cleared one by one. The moist air was stifling and reeked of cordite, burnt wood, rotting garbage, and the stench of dead bodies. Occasionally, the men had to hold their fire as fleeing civilians ran down the street attempting to get out of harm's way. It was a scene reminiscent of World War II street fighting in Manila, Salerno, or St. Lo.

At 1015 hours, Alpha Company's lead element linked up with a group of US MPs. The MPs, who had fought for their lives throughout the night and on through the early morning hours, were more than happy to see the grunts. The lightly armed MPs reported that they had been under heavy fire until 15 minutes before the Cottonbalers arrived. They pointed out the buildings where the VC had their strongpoints, and Captain Smaldone radioed for the ACAVs to move forward. After a short break, Alpha Company moved out, leaving the five VC prisoners they had captured with the MPs. The ACAV with the mounted 106mm recoilless rifle moved alongside Smaldone's lead platoon. Sniper fire was sporadic, but the closer the column moved to the racetrack the heavier it got. At 1120 hours, the advance was stalled by heavy fire, and Alpha Company reported that they were pinned down.

Major MacGill was still on the rooftop with his artillery LNO and the two MPs. He'd been in radio contact with Smaldone directing Alpha Company's advance. Both officers knew the Cholon area well from their previous Vietnam tours, and MacGill used landmarks they both knew, bars and night clubs, as reference points to direct the advance. A gunship team finally arrived to support the Cottonbalers. However, after a couple of passes at the VC positions on the rooftops surrounding MacGill's building, the gunships departed the area after reporting mechanical problems. No replacements were available. Most of the US gunships in the Saigon area that morning were supporting US and ARVN troops battling around Tan Son Nhut.

When he was notified that his OH-23 helicopter had refueled and was inbound, Major MacGill decided to go airborne again to direct the final assault on the racetrack. At 1130 hours, MacGill and his artillery LNO ran to their chopper that had landed on the rooftop. The major had just pinpointed the location of an enemy 12.75mm machine gun on a nearby rooftop for Captain Smaldone, ordering him to take it out. As MacGill's chopper lifted off the rooftop, the 106mm recoilless rifle track blasted the building where the enemy machine gun was positioned. The blast sent chunks of cement and shards of metal for hundreds of feet in all directions, some narrowly missing MacGill's helicopter. MacGill recalled that after several secondary explosions the building erupted in flames and smoke. He feared that the whole neighborhood might be set ablaze.

The Alpha Company advance continued building by building, block by block. Specialist McCabe moved at the rear of his squad, turning around every few steps to cover the squad's rear.

After crossing an intersection where an alley opened onto the street, McCabe turned around and saw four VC walking out of the alley. He wrote, "One had an RPG on his shoulder, the others had AK-47s, and they were all wearing bright red armbands and scarves around their necks. I yelled to our guys, who were all looking the other way, and raised my M16 to fire, but the damned thing jammed . . . the guy with the B40 fired it at me . . . and the rocket sailed over our heads and exploded against a building . . . our M79 gunner . . . lobbed an HE round and hit them as they reached the other side of the street. It was a perfect shot. We opened up on them and finished them off."

Twenty minutes after Major MacGill's helicopter lifted off, Alpha Company's grunts reached the southeast corner of the racetrack. Heavy machine-gun, small-arms, and B40 fire from the grandstands and concrete towers cut down some of the men as they attempted to cross the main avenue south of the track. Eight more of Smaldone's grunts were wounded. The men were evacuated to the 3d Field Hospital in Saigon.

Seizing the racetrack was an easy matter. Major MacGill received clearance from CMD to fire artillery into the racetrack if necessary; however, the 105mm howitzers with concrete-piercing ammo were still at the Cottonbaler firebase in Binh Chanh, well out of range of the racetrack. Captain Smaldone's Alpha Company, supported by the ACAV platoon, were on their own.

Smaldone ordered his ACAV forward to pound the VC positions in the racetrack with .50 caliber machine-gun fire and 106mm recoilless rifle fire, while he organized his men for an assault. The Captain's plan was to assault the southeast corner of the racetrack. An ACAV would smash through the eight-foot-high wall that bordered the southern end of the track, and the Cottonbalers would pour through the opening, fan out, and rout the enemy from their positions in the towers and grandstands. Smaldone was counting on shock, speed, and surprise to overwhelm the defenders.

The Alpha Company assault kicked off at 1435 hours, when an armored cavalry gunner took aim and fired a 106mm high-explosive anti-tank round into the racetrack's cement wall. A 12- ton ACAV then sped across the intersection and smashed its way through the breach. Cottonbalers moved at double time behind the tracked vehicle and swarmed through the breach behind the ACAV. The grunts then fanned out and ran toward the grandstands, firing as they ran. Most were too pumped with adrenaline to notice the half-dozen or so terrified racehorses that were loose from their stables and stampeding around the infield. Once the grunts reached the grandstands, they began ascending the stairwells in the towers, clearing rooms as they went.

Lieutenant Bill Starrett recalled tossing frag grenades into rooms before entering and spraying them with his CAR15. One of the rooms was a men's restroom with cement walls and a recessed trench in the floor with brass foot plates for those using the facility. Starett recalled that his rounds ricocheted off the cement floor and he narrowly missed wounding himself with his own fire. Seven VC who were trapped in the grandstands were killed and four weapons were captured, but the remainder escaped through the racetrack's rear gate when the US troops breached the south wall. They didn't go far, but instead took cover in buildings that bordered the north end of the track. At 1555 hours, Captain Smaldone reported that the racetrack was secure at a cost of three US dead and fifteen wounded.

The Alpha Company Cottonbalers were not surprised to see their CO seated in a folding chair in the infield, calmly reading a copy of the Wall Street Journal as he awaited the arrival of the rest of the battalion. They'd seen it before, and according to Cottonbaler Lieutenant Bill Trotter, "It had a calming effect on the men to see the old man reading his Wall Street Journal while chaos was running wild."

LTC Gibler had his Bravo and Charlie Companies standing by on a pick-up zone (PZ) near Binh Chanh, waiting for the racetrack to be cleared. Fifteen minutes after Smaldone gave the all clear, Charlie Company lifted off the PZ, landing at 1618 hours on the infield. Gunships hovered around the periphery of the racetrack like hungry sharks ready to strike the VC with rockets and machine guns. A few green tracer rounds from the enemy arched skyward from the surrounding rooftops in a defiant gesture. The enemy fire was quickly answered and suppressed by the gunships. The lift ships returned to Binh Chanh to pick up more Cottonbalers, and by 1715 hours, Bravo and Charlie Companies were on the ground at the track.

When LTC Gibler arrived, he set up his forward command post in the racetrack director's office where there was a large TV. Gibler and his officers tuned in the Armed Forces Network to catch the latest news on the fighting in other parts of the city. They were amused when the commentator announced that the VC still held the racetrack. As darkness fell over the tense city, the Cottonbalers steeled themselves for a counterattack. One of the grunts commented that "it had been a helluva long day."

CHAPTER 11

NIGHT OF FIRE

Phu Tho Racetrack, 3/7th CP—0030 Hours, 1 February 1968

Darkness brought little relief from the swamp-like heat and humidity of Cholon. The smell of smoke from fires smoldering throughout the district spread through the night air. From atop the grandstands, the Cottonbaler riflemen peered through their Starlight scopes at the streets below and across the rooftops of nearby buildings. Occasional shots rang out, as the grunts traded fire with VC snipers.

While Gibler's men braced themselves for a VC counterattack at the racetrack, the grunts at the battalion's fire support base at Binh Chanh prepared for the long night ahead. The 3/7th support staff and the battalion's direct support artillery battery remained at FSB Zindernuef. When the Cottonbaler rifle companies deployed to Cholon, the battalion's Echo Company was left behind to secure the firebase perimeter. The battalion XO, Major John Borgman, was the officer-in-charge at Zindernuef. Borgman breathed a sigh of relief when Bravo and Charlie Companies of the 5/60th Infantry, nicknamed the "Banditios," rolled into Binh Chanh on the evening of 31 January after a long road march from their base in the Mekong Delta. Upon their arrival, the two companies were attached to the 3/7th Infantry at the direction of Major General Ware. As darkness fell, the Bandito APCs rolled into positions along the perimeter of FSB Zindernuef, significantly enhancing the defensive posture of the base. The deployment of the two mech infantry companies to Zindernuef was a timely move.

167

A few hours later, the perimeter of the Cottonbaler firebase was attacked with RPG, machine-gun, and mortar fire, resulting in three WIA in Echo Company and seven WIA in the Bandito Bravo and Charlie Companies. The troops along the perimeter returned fire with small arms and the mech infantry's .50 caliber machine guns to break up the ground attack, while artillery fire knocked out the enemy mortars. The attack was part of a larger enemy effort to pin down the US troops outside Saigon to prevent their deployment into the city.

At 0030 hours, Major General Ware radioed the Cottonbaler CP at the racetrack to coordinate a plan of action for February 1st. The General directed LTC Gibler to begin clearing Cholon, starting with the area around the Phu Tho Racetrack. Bravo and Charlie Companies from the 5/60th Infantry were ordered to road march from FSB Zinderneuf at first light to reinforce Gibler's battalion. The remainder of LTC Bill Steele's 5/60th Infantry was ordered to conduct operations in the Binh Chanh area. Echo Company, 3/7th was attached to Steele's battalion. After his conversation with General Ware, LTC Gibler and his S3, Major MacGill, formulated a plan for clearing the area around the racetrack.

Bravo and Charlie Companies, 3/7th were ordered to search and clear the area west of the track. The two companies were directed to move north from Highway 4 on the west side of Highway 235, while Captain Smaldone's Alpha Company stayed behind as battalion reserve. When the two 5/60th mech companies arrived in Cholon, they were under orders to conduct a reconnaissance-in-force to the northwest of the racetrack, while the 33d ARVN Ranger Battalion, operating under the control of the 3/7th, was assigned the mission of clearing the area to the east.

Bravo and Charlie Companies of the 5/60th Mech departed Binh Chanh for Cholon at 0642 hours on the morning of 1 February. The Banditios were the first 9th Division units ordered to the capital city in response to the Tet attacks. Following Highway 4, the long column of Armored Personnel Carriers rumbled past the same scenes of devastation witnessed by Smaldone's company the day prior. As the column crossed a bridge on the outskirts of the city, the tracks took small-arms fire, but the column raced on toward Cholon. When the column entered the southern part of Cholon, the mech infantry companies halted at a street intersection where an MP truck had been overturned. Several dead MPs lay beside the vehicle, and the survivors had taken cover in a building. The MPs related that their truck had been hit with a large command-detonated explosive device. After rescuing the badly shaken MPs, the mech infantry moved out toward the racetrack. When they arrived, the Bandito COs were briefed by the Cottonbaler S3, Major MacGill, on the reconnaissance-in-force mission.

Cholon—1500–1800 hours, 1 February

Captain James Scarboro's Bravo Company, 5/60 Mech, began a reconnaissance-in-force northwest of the racetrack at 1500 hours, moving out on the west side of Highway 235. It was their first taste of urban combat. Moving cautiously, Scarboro's infantrymen halted frequently to dismount their tracks and search suspicious buildings, covered by the APCs' .50 caliber machine guns By 1600 hours, Bravo's mech infantrymen were about a kilometer northwest of the racetrack. As the company turned a corner, the men noticed a number of Vietnamese civilians departing the area while others ran into the houses that lined the street. Although the Vietnamese told Scarboro's troops nothing about what lay ahead, it was obvious to the Americans that they were headed into trouble. Captain Scarboro, in a 1968 interview with the 9th Division's Old Reliable magazine, told what happened next.

"As we moved slowly along the street, I noticed women pulling their children into the houses, and people covering their ears with their hands. I knew something was waiting for us."

Scarboro then related how his company continued cautiously about one third of the way down the street until they neared a large cemetery off the right side of the road. As he scanned the buildings along the road, a small Vietnamese boy ran alongside his command vehicle, shouting "VC, VC, VC!"

The Captain reported that, "Near the edge of the cemetery, I saw a flash from behind one of the many large trees growing in the cemetery. Then a B40 rocket hit the second track in my column." Then all hell broke loose.

The M113 burst into flames as a murderous barrage of rocket and machine-gun fire raked the column. The VC were firing from buildings to the southeast and northwest, and from the cemetery. Rounds ricocheted off the street around the tracks, showering the area with concrete shards. Captain Scarboro immediately deployed his tracks in a battle formation and returned fire with .50 caliber machine guns, while the remainder of his infantrymen dismounted and took up firing positions around the tracks. While his men returned fire, Scarboro ordered the driver of his command track to move forward through the intense fire to rescue the wounded from the burning vehicle.

Scarboro stated in his interview that "The VC were firing down on us from the treetops. You could see them tumble out of the trees as our shots found their mark. They were using B-40 rockets and had a recoilless rifle set up in a shack at the center of the cemetery."

As Scarboro's command track rolled forward toward the burning M113, it was hit on the left side with a recoilless rifle round. The Captain received multiple fragmentation wounds from the blast, and the vehicle's radios were destroyed. In the magazine interview Scarboro recalled, "I was grazed by the shrapnel and was helped out of my track to a building nearby. My men continued to return fire. Some dismounted to check the buildings adjacent to the cemetery."

First Lieutenant Bruce Mills, Bravo's 2nd Platoon leader, then moved forward with his men to aggressively engage the enemy in the cemetery. When he learned that his CO was out of the fight, the Bravo Company Executive Officer, First Lieutenant Robert Whitworth, assumed command. Unaware that the VC were rushing reinforcements into the cemetery, Whitworth ordered an assault on the enemy positions. A few minutes after the Bravo Company attack began, it stalled when the VC unleashed a volley of rocket fire. At that point, Bravo Company had three men KIA and 12 wounded.

The casualties were loaded onto two Bravo Company APCs for evacuation to the racetrack, the nearest location where a dust-off could land. Lieutenant Bill Starrett from the 3/7th had set up an emergency evacuation LZ at the track's "winners circle," when he learned that the Bandito casualties were en route. Starrett stated, "The M113s rumbled into the racetrack, lowered their troop compartment ramps, and the wounded troops, many with chest wounds, were carried off on stretchers by the medics." Starrett also recalled that the APCs that were used to evacuate the wounded had "50-cent-size holes in them."

The casualties were flown from the racetrack to 3d Field Hospital in Saigon.

Meanwhile, LTC Gibler and Major MacGill flew overhead of the Bravo Company fight and took control of the battle. MacGill thought that Bravo Company was blocked in, and he was concerned about losing the entire company. LTC Gibler requested artillery support and air strikes to smash the enemy force in the cemetery, but his request was denied due to possible civilian casualties and collateral damage. Frustrated by the restrictions, the Cottonbaler commander ordered the Banditos' Charlie Company, 5/60th to reinforce the embattled Bravo Company. A "Razorback" gunship team was also diverted to the area to provide fire support to the ground troops.

As Charlie Company raced toward the cemetery, the Razorback gunship team began to rake the enemy positions with rockets and machine-gun fire. Rumbling down the streets of Cholon at breakneck speed, Charlie Company's column soon reached the northeast corner of the cemetery. The Charlie CO brought his tracks of on-line, and opened up on the enemy's exposed flank with .50 caliber fire, tearing the VC positions to pieces. Taking advantage of the overwhelming firepower, Bravo Company launched a frontal assault on the VC stronghold in the cemetery, routing the enemy from their positions.

After the savage fighting, an estimated 128 enemy bodies lay strewn in and around the cemetery along with numerous weapons and munitions. The Banditos had no time to police the battleground. They were ordered by LTC Gibler to mount up and return immediately to the racetrack. A Viet Cong force was preparing to attack the track from the west. There was no time to recover the badly damaged M113s. Gibler ordered the Razorback gunships to completely destroy the damaged M113s with rocket fire to prevent their capture by enemy forces.

Phu Tho Racetrack—1700–1900 Hours, 1 February

The evacuation of the Bandito Bravo and Charlie Company casualties was still in progress when Colonel Davison, the 199th LIB's acting commander, attempted to land his C&C ship at the racetrack. Lieutenant Starrett recalled that the enemy fired RPGs at Davison's helicopter as it made a final approach to an LZ set up in the infield. The enemy gunners aimed their rockets at a gap between the grandstands. As the rockets exploded in the infield, Starrett radioed the pilot directing him to land closer to the winners circle area near the stands. When Colonel Davison landed safely, Starrett asked the Colonel's permission to use the C&C ship to evacuate some of the wounded to 3d Field Hospital.

After giving his OK, Davison ran toward an ACAV that was buttoned-up and idling in front the grandstands. According to Starrett, the ACAV was "just sitting there and not returning fire at the VC RPG gunners, who were firing into the racetrack from across the avenue." As the rounds exploded a few yards in front of the ACAV, Davison climbed onto the track and banged on the commander's hatch until it opened. According to Starrett, "The Colonel then proceeded to give the cavalrymen a pep talk." The ACAV commander, taking his cue from Davison, quickly put his .50 caliber machine gun into action against VC across the avenue. Standing on the deck of the ACAV, Colonel Davison continued to pick out targets for the machine gunner for several minutes before heading for the Cottonbaler TOC for an update on the situation.

While the 199th LIB commander received his briefing, Bravo and Charlie Companies, 5/60th Mech were rolling at maximum speed toward the racetrack. Meanwhile, atop the grandstands, Smaldone's Alpha Company grunts were in an intense firefight with VC concealed in buildings across the avenue. Two Alpha Company grunts were wounded in the exchange. Lieutenant Starrett grabbed a couple of headquarters troops and ran a resupply of M60 ammo and M79 rounds up the stairwells of the grandstands to the embattled Alpha Company grunts. Moments later the Bandito mech infantry companies rolled into racetrack in the nick of time. The VC broke off their attack. As darkness approached, the Cottonbalers and Banditos settled in for the long night ahead.

Cholon—2–4 February 1968

The 3/7th Infantry task force continued to clear the neighborhoods around the Phu Tho Racetrack on the 2d and 3d of February. Only light contact was made with VC units in and around the racetrack during this period. The VC units operating in Cholon had "gone to ground" in the face of overwhelming US firepower. Local Force VC commanders awaited reinforcement by main force VC and NVA battalions. They were never told that the Communist high command (COSVN) had, for the moment, decided not to commit additional units to the fight. Under relentless pressure from US and ARVN forces, the local force VC commanders switched tactics and ordered their troops to blend in with the civilian population and fight only when cornered.

At the request of the South Vietnamese Joint General Staff, General Ware began shifting the responsibility for clearing Saigon, including Cholon, to the Vietnamese. A realignment of the Capital area of operations was agreed upon. The Vietnamese armed forces were assigned responsibility for searching and clearing Saigon, and US forces began to move to the districts around the city to prevent Communist reinforcements from reaching the capital.

The ARVN 5th Ranger Group was assigned the mission of clearing Cholon, and on 4 February Gibler's 3/7th Infantry terminated its operations and returned to Binh Chanh to fight in its former area of operations. Bravo and Charlie Companies of the 5/60th Mech returned to control of their parent unit. The Cottonbaler battalion's efforts to seize control of the Phu Tho Racetrack and surrounding neighborhoods were successful. No one anticipated that the battalion would have to return to Cholon within a few days.

AO South Uniontown—0100 hours, 2 February

It was shortly after 0100 hours on 2 February. Specialist Bob Archibald, still carrying a small piece of shrapnel in his right leg, squinted as he looked down the road trying to focus on the scene unfolding before his eyes. Through the dense smoke that covered the hilltop, he could just make out a column of infantry approaching the Charlie Company perimeter.

Archibald wrote: "The thing that impressed me the most was the walking red curtain of gunship tracer rounds protecting them as they came up the road to us. I can still see the jets dropping the napalm just outside our lines." Ten minutes later, a relief column entered Charlie Company's perimeter ending a long night of fighting.

Ho Nai Village—1500 Hours, 1 February

Captain Tonsetic was concerned about his company's latest mission. Charlie, 4/12th was attached to the 2/3d Infantry after the heavy fighting in Ho Nai village on the night of 31 January. The Charlie Company grunts were exhausted. After the heavy fighting north of the village, Charlie Company spent the afternoon of 1 February searching Ho Nai village for VC. No one in the company had had more than an hour or two of sleep over the preceding two days.

LTC Carper, the 2/3d battalion commander briefed his company commanders and Captain Tonsetic on his plan for the night of 1–2 February. He started by briefing the company commanders on the latest intelligence. One VC battalion was still unaccounted for, and it was highly probable that it was located north of the Long Binh base complex and Ho Nai Village.

The 2/3d commander outlined his plan. Three rifle companies from the 2/3d were ordered to dig in and defend Ho Nai village, while Charlie, 4/12th was directed to move two kilometers north and establish a night defensive position. Pointing to a piece of high ground on his map, the Old Guard Commander said, "That's where Charlie Company will dig in, and block any enemy movement through the area." Tactically speaking it was a good plan. A company-size strongpoint on the high ground would provide early warning of another enemy attack through Ho Nai village, and it would also interdict any east–west movement of enemy units attempting to reinforce the attacks on Bien Hoa. Nonetheless, the Charlie Company commander had doubts whether his two depleted platoons of infantry and five ACAVs could successfully defend the hill against a battalion-size attack. LTC Carper told Captain Tonsetic that he would try to get Charlie Company's 1st Platoon released from its mission at the POW compound.

The Charlie Company grunts trudged northward in a double column up the dirt road, reaching the designated NDP shortly after 1800 hours. The jungle was bulldozed back about 75 yards from the center of the perimeter. The road continued on down the northern slope of the hill toward the Dong Nai River. Charlie Company's 3d and 4th platoons set up a 360-degree perimeter around the military crest of the hill. The five ACAVs from D/17th Cav were positioned around the perimeter to support the infantry. The ground was rocky, making it all but impossible for the grunts to dig in. They scraped away the topsoil and filled a few sandbags to complete their fighting positions before wolfing down a supper of cold C rations.

Captain Tonsetic was concerned about artillery support. Over the past 24 hours, artillery fire missions had poured in to the firing batteries, and the FDCs were forced to prioritize the missions. The Captain wanted his company's 81mm mortars on the hill. Firing from the company's perimeter, the 81mm's could engage targets out to a range of 4,000 yards, and as close as 50 meters to the perimeter. However, Charlie Company's mortars were at FSB Concord.

The Captain radioed his battalion CO, LTC Mastoris, to request that Charlie Company's 81mm mortars be flown in immediately. The Warrior battalion commander agreed to send one of the mortars. The other two were needed to defend FSB Concord. The 81mm mortar, along with 60 rounds of ammo, were flown to Charlie Company's NDP just before dark. Platoon Sergeant Jaynes had the mortar set up in a matter of minutes. He hoped that 60 rounds of ammo would see the company through the night.

At dusk, Lieutenant Tuber's 1st Platoon rolled into the perimeter with five ACAVs and two jeep-mounted 106mm recoilless rifles. Weary from their fight at the POW compound, the 1st Platoon grunts were rushed to positions along the perimeter.

Charlie Company—NDP, 2030–2400 Hours, 2 February

At 2030 hours, a group of VC were spotted crossing the road about 150 meters north of Charlie Company's perimeter. Almost simultaneously, enemy automatic weapons fire was received from the south and west. Captain Tonsetic ordered his lone 81mm mortar to fire on the group north of the perimeter, while he called for artillery and gunship support to silence the enemy positions to the west. The mortar was not completely dug in, and the crew was exposed to heavy incoming fire.

One of the men recalled that the gunner was laying on his back adjusting the elevation on the mortar, while the other gunner lay beside the tube preparing each round for firing. The gunner would then raise his body just enough to drop a round down the tube. The mortar rounds impacted 150 meters north of the perimeter with bright flashes and thunderous explosions, scattering the enemy in all directions. However, the preplanned artillery fires that the Captain plotted to the west of the perimeter required significant adjustments to get the rounds on target. Meanwhile, Jayne's mortar fire and .50 caliber machine-gun fire from the ACAVs broke up the attack from the north. However, the supply of mortar rounds was running low.

A few minutes later, a pair of gunships arrived overhead, followed shortly by a C-47 "Spooky" flare ship. Flying in a high orbit over the rocky hillock, the C-47 illuminated the area with flares. Tonsetic radioed his platoon leaders to mark their locations with strobe lights, as he directed gunship strikes on the enemy. The helicopter gunships pounded the jungle with machine guns and rockets on the west side of the perimeter, while the Air Force C-47's Gatling gun hosed down the enemy to the east.

Small-arms fire continued for the next hour as the enemy probed the perimeter looking for a weak spot. Spooky and the gunships were shooting at anything that moved outside the perimeter. At 2300 hours, the battle began to intensify on the east side of the perimeter. A barrage of RPG fire slammed into the perimeter, showering the ground with shrapnel but missing its intended targets, the ACAVs. One of the RPG teams moved forward to get a better shot and scored one direct hit on an ACAV, seriously wounding six members of the crew. An M79 gunner on the perimeter lobbed a 40mm round on the RPG team before they got off a second shot. Spooky shifted its fires closer to the perimeter, and was soon spraying the jungle with a wavy stream of red tracers like a garden hose. Each burst of the C-47's Gatling gun sounding like a buzzsaw.

With Spooky and the gunships on station, Captain Tonsetic radioed for a dust-off for the six seriously wounded troopers. The chopper arrived a few minutes before midnight. On his first attempt to land, the pilot was driven off by a barrage of enemy fire. After the gunships shifted their fires to cover the dust-off, the pilot made a second attempt to land. In the darkness, he started to touch down outside the perimeter. Tonsetic radioed the pilot, telling him to abort the landing. The pilot pulled pitch and took off through a hail of enemy fire that ripped through the medevac chopper's tail boom.

Undeterred, the dust-off pilot returned and landed inside the perimeter on his third attempt under heavy incoming fire. A medic who was helping to load the wounded aboard the ship was hit, and was himself pulled aboard by a crewmember. After the wounded men were on board, the pilot lifted off under intense fire. Despite sustaining several more hits, the dust-off ship cleared a tree line and raced to the 93d Evacuation Hospital in time to save the men on board.

The battle continued unabated. Tonsetic was concerned about an all-out attack on the eastern side of the perimeter. All of the 81mm mortar rounds had been fired, and the Captain knew his men were running low on rifle and machine-gun ammo. He radioed LTC Carper for assistance. Carper ordered Charlie Company, 2/3d, and another platoon of ACAVs to move north and reinforce Captain Tonsetic's embattled company.

Charlie Co. Night Defensive Position—0100–1400 Hours, 2 Feb.

A Forward Air Controller (FAC) and two U.S. F-4s were on station over Charlie Company's night defensive position at 0130 hours. Captain Tonsetic requested that the high-performance aircraft strike the enemy positions in the dense jungle 100 yards east of his perimeter, using a south to north approach. Seconds later, the Phantoms soared in at treetop level dropping napalm canisters. Cliff Kaylor, Captain Tonsetic's radio operator, recalled "a blast of heat as the napalm ignited." The grunts on the eastern side of the perimeter saw several VC run out of the burning jungle. Their uniforms were on fire and the men were screaming as the Phantoms began a strafing run. Firing their 20mm automatic cannon, the jets roared over the jungle and started their afterburners. The air strike broke the backbone of the enemy assault, although the perimeter continued to receive sporadic fire.

With the night sky illuminated by flares and the burning napalm, the Charlie Company grunts saw the point element of their relief force approaching from the south. Ten additional ACAVs accompanied the relief column. Gunships flew along the flanks of the column firing at the insurgents. The relief column suffered only two casualties during their approach. After the Old Guard's Charlie Company entered the perimeter, a medevac was called to evacuate the casualties.

Moments later, a wounded enemy soldier stumbled into the Charlie Company perimeter and was taken prisoner. Specialist George Hauer, one of the Charlie Company medics, began to apply a pressure bandage to the man's gunshot wound. Nearby, two Charlie Company grunts began to rebuke Hauer for treating the enemy soldier. Hauer reminded the men that his job was to "treat all the wounded, both friendly and enemy, in accordance with the Geneva Convention." The wounded VC was put aboard the same dust-off with the Charlie Company wounded.

At first light, the company's grunts scanned the area around their perimeter. Smoke from the burning jungle and damaged ACAVs hung low over the hillock. The air was polluted with the odor of cordite, napalm, and burnt human flesh. Three dazed and terribly burned VC wandered into the perimeter and were taken prisoner. A patrol was sent into the battered jungle to the east, and they radioed back that they'd found more than fifty bodies burned beyond recognition. Other Charlie Company grunts swept the area just outside the perimeter to claim the weapons laying beside enemy corpses. Almost every Charlie company grunt now carried a captured AK-47 in addition to his assigned weapon. Nowhere had the VC actually breached the perimeter, but some bodies were found within 25 meters of the company's fighting positions..

Charlie Company spent the remainder of the morning on the hill, patrolling in the vicinity, and finding more weapons and bodies, taking one additional prisoner. At 1330 hours Charlie Company was released from operational control of the 2/3d Infantry and ordered to return to FSB Concord.

An hour later, the ACAV column with Charlie Company's infantrymen on board rolled into the firebase. They were met by LTC Mastoris and Sergeant Major Moon. As the exhausted Charlie Company Warriors dismounted the tracks, the Warrior commander began shaking hands with his men as his Sergeant Major distributed cases of beer to each platoon. During three days of intense combat, Charlie Company had played a key role in repulsing the enemy attacks on Camp Frenzell-Jones and the POW compound near Bien Hoa. Two Distinguished Service Crosses, three Silver Stars, and numerous other awards for valor were awarded to the men of Charlie Company for their heroism during the Tet Offensive of 1968.

CHAPTER 12

COTTONBALER HOT LZ

Binh Chanh District—4–5 February

The 3/7th task force completed their movement from Cholon to Binh Chanh District on the evening of 4 February. The Cottonbalers and the two attached 5/60th mech infantry companies needed rest and recuperation after four days of heavy urban combat, but the fighting was far from over. The rifle companies of the Cottonbaler battalion were ordered to establish platoon-size night ambush positions throughout AO Haverford. Lieutenant Bill Trotter, Bravo Company's 2nd Platoon leader, later wrote, "It was so dark that we had to move in a file formation with each man holding on to the LBE of the man in front." The exhausted grunts moved into night ambush positions and waited for dawn.

While the rifle companies sent out their ambush patrols, Lt. Colonel Gibler and Major MacGill planned the next day's operations. The battalion's new mission was to block and disrupt the enemy infiltration routes into the Saigon area to prevent reinforcements from reaching the city. Two highways, QL-4 and 233, ran through the district. These roads ran from the Mekong Delta to Saigon, and were used to infiltrate men and supplies into the city prior to Tet. The mission of interdicting enemy infiltration along road networks was assigned to the attached 5/60th mechanized infantry companies.

The insurgents also used the Kinh Sanh Canal that ran through the northern portion of Binh Chanh District. This canal was used by the enemy to move men, weapons, ammunition, and other supplies into

Saigon. During daylight hours, the men and supplies were hidden in small base camps and villages along the canal. At night, sampans loaded with men and supplies slipped silently up the canal headed for the city. Intelligence reports pinpointed the village of Tan Nhut, as a major enemy waystation along the canal. Gibler and MacGill planned to cordon and search the village. The plan called for Bravo Company to conduct an airmobile assault just east of the village before moving overland to establish a cordon and conduct the search. In the event of a major contact, Alpha, and Charlie Companies were on call to reinforce Bravo Company. Major MacGill requested an airmobile assault helicopter company from Task Force Ware. He wanted the company available from 0730 hours to 1700 hours on 5 February. MacGill's request was approved, and the tasking was given to the118th Assault Helicopter Company stationed at Bien Hoa. The 118th was nicknamed the "Thunderbirds."

February 5th started badly for the Cottonbaler battalion. Shortly after midnight, the Cottonbaler TOC received a call from the Binh Chanh advisory team that their compound was under heavy mortar attack and needed assistance. Major MacGill ordered one platoon from Charlie Company with a team of medics to evacuate the casualties. When the Cottonbalers arrived at the compound, they found three ARVN KIAs and six WIAs. They evacuated the casualties to FSB Zinderneuf for further treatment.

Shortly after 0300 hours, Charlie Company, 5/60th Mech, was attacked in a night lager position. The company was hit with mortar and B40 rocket fire. One M113A1 was destroyed and another was damaged by the enemy fire. The Banditos returned the fire with machine guns and small arms, and the CO requested artillery and gunship support. When a gunship team reached the area, the mech infantrymen marked the enemy targets with .50 caliber tracer rounds. On each strafing run, the gunships fired salvos of 2.75mm rockets, finishing up with machine-gun fire. Artillery flares illuminated the dry rice paddies, silhouetting the fleeing VC. The attack ended as suddenly as it began as the remnants of the enemy force faded away into the night shadows. When a dust-off landed, six wounded and two dead from Charlie Company were loaded aboard. Shortly thereafter, LTC

Gibler was notified that the two 5/60th mech infantry companies were to return to control of their parent unit the following morning.

When MacGill received approval for the airmobile assault, he alerted the Bravo Company CO. Captain Kent Pietsch, a 1964 West Point graduate, who was an experienced commander with four months of combat behind him. First Sergeant Bobby Dalrymple was the company's Top Sergeant. He wore the CIB with star, a veteran of both the Vietnam and Korean Wars. During the latter, he had been a member of an elite airborne ranger company. Captain Pietsch picked his two most experienced platoon leaders, Lieutenants Joe (Scotty) Burgett and Bill Trotter, to lead the airmobile assault. The two lieutenants had gone through officer candidate school together, and trusted each other implicitly. Both were highly regarded by grunts in the Cottonbaler battalion.

By 1000 hours, the weary Bravo Company grunts were lined up by chalk load on the rice paddy PZ. Captain Pietsch and First Sergeant Dalrymple were going in with the first lift along with Burgett's 1st Platoon and Trotter's 2nd. Bill Trotter later recalled that his platoon had very little advance notice of the airmobile operation, and he was unsure of the exact location of the LZ. It was on a different map sheet than the one he carried.

A flight of nine UH-1Ds flying in tight trail formation appeared on the horizon and began their descent toward Bravo Company's PZ. The 10th lift ship had mechanical problems, and its pilot was forced to abort the mission. The two Bravo platoons and Pietsch's command group were lined up in ten chalk loads, one for each lift ship. When only nine ships landed on the PZ, the loading became confused and several personnel were left on the ground to await the second lift. Among those left behind on the PZ was Glen Pagano, one of Captain Pietsch's radio operators. The lack of one of the company's radios added to the command and control problems experienced during the airmobile assault.

The grunts jostled each other for space on the lift ships' studded metal floors as they climbed aboard. Most had made numerous airmobile assaults, but the grunts still experienced the same adrenalin rush. The crew chiefs and door gunners wore deadpan expressions as they pointed their M60 guns toward the ground. When the loading was complete, the flight leader ordered his pilots to lift off. Each Huey's turbine whined as it picked up torque, and the ships began to rise in a trail formation. The time was 1025 hours.

The grunts welcomed the cool rush of air that flowed through the open bay as the ships lifted off and picked up speed. Glancing downward, they saw a broad expanse of rice paddies, crisscrossed by canals and tree-lined streams. The flight took a northwest heading toward an LZ near Tan Nhut village on the Kinh Sang canal.

As the flight neared the LZ, the men could see bright orange flashes of artillery rounds exploding in the nipa palm growth along the canal. Gunships circled like hungry sharks around the LZ, staying clear of the artillery gun-to-target line. When the lift ships made their final approach into the LZ, the gunships flew along the flanks of the formation ready to open fire on any enemy near the LZ.

As the aircraft began their slow descent, all bantering and wisecracking among the grunts abruptly stopped as they made a final check of their weapons and equipment. Some fidgeted with the selector switches on their M16s, moving them from semi-automatic to automatic fire. The door gunners aimed their M60s at the LZ and moved their safety switches to the fire position. As the choppers approached the LZ, the grunts slid their bottoms across the floor until their legs dangled outside the open doors.

The door gunners and a few of the seasoned Cottonbalers picked up the bright green tracer rounds that reached skyward toward them, as the pilots flared the noses of their ships upward in preparation for a touch down. The door gunners returned fire with their M60s. Shell casings flew out the ejection ports of the machine guns as the door gunners sprayed the rice paddies, hedgerows, and tree line just off the LZ. With lips pursed, the stern-faced grunts waited until their lift ships were close enough to the ground to jump. Then, they lunged out the doors toward the rice paddy below. Their worst nightmares were playing out in real time. It was a hot LZ.

The UH-1D carrying Captain Pietsch and 1st Sergeant Dalrymple was hit with automatic weapons fire as it flew into the LZ. An AK-47 round tore through the Captain's lower left leg severing a nerve. Another slug wounded the captain's RTO. As the pilot flared the nose of the ship upward, preparing to land, 1st Sergeant Dalrymple slid to the door and began firing downward toward the enemy with his .45 caliber pistol. Before the ship touched down, Dalrymple took an AK-47 round through his foot. Dalrymple spotted his assailant from the air and dropped him with a pistol shot. When the ship touched down, the Captain, his 1st Sergeant, and the RTO took cover on the LZ. Then 1st Sergeant Dalrymple crawled over to the VC he had just shot and grabbed the man's AK-47, figuring it would be more useful than a .45 caliber pistol in the fight on the LZ.

Twenty-year-old Sergeant Ron Whelan's platoon was first to arrive at the PZ. Whelan carried an extra radio on the airmobile assault. He recalled that the men were very tired and the movement to the PZ had been very rushed, so much so that Captain Pietsch's radio operator missed getting on the command group's lift ship. Whelan himself was ordered to get on any ship he could find room on. He ended up on a Huey in the middle of the flight formation. As the flight began to land, he saw that the first "two or three" lift ships were disabled and "smoking" on the LZ, unable to take off. When his lift ship was 15–20 feet off the ground, the pilot decided to abort the landing, and according to Whelan, "We were ordered to jump, since many of our fellow soldiers were already on the ground . . . . I jumped with full gear and a 25-pound radio on my back." Fortunately, the muddy rice paddy cushioned Whelan's fall. The grunts from Whelan's ship took cover behind a dike. Whelan recalled that the machine-gun fire from the village was so intense that the bullets and RPGs "kept us pinned down behind the dikes for what seemed an eternity . . . nobody could move or even raise his head without becoming an easy target."

Lieutenant Bill Trotter, the 2nd Platoon leader, was aboard the eighth UH1D in the formation. He later wrote, "On our approach to the LZ, we saw a lot of smoke and the gunships were going in on strafing and rocket missions. . . .The LZ was a rice paddy. We had automatic gun fire and B-40 rockets coming at us. The incoming fire was so hot that a lot of the choppers didn't go all the way to the ground."

Lieutenant Trotter's good friend and OCS classmate, Lieutenant Scotty Burgett, was aboard the third chopper in the flight. Burgett was 1st Platoon leader. His platoon sergeant was riding in another Huey that had to turn back due to mechanical problems. Burgett's helicopter hovered over the hot LZ unable to touch down because of the intense fire. The lieutenant, his RTO, an M60 machine gunner, and three rifle-men leapt from the helicopter when it was about 20 feet above the rice paddy. They landed hard in the paddy mud as did many others. Some were injured in the fall.

Bill Trotter wrote that Burgett's M60 machine gunner injured his back when he hit the ground and was stuck in the paddy mud. "Scotty was on the ground. He saw what the situation was, and knew that he had to get his men to cover and return the fire. Scotty ran over to help his M60 gunner who was stuck in the mud. He was going to get the M60 to lay down effective fire to cover his platoon. The whole LZ was hell."

Trotter further recalled that "While Scotty [Lieutenant Burgett] was doing this, he caught a round in the chest close to the heart from an NVA who was about 30 yards away with an AK-47." Trotter spot-ted the NVA who shot his friend, and ran forward to get a shot at him from a rice paddy dike. Meanwhile, Lieutenant Burgett's men carried him to cover. The lieutenant was unconscious and died moments later. Burgett's RTO took over for his lieutenant and began directing his pla-toon's fire on the enemy positions.

Captain Pietsch fought to bring the situation under control. Despite a painful leg wound, he began to direct his men's fire toward a tree line just off the LZ where the enemy were dug in. He was assist-ed by 1st Sergeant Dalrymple, who crawled through the incoming fire to organize his company's defense of the LZ. Like his Captain, Dalrymple refused medical treatment until the other wounded were treated. First Sergeant Bobby Dalrymple was awarded the Silver Star for his courageous actions that day.

Overhead in the battalion C&C ship, Major MacGill radioed the TOC to report that there were three choppers still on the LZ. All three were heavily damaged and unable to take off. According to MacGill, the only lift ship that was not hit by enemy fire was the trail ship in the formation. Its pilot, WO William Moline, managed to land, offload the grunts, and lift off unscathed. Only after he was airborne did Moline realize that the aircrews from three downed UH1Ds were stranded on the hot LZ. When he became aware of the downed crew-men, he flew back into the LZ to pick them up. From his C&C ship,

Major MacGill saw a VC charging toward Moline's ship with his AK-47 on full automatic as the helicopter touched down. Moline's door gunner fired a burst from his M60 machine gun, killing the VC at pointblank range. After picking up the crewmembers from one of the downed ships, Moline flew to the other two ships and picked up the survivors before leaving the LZ. William Moline was awarded the Distinguished Flying Cross for his heroism and flying expertise, and later received an appointment to West Point.

Another Thunderbird pilot was shot in the leg during the landing and his ship was badly damaged. Ignoring his painful wound, the pilot lifted off and flew to FSB Zinderneuf where he safely landed his aircraft. After landing, he was rushed to the battalion aid station where the battalion surgeon worked to save his leg.

Back at the LZ, Major MacGill radioed for additional gunship support, and another airmobile assault company to insert Alpha Company into the area to reinforce Bravo. However, the Thunderbird company was too shot up to conduct another airmobile assault that day. Only one of the lift ships that left the LZ under its own power made it back to Bien Hoa without incident.

MacGill was also concerned about Bravo Company's casualties. After he radioed the brigade TOC for a dust-off, he also called upon the battalion's resupply bird to assist in the evacuation. There were more than a dozen Bravo Company wounded on the LZ, along with a number of others with back and leg injuries sustained from jumping from the lift ships.

On the ground, the fight for the LZ continued. First and second platoons were pinned down by a heavy volume of small-arms and rocket fire. Coordination between the two platoons was minimal since both platoons' radios were hit with incoming fire and rendered inoperable. Radio communications between the C&C ship and the ground commander was also a problem. According to Bill Trotter, the artillery FO had the only working radio, and he insisted that it be kept on the artillery frequency.

A few minutes before noon, a dust-off pilot radioed the LZ on the artillery frequency, saying that he was in-bound to medevac casualties. Braving the insurgent fire, the dust-off touched down on the LZ and a number of the most seriously wounded were loaded aboard. Moments later a second dust-off landed and evacuated the remainder of the wounded, including Captain Pietsch.

After Pietsch was evacuated, there was confusion about who was in command on the LZ. There were only two surviving officers, Lieutenant Trotter, the 2nd Platoon leader, and the artillery forward observer, who was also a lieutenant. Trotter recalled that the FO was senior to him based on date of rank. When the FO refused to take command, Trotter grabbed the FO's radio, switched to the battalion frequency, and took command of the remaining 45 men struggling to hold the LZ.

While the fight on the LZ continued to rage, Alpha and Charlie Companies were ordered to reinforce the embattled Bravo Company. Major MacGill directed the companies to move to nearby PZ s and await the arrival an airmobile lift company. MacGill selected an LZ to the west of Bravo Company for Charlie Company's insertion. Alpha Company's LZ was to the north. Both Alpha and Charlie Company landed on "cold LZs," and the Cottonbalers moved out quickly toward the embattled Bravo Company.

Shortly after 1500 hours, Captain Tony Smaldone's Alpha Company arrived at Bravo Company's location. Bravo's two depleted platoons had fought the VC for more than five hours before the reinforcements arrived. With a resupply of ammunition and reinforcements, the momentum of the battle shifted in the grunts' favor.

Captain Smaldone quickly organized his platoons to assault the enemy-held positions. The VC were dug in along a tree line about 150 meters off the LZ. With fire support from "Silver Spur" and "Razorback" gunship teams and a pair of Vietnamese gunboats, the Cottonbalers surged across the paddy to assault the enemy positions. Gunships swooped down on the tree line, firing rockets and machine guns at the enemy fortifications. Smaldone's grunts fired short bursts from the hip, switching to longer bursts as they neared the tree line. The nipa palm and bamboo shook as if blown by a violent windstorm when hit with the barrage of fire. When the skirmish line reached the trees, the Alpha Company grunts fought with a frenzy to destroy the VC bunkers with hand grenades and small-arms fire. The VC who were pinned down in the bunkers returned a ragged, inaccurate fire.

The Cottonbalers advanced relentlessly, taking out bunker after bunker.

Sergeant Ronald Burkhart led one of the Alpha Company squads into the tree line. Exposing himself to intense enemy fire, he moved from position to position, directing his squad's fire and encouraging his men. After destroying two enemy bunkers and killing ten enemy soldiers, Sergeant Burkhart was seriously wounded while pulling an injured squad member to safety. Despite his wounds, Burkart managed to continue placing fire on the VC, killing two more. For his exceptional courage under fire and intrepid leadership, the 19-year-old Sergeant from Albany, Oregon was awarded the Silver Star. Sergeant Burkhart recovered from the wounds he sustained on 5 February and returned to Alpha Company, only to be killed in combat during the following month.

The savage fighting continued for two hours, ending only when the remaining enemy were killed or fled the area. Forty-nine enemy bodies lay strewn through the wood line, and two prisoners were taken. Alpha Company lost three men in the savage fighting.

When the battle ended, Lieutenant Trotter located Lieutenant Burgett's body. Trotter later wrote, "I closed Scotty's eyes and said a prayer. We were very close." Before the air assault, Bill Trotter and Scotty Burgett had shared a C-ration breakfast. The OCS classmates had been on twenty air assaults together. Sadly, the twenty-first assault was their last.

CHAPTER 13

TO SNARE A GENERAL

9 February—Cholon

After the 5 February airmobile assault, Bravo Company, 3/7th returned to FSB Zinderneuf and was assigned the base security mission. LTC Gibler looked around for a replacement for Captain Pietsch, who was too badly wounded to return to duty. He found one in short order. Captain John Hershel South was the Cottonbaler S4 and had demonstrated superb abilities as the logistics staff officer, and a strong potential for command . His was on his second tour in Vietnam, having spent his first tour with the 5th Special Forces Group. The 25-year-old Regular Army Captain was a soft-spoken man, respected by all. Retired Lt. Colonel Bill Trotter, reflecting on the time he spent under South's command, wrote, "He was the only commander I ever had who took the time to teach me leadership." Captain South did not have much time to get his feet on the ground with Bravo Company before the unit was thrown back into the fray.

On 9 February the Cottonbalers were ordered by Major General Ware to return to Cholon. The South Vietnamese Joint General Staff requested the redeployment of a US battalion to reinforce two ARVN Ranger battalions that were engaged in heavy fighting in Cholon. The 2/3d Infantry was ordered to move to the Binh Chanh district to replace the Cottonbalers.

Moving by a combination of CH-47 Chinook helicopters and overland convoy, the 3/7th closed on the Phu Tho Racetrack by 1630 hours, 9 February. Major General Ware and Colonel Davison, the act-

191

ing 199th LIB commander, flew into the racetrack moments later to give LTC Gibler his mission for the next two days.

There were intelligence reports indicating a second wave of Communist attacks was imminent, and the TF Ware commander wanted Gibler's Cottonbalers to provide security at the Phu Tho Racetrack, and to assist the 33d ARVN Ranger Battalion in searching and clearing the area west of it. The Rangers were reinforced with three tanks and twelve M113 Armored Personnel Carriers.

After conferring with Ware and Davison, LTC Gibler deployed three rifle companies to the west of the racetrack. Charlie Company and an armored cavalry platoon remained at the racetrack to provide security and serve as a ready reaction force. A 40mm Duster platoon and a pair of quad .50 machine-gun tracks were attached to Gibler's battalion for the mission. These direct fire weapons were capable of delivering deadly accurate fire on targets without inflicting collateral damage on surrounding buildings. General Westmoreland was concerned about the use of artillery in the urban areas, and stringent restrictions were imposed on its use. Unlike artillery, the Dusters and quad .50s were better suited for urban combat.

Throughout the remainder of the day, intelligence reports were received indicating a strong enemy presence west and northwest of the racetrack. LTC Gibler and Major MacGill developed plans to search and clear those areas over the next two days. Both men knew that some tough fighting lay ahead for the Cottonbalers.

Mike Swearingen, a 199th LIB Public Information Officer (PIO), accompanied the Cottonbaler battalion on its second trip to the racetrack. Swearingen, who escorted members of the media covering the fighting in Cholon, recalled, "There were so many news media types trapped in Saigon for Tet that we literally were hauling them around by the deuce-and-half loads to get them to the action." When a reporter accompanied a unit on patrol, Swearingen usually went along to insure things went smoothly.

Describing one patrol, the former PIO wrote, "The infantry companies moved out in two columns, one on each side of the street, just like in the WWII movies. . . .The door-to-door stuff was new to everyone. I tossed my first frag grenade there during Tet." Swearingen further wrote, "On one sweep with the 3/7th in Cholon, the VC had weighted down an NVA flag in the middle of the street as sniper bait. Nobody was dumb enough to fall for the bait of course, and the VC snipers were quickly engaged and killed up in higher buildings on both sides of the street. I was planning on going back and snagging that flag after the fighting, but someone beat me to it."

When he was not ferrying the press around Cholon, Lieutenant Swearingen set up a makeshift office at the racetrack. As he described, "There was a great overview of the city from the top of the grandstands, which is where I slept in a VC hammock. . . .There was a knocked out ACAV out in the racetrack infield and an empty yellow three-hatch South Vietnamese water truck just outside the track." He later found out that the VC had used the truck to smuggle their men into Cholon and the racetrack before the offensive.

On 10 February, the Cottonbaler companies swept through the areas to the northwest and west of the racetrack. There was only light contact with small enemy units and individuals during the daylight operations. As darkness fell, the rifle platoons established ambush positions throughout the areas to the west.

Chester Porter was assigned to 3rd Platoon, Delta Company. Describing his platoon's activities that day he wrote, "We found some weapons caches but nothing significant. At dark we set up in a three-story building." The platoon leader positioned two squads on the third floor of the building and two on the second floor to cover the street below. Two men were left to cover the first floor entrance that was booby trapped with a grenade, and a Claymore mine was placed in front of the door. The platoon leader put the men on 50 percent alert with half the men trying to catch a few hours sleep while the other half stood guard."

Porter continued, "Around 2200 hours, we heard someone on a loudspeaker speaking in Vietnamese. Our Kit Carson scout said it was an enemy commander calling his units together. Shortly after that, North Viet Regulars started coming out of the alley across the street. We opened up on them from the third floor. . . . As soon as we opened up an RPG round came through the wall and went out the ceiling where it exploded. It was followed by a second RPG round."

Porter's squad was sprayed with bits of concrete, plaster, and small bits of shrapnel, but no one was seriously wounded. The firefight continued for several minutes, and several enemy were cut down as they tried to rush the building where Porter's platoon was holed up. Similar actions were going on all over Cholon, as both sides battled for control of the streets.

Late in the afternoon of 10 February, LTC Bill Schroeder, Task Force Ware's G-3, choppered into the racetrack to confer with LTC Gibler. Bill Schroeder recalled that when he entered Gibler's command post at the racetrack, the Cottonbaler commander was heating a can of C-rations, and joked with Schroeder, "You sonofabitch, I just heated up my C-rations." Schroeder told him, "You better put them aside because I've got a big one for you."

Schroeder and Gibler were friends from the days when Schroeder commanded the 4/12th Infantry. Schroeder passed the latest intelligence to Gibler. The ARVN were convinced that they knew the location of the Communist command post that was directing the attacks on Saigon. ARVN intelligence officers had informed their US counterparts that Major General Tran Do of the South Vietnamese People's Liberation Forces was directing the offensive from the command post. Schroeder also revealed that the command post was located in a small village just three kilometers west of Gibler's CP at the racetrack. According to the ARVN, the enemy CP was housed in a concealed bunker and tunnel complex beneath the village.

After pinpointing the location of the VC command post on his map, Schroeder told Gibler that the ARVN wanted to attack the Communist CP and had asked for the 3/7th to provide a blocking force for the operation. According to Schroeder, Gibler wanted the mission of attacking the CP. With the attached Dusters and quad-fifties, the Cottonbaler commander was confident that his battalion was better suited for the mission. Schroeder agreed to present Gibler's proposal to General Ware and the Vietnamese authorities.

Major General Ware convinced his ARVN counterpart to let Gibler's task force lead the attack. The 33d ARVN Ranger Battalion was ordered to provide a blocking force south of the village. The Cottonbaler commander and his S3 quickly formulated a plan for the assault. Captain South's Bravo Company was assigned the mission of blocking the area north of the village, while Captain Jeffrey Delia's Charlie Company was ordered to sweep into the village from the east. A platoon from Delta Troop, 17th Cav, reinforced by two M42 Dusters with 40mm cannons, was ordered to move to positions west of the village to bloc that escape route.

It was mid-afternoon on 11 February before Delta Company, Bravo Company, and the 33d Ranger Battalion were in position to begin the operation. In the sweltering heat of that Sunday afternoon, Captain Delia's Delta Company crossed their line of departure, moving west toward the village.

Brad Huffman was a rifleman with Delta Company. He wrote, "We were on patrols in the streets around the racetrack . . . about all the time and never got enough sleep. We were sent to a little village a couple of clicks out of town. I think maybe 6 or 7 hooches is all. We found nothing except old women and kids. We were about to turn around and go through again when all hell broke loose. The VC came out of the ground. They were in underground bunkers and tunnels and the entrances were very well hidden."

Chester Porter, who was assigned to Delta Company's 3rd Platoon, wrote, "Second and third squads were sent to sweep the village, the French lady (a magazine reporter) came with us. We swept the village and found nothing. Both squads took a break while the officers planned the next move. The village had several large haystacks, and the reporter wanted some pictures of the men tearing down the haystacks. There were five men standing next to one of the stacks, and one of them picked up a long pole and attempted to stick it into the stack. The haystacks were camouflage for bunkers, and as soon as the grunt stuck the pole into the stack, a machine gun opened up."

Specialist-Five Ronald Bagen's squad took the brunt of the fire. The 20-year-old Ohioan was wounded along with several men in his squad. Bagen moved forward to evacuate two of the men and was hit again. This time the wound was fatal. Twenty-year old Specialist James Tinsley from St Louis, Missouri, who was providing covering fire for his squad leader, was also shot and killed. Fire team leader, Sergeant Donald Colson was the third member of the squad to fall. The 24-year-old Louisianan was Regular Army, and had completed three months of his tour when he fell. As the squad withdrew, one of the grunts fired a burst into the haystack, setting it on fire. Two enemy soldiers fled from the burning haystack. Chester Porter, his buddy Barnes, and an M60 gunner cut down the fleeing VC as they ran toward 3rd Platoon's positions. As the embattled squads withdrew to a rice paddy dike on the edge of the village, the enemy started firing from spider holes and trees in the village. The Delta Company grunts returned fire and managed to set several more haystacks and hooches on fire.

Captain Jeff Dalia, the Delta CO, repositioned his men to gain fire superiority. Brad Huffman's squad took cover behind a rice paddy dike and began to return the enemy fire. An M42 Duster rolled up behind Huffman's squad and began firing its twin Bofors 40mm cannon at the VC positions. The enemy fire began to slack off as the 40mm point-detonated HEIT projectiles slammed into the enemy bunker positions at a rate of 240 rounds per minute. The noise was deafening as the exploding rounds reverberated through the village. The insurgents returned fire with small arms and RPGs.

Chester Porter's platoon used the covering fire from the Dusters to work their way around to the west side the village where they gained a foothold. One of the platoon's machine gunners, PFC Waller, laid down a base of fire for his platoon's advance until an RPG round exploded in front of his gun, spraying his face with tiny bits of white-hot shrapnel. After checking that his M60 was still capable of firing, the wounded machine gunner loaded another belt of ammo and resumed firing. According to Porter, 3rd Platoon's advance stalled when "we found ourselves pinned down by an NVA soldier in a well. We hit the well with LAWs, but he kept us pinned down till dark when we pulled back to the dike."

Under heavy fire, small groups of enemy soldiers attempted to flee to the north where they ran into Captain South's Bravo Company. Other more diehard VC fought it out in their bunkers in the village. The Delta Company grunts were taking out the enemy bunkers one by one, using fire and movement, but it was costly work. Sergeant Jerry Bowling and Specialists Gary Vickery, Adalberto Caceres, and James Tinsley from Delta Company were killed as the heavy fighting continued.

Enraged by the enemy's stubborn resistance, the Delta Company grunts continued pouring fire into the village, burning up magazine after magazine of the their basic load of ammo. When he learned that his rifle squads were almost out of M16 and M60 ammo and grenades, Captain Dalia radioed for an emergency resupply of ammunition. The battalion resupply helicopter was enroute to Long Binh when it was diverted back to FSB Zinderneuf to pick up a load of ammo for Delta Company. The headquarters troops loaded the Huey with crates of small arms ammo, grenades, and LAWs, and the pilot lifted off the resupply pad en route to the embattled Delta Company.

First Lieutenant Gerard Doiron's platoon held the right flank of Bravo Company's blocking position. A group of fifteen heavily armed enemy soldiers ran right toward Dorion's platoon. Specialist Dennis Spearman spotted the VC first, and moved his fire team into a position to take them under fire. He had his men hold their fire until the VC were within 30 meters of his team's position, and then they delivered a deadly volley. When Lieutenant Dorion saw his right flank was about to be overrun, he fired his grenade launcher into a group of five VC, killing or disabling all of them. Then he ran toward the platoon's endangered flank, distributing ammunition to each position. More fleeing VC ran directly into Dorion's platoon as they attempted to break out of the encirclement. Two of Dorion's men, Specialist Ronald Woody and PFC Richard Acker, were wounded, but the platoon managed to kill seven VC and take one prisoner. When the lieutenant moved forward to check the enemy bodies and recover their weapons, three of the VC who were feigning death opened fire on him. Doiron, who was wounded, managed to kill all three.

Ron Whelan was on one of Bravo Company's radios calling in medevacs for the wounded when a group of NVA attempted to break out of the village. Whelan estimated that a hundred or so uniformed NVA fled across the open rice paddies toward Bravo Company's blocking position. He wrote, "Thankfully, some helicopter gunships showed up to attack them in the open paddies to help us out." While the gunships cut down a number of the fleeing enemy, a number of others rushed right toward the dike where the Bravo Company grunts were positioned.

Bill Plains, another Bravo Company soldier, spotted "four or five"

NVA running out of the village "with AK's in both hands." The enemy soldiers were headed for a patch of woods that stretched along Bravo Company's flank, then bent around to the company's rear. Seizing the initiative, Plains moved down the dike toward the flank to cut them off. He wrote, "I headed down the dike knowing if they made the woods we would be in deep shit, they would be behind us. I know none of them made the woods."

Back at the village, Brad Huffman's squad was ordered to send a five-man detail to the LZ to retrieve the ammunition which was inbound on the resupply bird. Staying low, PFC Huffman and four other men headed for the LZ, accompanied by two of the company's wounded. On the way they captured a VC who was running from the village. After tying up their prisoner, the detail continued on to the LZ, where they popped a smoke grenade signaling the resupply Huey where to land. As the ship touched down, it drew fire, and the S4 troops began tossing the ammo crates out the doors as quickly as they could, unloading the chopper in record time. The two WIAs and the POW were then put aboard, and the Huey lifted off for the 3d Field Hospital in Saigon. Huffman and his resupply detail then made their way back to the village and distributed the badly needed ammo to the rest of the company.

In the meantime, gunships and the M42 Dusters continued to pound the enemy positions. When movement was detected near a hootch a few meters away from Huffman's location, a Duster slammed four rounds into it. Huffman's buddy, nicknamed Cowboy, was wounded in the left arm and Huffman felt a burning sensation on his back. A piece of white hot shrapnel from one of the 40mm rounds had landed on his back and set his shirt on fire. His buddy, Cowboy, reached over and put the fire out, and the pair resumed firing. As Huffman described, "Seemed like there was NVA running back and forth in there, and we would send out a wall of lead in their direction, which must have been pretty effective . . ."

In the failing daylight, Major MacGill landed just outside the village to take command of the operation. His ship was fired on as he touched down. MacGill leapt from the door and sprinted for the Delta Company positions amid a volley of small-arms fire. Jim MacGill recalled that the Dusters were positioned on the edge of the perimeter where they were blasting the enemy bunkers with round after round of 40mm cannon fire. The explosions were deafening.

Major MacGill ordered Captain Dalia to prepare for a final assault on the VC positions. As darkness descended, the exhausted Delta Company grunts began their final assault to finish off the remaining enemy soldiers. When the fighting ended around 2000 hours, Delta and Bravo Company called dust-offs for their dead and wounded. Five Cottonbalers had been killed and 12 were wounded. A ghastly pall hung over the area, and the night had grown fully dark as the Cottonbalers began their search of the village.

Twenty-four enemy bodies were pulled from the battered bunkers and tunnels. Only three enemy soldiers were found alive to be taken prisoner. Brad Huffman wrote, "We spent quite awhile gathering up bodies, weapons, papers, and I remember finding a lot of maps." Chester Porter recalled, "There were numerous sacks of money. . . found in the bunkers." Several of the enemy casualties were officers, indicating that the village had indeed been a command post. One of them appeared to be a senior officer. Huffman recalled, "We all had to check out this NVA General in his uniform, and then we burnt the whole place."

The Cottonbalers were later told that the body of the high-ranking officer was not that of Major General Tran Do. This was later confirmed by ARVN authorities after a full investigation and follow-on reports concerning General Do's whereabouts. While they had failed to kill or capture the Communist general, the Cottonbalers did destroy his command post that had been directing the insurgent forces fighting in the Cholon area.

The fight on 11 February was the last major contact for the Cottonbalers during the Tet Offensive and its aftermath. Of the 199th LIB's three infantry battalions, the Cottonbalers suffered more casualties than the other two battalions combined. For actions in Cholon during the Tet Offensive, the 3/7th Infantry Battalion received the Army's Valorous Unit award.

The Cottonbalers remained in the Cholon area for another week, conducting sweeps and patrols. Snipers remained a constant threat during these operations. On 18 February, the 3/7th Infantry was released from the operational control of Task Force Ware and returned to the 199th LIB's control. Responsibility for the Cholon area was once again assumed by ARVN forces. The Tet Offensive of 1968 was at an end for the officers and men of the Cottonbaler battalion.

CHAPTER 14

APRIL 1968—
A CRUEL MONTH

The 199th Light Infantry Brigade's participation in the Long Binh/
Saigon Tet Campaign ended on 18 February 1968, when the 3/7th
Infantry ended operations in Cholon. In recognition of its role in
defeating the Communist attacks on Long Binh and Saigon, the 199th
LIB was awarded the Valorous Unit Award. When the Tet Campaign
ended, no one anticipated that the Communists would launch another major offensive in less than three months.

In the interim, the light infantrymen of the 199th LIB relentlessly
pursued the Communist forces as they withdrew back to their jungle
sanctuaries. During operations UNIONTOWN III, VALLEY FORGE,
BOXSPRINGS, and WILDERNESS, the grunts searched for and
destroyed NVA and VC units and their base camps in areas stretching
from southern War Zone D to an area west of Tay Ninh along the
Cambodian border. It was tough, demanding, and dangerous work
without any major victories. There was little, if any, respite between
these operations, and attrition took its toll on the rifle companies.
More than 80 brave men were killed between the Tet Offensive of
January–February 1968 and the May Offensive of that year. Hundreds
more were wounded. Two of the most costly battles occurred in late
April of 1968 during Operation TOAN THANG.

On 11 April, the 199th LIB concluded its operations in the Tay
Ninh area. The 3/7th Cottonbalers moved by air back to the brigade's
main base at Long Binh, while the 4/12th Warriors moved by land
convoy. The 2/3d Infantry remained under the operational control of
the US 9th Division south of Saigon.

The operation west of Tay Ninh took its toll on the Warrior and Cottonbaler battalions, and the rifle companies were in bad need of rest and refitting. Although no significant engagements with enemy forces occurred, the daily treks through the jungles, some less than a kilometer from the Cambodian border, were tiring and stressful for the troops. An outbreak of diarrhea and gastroenteritis swept through the brigade in March, resulting in a high number of medical evacuations. Replacements arrived in the battalions at a steady rate, but it took time before the men were ready to join their companies in the field. In early April, a fourth infantry battalion joined the brigade. The 5th Battalion, 12th Infantry arrived fresh from Fort Lewis, Washington. However, the battalion was untrained in jungle warfare and it took several weeks before it was fully combat ready.

The officers and men of the 3/7th and 4/12th Infantry were promised a five-day stand-down at Camp Frenzell-Jones upon their return from Tay Ninh. They were more than a little disappointed when the stand-down was abruptly cut short one day after their return. The Warrior battalion was ordered to move to AO Columbus, east of Long Binh, on 13 April, and the Cottonbalers followed a day later.

During the one-day stand-down, the men were issued a clean set of jungle fatigues, showered, and drank as much beer and whiskey as they could hold. The officer, NCO, and EM clubs were jampacked, and fistfights broke out between the grunts and the rear echelon troops. When the grunts saw all the amenities that the rear echelon troops enjoyed on a daily basis, they were soon fighting mad and it didn't take much to set them off. The short stay at the base camp did morale more harm than good.

AO Columbus encompassed parts of the Duc Tu and Cong Thanh districts of Bien Hoa Province south of the Dong Nai River. It also included portions of the Xuan Loc and Kiem Tan districts in Long Khanh Province. The mission of the 3/7th and 4/12 Infantry battalions was to interdict enemy movement from southern War Zone D into AO Columbus. The 5th VC Division had infiltrated troops along this same infiltration route during the January Tet Offensive

During early April 1968, most 5th VC Division units were still north of the Dong Nai River; however, according to intelligence sources, the 274th VC Regimental headquarters and the 3d Battalion of that regiment were south of the river. It was fairly easy for these units to stay hidden. With the exception of an abandoned rubber plantation in the northeast portion of the AO, most of Columbus was overgrown with thick jungle. The few inhabitants in the area lived in villages along Highway 1 in the AO's southern portion. Vehicular movement through most of the AO was limited. In the northern portion of AO Columbus, an unpaved road, LTL 24, followed the southern bank of the Dong Nai River, but only a few narrow unimproved logging trails crisscrossed the jungle to the west and south of the rubber plantation. Cross-country movement was also difficult, particularly in the Cottonbaler AO. A rifle company accustomed to this type of terrain could cover, at most, four kilometers in a day. Helicopter landing zones were few and far between, and little could be seen from the air due to the triple canopy jungle below. Therefore AO Columbus was an excellent staging area for VC and NVA units.

The Warrior battalion moved to the area by convoy and CH-47 helicopter on 13 April, establishing a fire support base, FSB Farrell, in the northeastern corner of the rubber plantation, about 500 meters south of the Dong Nai River. On the following day, the Cottonbalers conducted airmobile assaults west of the Warrior battalion's AO and established FSB New Orleans, some ten kilometers west of FSB Farrell, and about three kilometers south of the river.

AO Columbus, FSB New Orleans—17–18 April 1968

The first few days in their new AO were uneventful for the Cottonbalers. For three days the line companies of the battalion patrolled the jungle around the firebase without any significant contact with the enemy. Battalion commander LTC Ken Hall, and his S3, Major Jim MacGill, overflew AO Columbus on the afternoon of 17 February looking for signs of the enemy. On pass after pass, Hall and MacGill could see nothing below. The jungle seemed impenetrable from the air.

Lt. Colonel Hall assumed command of the Cottonbaler battalion in late February, after serving as the brigade S3 for four months. Hall was a West Pointer, Class of 1952, and a highly regarded infantry officer. One of his lieutenants later wrote, "LTC Hall was in a class by himself. His tactical skill, ability to get his men to follow him voluntarily in combat, and his genuine concern for the welfare of his men set him apart. . . . I can still see him jumping out of the LOG bird in cut off fatigues, and a Swedish K slung over his shoulder. He would come into the company area and call all the NCOs by their first names." Ken Hall was one of a rare breed of battalion commanders in Vietnam who was genuinely loved and respected by his men. He had only two months left to live.

On April 17th, Hall's rifle companies were deployed a few kilometers to the east of FSB New Orleans, while the battalion's Echo Company continued construction and security of the firebase. After a terrain analysis and aerial reconnaissance, LTC Hall concluded that a hill mass three kilometers to the east of FSB New Orleans was an ideal site for an enemy base camp. The heavily forested piece of terrain lay two kilometers south of the Dong Nai River. A stream flowed north toward the river on the west side of the hill mass. Days before, air cavalry scouts and LRPs had spotted enemy troops in NVA uniforms moving in the vicinity. Hall decided to commit his ground troops to search the area.

As dawn broke on 18 February, the Cottonbaler companies prepared to move out on their search and destroy mission. The sleep deprived grunts dragged themselves out of their hastily dug fighting positions, dusted themselves off, and groggily began their early morning routine. Some relieved themselves in hastily dug cat holes, while others brewed C- ration coffee or cocoa in their canteen cups, or wolfed down a can of ham slices or sliced peaches. Claymore mines and trip flares were retrieved from outside the perimeter and carefully packed in rucksacks. Rifles and machine guns were given a quick cleaning. For some it was to be their last morning in the "green hell."

Alpha and Charlie Companies were located a couple of hundred meters south of the unimproved road that paralleled the Dong Nai River. LTC Hall wanted the companies to move south on parallel routes up a long finger that led to a hill mass some 60 feet in elevation. Captain Tony Smaldone's Alpha Company moved out around

0730 hours, followed by Captain Brian Sneed's Charlie Company 45 minutes later. Captain South's Bravo Company and Captain Zimmerman's Delta Company patrolled the area between FSB New Orleans and the high ground to the east.

Alpha and Charlie Companies' progress was slow. The jungle itself changed subtly as the men trudged up a gentle slope. Patches of bamboo and coils of interlocking vines and undergrowth slowed the march. No breeze penetrated the thick vegetation, and even the morning air was oppressive. Insects buzzed around the unshaven, sweat-drenched faces of the grunts and they squinted to keep the gnats from their eyes. The point elements of both companies moved cautiously, and the columns halted every hundred meters to send out patrols in a cloverleaf pattern. Radios cackled as platoon leaders whispered instructions to their squad leaders and reported their progress to their CO's. The men sipped water slowly from their canteens, careful not to spill a drop. Overhead in their C&C ship, Lt. Colonel Hall and Major MacGill tracked the rifle companies' progress.

A few minutes before 1130 hours, Sneed's Charlie Company made contact when its point element approached the camouflaged perimeter of a 60-bunker base camp complex. The jungle in front of Charlie Company seemed to explode in simultaneous blasts of explosive devices, followed by a hail of bullets that flailed the foliage. The screams of wounded men and the cry of "medic! medic!" were heard above the crescendo of rifle and machine-gun fire. Ignoring a shrapnel wound, the Charlie Company commander quickly took control of the fight.

In a 199th LIB newspaper article published after the battle, Captain Sneed told a reporter, "They definitely knew what they were doing. They went for the radios and machine guns from the start. Every time you popped smoke to identify your position for the air support, you invited a rain of grenades and automatic weapons fire. They were throwing everything they had at us. I didn't hear anything but automatic weapons and rocket grenades going during the whole fight."

LTC Hall radioed Captain Sneed, telling him to mark his unit's front with smoke so he could adjust artillery fire on the enemy's positions. Then he radioed Captains Smaldone and South, directing them to move to Charlie Company's support. Within minutes, the 105mm howitzers of Bravo Battery, 2/40th Artillery were firing marking rounds over the heads of the Charlie Company grunts. As his FO adjusted the incoming artillery fire, Captain Sneed maneuvered his platoons to place maximum fire on the enemy base camp.

At 1230 hours, Captain Smaldone reported that Alpha Company was also in heavy contact. Smaldone thought that his company had hit another base camp a short distance away from Charlie Company. In fact, it was part of the same large base complex that covered several acres of ground. The Apha Company CO requested an urgent dust-off with a hoist capability. He had two KIAs, nine WIAs, and no LZ in the immediate area of the contact.

Convinced that his battalion was in a major fight, the Cottonbaler commander radioed an urgent request to brigade for an airmobile company. He wanted to air assault Captain Zimmerman's Delta Company into the area of Alpha and Charlie Company's contacts. MacGill spotted a PZ in the vicinity of Delta Company and ordered Zimmerman to get there as fast as possible. In the meantime, Sneed's Charlie Company had regrouped and was holding its ground. Therefore, LTC Hall ordered Captain South's Bravo Company to reinforce the hard-pressed Alpha Company.

Meanwhile, Alpha and Charlie Companies continued to slug it out with the enemy, desperately trying to gain a foothold in their entrenchments. Charlie Company's Sergeant Mel Ballard was moving his squad near the front of the company column when it came under small-arms and rocket fire. Ballard brought his men on line to assault the enemy bunkers. The gallant sergeant was seriously wounded in a hail of automatic weapons fire before he was ordered to withdraw.

The Company's FO was directing artillery fires onto the enemy positions. Ballard passed the order to his men, but remained behind to provide covering fire for the wounded. Moving about the forward area, Sergeant Ballard continued to search for and treat the injured until he was mortally wounded by fragments from an exploding enemy rocket. The 23-year-old Californian was posthumously awarded the Army's Distinguished Service Cross for his extraordinary heroism that day. Sergeant Mel Ballard was not the only hero in Charlie Company that day. There were many, but 19-year-old rifleman Jerry

Boyles was another who stood out among the rest.

The young Missourian was seen moving about the hottest areas of the fight, snapping off rifle shots at the enemy bunkers as he ran to pull he wounded comrades to safety. Even though painfully wounded himself, he repeatedly returned to the heaviest area of contact until he was wounded a second time. This time his wounds were serious. Frank Auer of Charlie Company wrote, "Jerry was full of life and just returned from stateside to see his very sick mom. We carried him out, and he was dying as we were trying to dust him off. The chopper pilot was nervous, saying there was too much fire in the area. Finally we just kept Jerry as he expired." Jerry Boyles was posthumously awarded the Silver Star for his gallantry.

It was mid-afternoon before Delta Company air assaulted into the area to support the embattled Alpha and Charlie Companies. Bravo Company continued to move overland to reach the scene of the fight. Meanwhile, the casualties continued to mount.

Captain Smaldone's Alpha Company suffered the most. By 1600 hours, five Alpha Company men were KIA. Specialist Doug McCabe later recalled, "Captain Smaldone got us into a tight perimeter around what might have been a bomb crater and called in a medevac and resupply. During the medevac, the NVA hit us again. . . . I was on the perimeter when an RPG exploded a few feet from me knocking me to the ground with shrapnel in my neck and shoulder. I was very lucky as I was on the edge of the blast, but the artillery FO and his RTO were hit bad. The FO was hit in the head from the blast, and the RTO was shredded by shrapnel and his fatigues were on fire. We jumped on him to smother the flames. I think he survived, but the FO was dead." Lieutenant Tom Carnegie died doing what he was trained to do.

Twenty-five year old Ernest Vetter, a native American from Oklahoma, also distinguished himself that day. Specialist Vetter was in the vanguard of his company when the enemy opened up. Instinctively, he returned fire and began to move forward before taking a sniper round. He spotted an enemy bunker as he went down. Arming a hand grenade, he crawled forward, still in intense pain, and tossed it into the enemy bunker, killing its three occupants. Then reloading his rifle, he began firing into the aperture of another bunker until he was mortally wounded. Specialist Vetter was posthumously awarded the Silver Star.

By mid-afternoon, Alpha Company had 19 men wounded, seven of whom were in serious condition. Making matters worse, the Company's indomitable CO, Captain Tony Smaldone, was among them. The Captain had suffered a painful gunshot wound to the lower forearm. Tony was still directing the fight, but he knew that his wound required hospital treatment. For the moment, however, there was way to evacuate Alpha Company's casualties. The company's positions were too exposed to enemy fire to lift the wounded out by hoist, and there was no suitable LZ in the vicinity.

Charlie Company was more fortunate. With a gunship team providing covering fire, a dust-off ship landed on a small LZ and evacuated seven of the company's most seriously wounded. Nineteen of the less badly wounded had to wait. Most ignored their wounds and returned to the fight after they were patched up by the company medics.

Captain South pushed his men up the high ground, arriving in Alpha Company's vicinity at around 1700 hours. South had pushed his men hard on their 2,700 meter trek to reinforce the hard pressed Alpha Company, but there was no time for a rest. Bravo went quickly into the fight. One Cottonbaler recalled that South "literally ran" the company to get there. The Captain, who carried Army Field Manuals on tactics in his rucksack and studied them each night, was moving with his command group directly behind his lead platoon. When the platoon was pinned down by enemy fire, the Captain skillfully maneuvered his 1st and 3rd Platoons to the left to take the pressure off Alpha and Charlie Companies. After repositioning his platoons, Captain South led an assault along the crest of the hill, driving the enemy back and moving his company into the gap between Alpha and Charlie.

Ron Whelan, one of South's RTOs, described Bravo Company's link-up with Alpha Company. "Captain South never stopped to take cover as we were dancing through machine-gun fire all around us, while jumping over our dead and wounded soldiers. We arrived at a large bomb crater and jumped in to join the Captain of Company A [Smaldone] . . . he had been wounded. There were many dead bodies from the fighting prior to our arrival." Captain South's other RTO,

Glen Pagano, recalled that he had to struggle to keep up with his CO. In addition to the radio, Pagano was carrying an M79 grenade launcher and a basic load of 40mm grenades. Pagano temporarily lost sight of Captain South as the command group sprinted forward. He later recalled that he was following two grunts when an RPG struck the ground a few meters to his front. Both of the grunts were peppered with shrapnel in their torsos and faces, but Pagano, partially shielded by a tree, took only a few fragments in his arm. Despite his wounds, Glen Pagano continued to advance until he caught up with his Captain. The Captain and his artillery FO were pinned down by enemy fire from a bunker that they'd passed. Pagano began firing M79 rounds at the bunker until he finally put a 40mm round through the aperture, killing the occupants. Glen Pagano received a Bronze Star for Valor for his heroic actions.

While Captain Smith fought his way into the beleaguered Alpha and Charlie companies, Captain Zimmerman's Delta Company was approaching the enemy positions from the northeast.

Platoon Sergeant Roberto Rangel's platoon was first to make contact, running headlong into the bunker complex. During the initial contact, four of Rangel's men were seriously wounded, but Rangel continued and led his men in an assault deep into the bunker complex, killing a number of enemy. When he saw his commander's RTO fall fatally wounded 15 meters in front of an enemy bunker, Rangel charged the bunker and destroyed it with a hand grenade. Then Rangel grabbed the CO's radio and continued to engage the enemy. The VC quickly counterattacked the penetration of their perimeter. After realizing that the rest of the company was withdrawing under enemy pressure, Rangel gathered his men about him, including the wounded, and fought his way back out of the enemy base camp, leaving no one behind.

With the arrival of Bravo and Delta Company, the Cottonbalers began to gain control of the situation. The Cottonbaler commander also requested that another rifle company from the 5/12th Infantry be flown in to reinforce his battalion. The 5/12th was new in country, but Hall knew he needed to get as many men on the ground as possible.

As dusk settled around them, the embattled Cottonbalers began to dig in. Intermittent firing continued as the enemy traded shots with the grunts. The men dug and scraped as hard as they could, ending up with fighting positions barely deep enough to lie down in.

Ron Whelan wrote, "I remember digging in . . . we had no sandbags and had to stack bodies in front of our positions as defenses to stop incoming bullets." The grunts made sure to reload all of their magazines with ammo and laid them out beside their grenades where they could reach them. After crawling forward and placing Claymores and trip wires in front of their positions, the grunts laid down in their shallow holes facing out, their M-16s pointed in the direction of the enemy.

It was full dark as the commanders crawled around to each of their platoons to check their perimeters and get an accurate count on their losses. There were a total of 12 KIAs and 58 WIAs in the four companies. Twenty-one of the wounded men remained with their companies awaiting evacuation. Dust-offs were put on hold for the night. The LZ was too small to risk a night landing, but it was used to drop supplies into the companies. Ron Whelan wrote, "The resupply ships, with no lights turned on, would hover at treetop level and kick out full boxes of ammo and drop bladders of water that came crashing down through the trees."

The Cottonbalers continued to trade sniper fire with the enemy as a flareship provided illumination. One grunt recalled, "On command we were ordered to fire at will every 30 minutes throughout the night to prevent the NVA from moving back into our perimeter defense."

When dawn broke, the Cottonbalers assaulted the enemy base camp and found it deserted. The stench of battle permeated the area. The enemy had withdrawn during the hours of darkness, but left behind 59 of their fallen comrades. The grunts also recovered fourteen individual and crew-served weapons, along with an assortment of ammunition. Searching further, the Cottonbalers found a cache of over 400 lbs. of C-4 explosive. Based on the number of bunkers, the camp was large enough to have accommodated a full battalion. The fortifications were in a good state of repair and the various positions were prepared to provide all around observation and support. Extensive use had been made of command-detonated mines and booby traps. From documents left behind, it was later determined that the enemy unit that defended the base camp was the 4th NVA Sapper

Battalion, with 318 men assigned, including three lieutenant colonels. The presence of a newly arrived NVA sapper battalion in AO Columbus was an ominous sign.

AO Columbus, Fire Support Base New Orleans—23 April

The 3/7th and 4/12th Infantry received orders from Brigadier General Forbes on 23 April to close out their fire support bases the following day and move to FSB Tri-Corners. Tri-Corners was located in the southern portion of AO Columbus, about two kilometers north of the village of Trang Bom on Highway 1. The firebase was midway between Bien Hoa and Xuan Loc. Forbes had become fully aware of the latest intelligence.

After reviewing numerous agent reports, aerial observer and LRP sightings, and signal intelligence reports, intelligence analysts were certain that the Communists were about to launch another major offensive. General Forbes wanted the 3/7th and 4/12th positioned near Highway 1 to facilitate their movement by ground transport or helicopter to any threatened area in a minimum amount of time. From positions near Highway 1, the infantry battalions would also be capable of interdicting enemy forces moving west to attack targets in the Long Binh–Bien Hoa areas. The 199th LIB commander also wanted Hall's Cottonbalers to search the southern portion of AO Columbus north of FSB Tri-Corners.

The movement plan called for the 3/7th CP and B Battery 2/40th Artillery to displace from FSB New Orleans to FSB Tri-Corners by air, while the rifle companies leapfrogged toward the south in a series of airmobile assaults. Major MacGill was charged with the responsibility of closing out the fire support base, while Lieutenant Colonel Hall displaced with his CP to FSB Tri-Corners on 23 April.

Major Jim MacGill recalled a conversation he had with Captain John Hershell South, the Bravo Company commander on the evening of 23 April. The two were discussing the Alpha Company commander, Captain Tony Smaldone, who had once again cheated death on 18 April. Smaldone was still in the hospital recovering from his wound. They spoke of the Captain's habit of moving forward without concern for his own safety during firefights, and rarely bothering to take cover from incoming fire. Smaldone seemed to have a sixth sense about that. MacGill thought that the Alpha Company CO was particularly adept at listening to the rounds as they whizzed by and timing his moves accordingly. He had been wounded on several occasions, but never received a mortal wound. MacGill told South to be a bit more cautious than his fellow company CO. The Cottonbaler S3 did not want to lose another good commander.

On the morning of 24 February, Companies A, B, and D of the 3/7th conducted airmobile assaults into LZs in an area roughly seven kilometers north of FSB Tri-Corners. Charlie Company was designated the battalion reserve. The airmobile insertions came off without a hitch, and by 1100 hours all three companies were on the ground. LTC Hall controlled the airmobile assaults from his C&C ship, while Major MacGill supervised the closing of FSB New Orleans. The firebase was a hub of activity as sortie after sortie of CH-47 helicopters lifted artillery tubes, ammunition, food, and other materials to the new location. MacGill had requested a CH-54 to bring out a D7 bulldozer that was too heavy for a CH-47 to lift. There were no CH-54s available, so MacGill ordered the engineers to remove the dozer's tracks to be airlifted out. The rest of the dozer was destroyed in place with C4 explosives.

Companies A, B, and D moved south from their LZs for several hours on parallel routes. The point elements of the three companies tried to stay on line, but they had to maneuver across difficult terrain and kept losing sight of each other. Scout dog handler Bob Himrod followed the point element of Bravo Company with his dog, Cracker.

Himrod wrote, "It was approximately 1400 hours when Cracker gave me a faint alert to the front. I stopped, and the Company commander, Captain John South, and his radio operator, Specialist Fourth Class Glenn Pagano, came to my position at point." South conferred with Himrod and instructed him to move forward cautiously. The dog continued to alert as they followed the trail. Himrod continued, "Just up this trail I found a dripping wet NVA shirt hanging over a bent tree branch . . . it was still bobbing up and down from someone having just thrown it over the branch." Beside the tree a small campfire smouldered. A ball of rice was dumped on the ground beside the fire, indicating someone's hasty departure. Eyeballing the surrounding area,

Himrod suddenly spotted a camouflaged bunker. He recalled, "We were cautiously checking out the area when all hell broke loose! Automatic weapons and rifle fire raked our position and pieces of tree bark flew from the trees as the bullets tore into them. . . .We jumped into a small bunker for cover and started returning fire."

When the enemy fire momentarily slackened, Captain South brought his platoons on line and the grunts began cautiously moving up the rising ground. Robert Himrod wrote, "We started up this small knoll when a huge explosion went off to the front and above me. The NVA set off a command-detonated explosive in this large tree. . . . It peppered the two soldiers in front of me with shrapnel, but because I was on the backside of the tree, I didn't get hit with any fragments."

Within minutes, Alpha Company, moving on Bravo Company's left flank, ran head-on into the bunker complex. Alpha's point man and another grunt were shot at nearly pointblank range. Doug McCabe, who was moving behind the point element, heard the wounded pair calling for help. McCabe crawled forward, taking advantage of the ground cover, and pulled the men back to safety.

Specialist Walter Baker was near the front of Alpha Company when the firing began. Spotting one of the enemy bunkers, Baker silenced it with a burst of M16 fire into the aperture. He then advanced toward a second bunker, but was hit before he reached it. As he lay on the ground, he saw a group of NVA repositioning a machine gun to fire down a trail toward his company. Ignoring painful wounds to his back and leg, Specialist Baker assaulted the machine gun position, killing the NVA soldiers, but he was hit again several times during his assault. Nonetheless, he was able to turn the captured machine gun around and begin firing on the enemy emplacements. Only after pointing out additional enemy positions to his comrades did he consent to evacuation and treatment of his seven wounds. Specialist Walter Baker was awarded the Army's Distinguished Service Cross for his extraordinary heroism.

The fighting continued as Captain Zimmerman's Delta Company pushed forward to close with the enemy. Two Delta Company grunts were hit immediately when a group of enemy soldiers tried to flank the company, but the Delta grunts drove them off with good marksmanship and raw courage. Delta Company continued to press the assault, taking some of the pressure off Alpha and Bravo Companies.

In the midst of the heaviest fighting, LTC Hall decided to commit his reserve company to the battle. Hall wanted Charlie Company airlifted in, so he sent an urgent request to the brigade commander for an airmobile assault company. He also requested additional gunship and medevac support. There were scores of wounded in need of medical evacuation.

The 128th Assault Helicopter Company, the "Tomahawks," were scrambled to insert Captain Brian Sneed's Charlie Company. An LZ some 900 meters to the east of the contact was selected for Charlie Company's insertion. Its first lift was in the air just after 1600 hours. As the Tomahawk lift ships headed for the LZ, the Gunslinger gunships pounded the jungle that surrounded the LZ. When the pair of gunships took small arms fire from the eastern side, they each unleashed a salvo of rockets into the area. The gunship and artillery prep continued as the lift ships made their final approach. When the helicopters neared the ground, the grunts leapt into the elephant grass and moved out to secure the landing zone. All three Charlie Company lifts were on the ground by 1645 hours. Wasting no time, Sneed ordered his company to move out.

The worst of the fighting was yet to come. A few minutes after 1700 hours, Lieutenant Colonel Hall learned that his Bravo Company commander, Captain John Hershell South, had been killed in action. The 25-year-old Captain had been hit as he moved forward to direct his men's fire.

Ron Whelan, who carried one of Captain South's radios, wrote, "Captain South and I were moving through a column of soldiers towards the bunkers. An RPG exploded when it hit a tree 20–30 yards ahead of us, and two GI s were wounded in the face and body. When we got to the edge of the ravine, two camouflaged bunkers buried in that hillside opened up on us with automatic fire. Capt. South was grabbing hand grenades from the back strap of my radio and lobbing them at the bunkers. . . . We had some of our soldiers already across that ravine and moving up the hillside above those enemy bunkers." Captain South and Whelan then crossed the ravine and started moving up the hill.

Bill Plains was one of the grunts who was across the ravine, trying to take out the bunkers. He wrote, "Started up the hill and there were two bunkers about 25 yards in front of me. I was carrying a 'thumper' [M79 grenade launcher] and put two rounds in each bunker. That's when I caught shrap metal in my right leg. South asked me how bad it was. I told him I don't know, I was scared to look . . . the Captain said put another round in each bunker then set them on fire. So I crawled up and lit some C4 at the edge of the first bunker then crawled up and did the same to the other one." After blowing up the bunkers, Plains' leg began to "throb and stiffen up," and a medic told him he was out of the fight and directed him back to an area where an LZ was being set up.

After the bunkers were destroyed, Captain South and his RTO continued to move forward until a sniper hidden in the foliage of a tall tree opened up with automatic weapons fire. According to Whelan, Captain South was killed instantly, and a medic moving behind him was wounded in the left arm and shoulder. Whelan was amazed that he was spared. After propping his Captain's lifeless body against a tree, Whelan assisted the wounded medic to move back down the hillside. Leaving the medic in the care of another soldier, Whelan returned back up the hillside to where he had left Captain South's body. As he approached the area, he scanned the trees for the sniper. He was soon joined by a group of riflemen. After they saw the lifeless body of their fallen Captain, the vengeful grunts moved forward and disappeared into the jungle foliage. Moments later, Whelan heard a heavy exchange of gunfire and M79 explosions. The grunts had avenged the death of their CO. Captain South was the fourth Bravo Company KIA that day, and the company also had 12 men wounded as the savage fighting continued.

Four separate dust-offs were called to evacuate the wounded. Bomb craters were used as LZs. C4 explosives were used to blow down trees around the perimeter of the craters to give enough clearance for the dust-off ships' rotor blades. Thirty-three badly wounded men from Cottonbaler rifle companies were evacuated to the 24th and 93d Evacuation Hospitals at Long Binh.

As dusk approached, LTC Hall flew over the scene of the contact and ordered his companies to pull back and form a night defensive position. From the air, he could see nothing of his men below, but he wanted to resupply them with ammunition before dark, and evacuate as many casualties as possible.

As night fell, an Air Force FAC orbited over the area of the contact and marked the enemy base camp with rocket fire for his attack aircraft. Two F-100s swept down from the darkening sky, dropping napalm and cluster bombs on the enemy fortifications. Once they had expended all of their ordnance, a second pair of fighter bombers followed up with a second air strike. The burning napalm illuminated the night sky.

While the jets pounded the enemy fortifications, the dust-offs continued at the makeshift LZs. Sergeant Robert Himrod described the scene: "The pilots had to hover and come straight down through the trees. . . . The battalion had called in TAC air support and the ground was shaking as each bomb slammed into the jungle. The helicopter gunships were making rocket and machine-gun passes at targets marked by our smoke. Their brass shell casings were raining down on us after each pass. . . . The dead were placed in an area covered with ponchos. . . . Also with the dead were body parts, a leg from the knee down, a hand and forearm, and a foot still in the boot. The medics were feverishly working on the wounded."

When all of the critically wounded were evacuated, the dust-offs returned to pick up the dead, but not all the KIAs were lifted out. One of the dust-off ships was hit by small-arms fire as it lifted off with several KIAs, and the night landings became too risky to continue. The remaining KIAs were moved by stretcher to an area near the CP. Sergeant Himrod, who was located near the CP, wrote, "Illumination rounds were casting strange shadows about the jungle through the trees. . . . I set up, watered, and fed my dog out of my overturned helmet. I ate a C-ration and thought about the two soldiers (KIAs) under the ponchos next to me. I laid out my poncho, tied my dog's leash to my foot, and settled back clutching my CAR15. I heard someone calling in the paragraph and line numbers of those killed and wounded on the radio as I fell exhausted off to sleep."

The following morning, four additional air strikes were called in on the enemy's base camp. After the air strikes, the Cottonbalers swept through the NVA camp. From captured documents it was determined that the base camp had housed a major enemy headquarters guarded by elements of the 4th NVA Sapper Battalion. The enemy headquarters exercised command and control over 21 different units, including a Flame Thrower Detachment that had conducted an infamous flame attack on a Montagnard village near Dak To. More ominous were sketch maps of rocket and recoilless rifle firing sites within the effective range of the Long Binh Base complex.

Two days later Bravo Company, 4/12th Infantry captured an NVA doctor who had been charged with setting up a forward hospital by 22 April. In his captured diary was an entry indicating the date for a new major offensive. The attacks were set to begin at 0001 hours, 28 April, 1968.

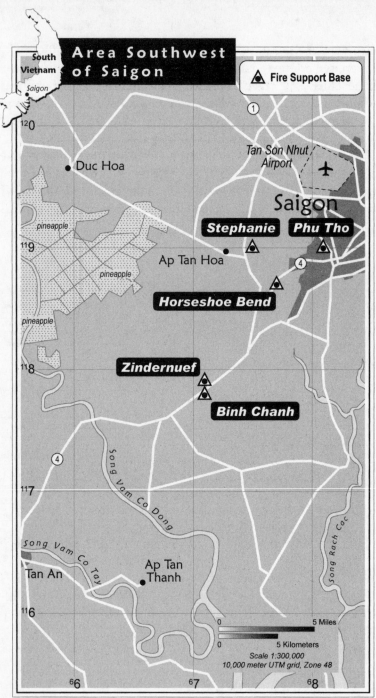

Area Southwest of Saigon

South Vietnam

Saigon

△ Fire Support Base

120

Duc Hoa

Tan Son Nhut Airport

Saigon

pineapple

119

Stephanie   *Phu Tho*

Ap Tan Hoa

4

pineapple

Horseshoe Bend

pineapple

118

Zindernuef

Binh Chanh

117

4

Song Vam Co Dong

Song Rach Cac

Song Vam Co Tay

Tan An

Ap Tan Thanh

116

0   5 Miles

0   5 Kilometers

Scale 1:300,000
10,000 meter UTM grid, Zone 48

66   67   68

Cartography by Michael Podolny

CHAPTER 15

THE MAY OFFENSIVE

Saigon—4 May 1968

Shortly before midnight on Saturday May 4th, a taxi loaded with more than a hundred pounds of TNT exploded outside the Saigon radio and TV station. The attack marked the beginning of the May Offensive in the Saigon metropolitan area. The offensive had been twice postponed by COSVN, pushing the date back from the last week of April to the first week of May 1968.

The ground offensive began on the eastern side of the city with attacks on the Binh Loi and Newport bridges. The K1 and K3 units of the Dong Nai Regiment attacked the Binh Loi bridge at 0500 hours, and the fighting continued until 1700 hours. At nightfall, the bridge remained intact and in friendly hands. Another attack was launched against the Newport bridge. After a 30-minute pre-dawn mortar attack on the bridge, two separate ground attacks were conducted by the units of the 4th Local Force Battalion and 2d Battalion, 274th VC Regiment. Both attacks faltered far short of the bridge itself. Attacks were also launched on the Tan My Tay area on the city's eastern edge, but in all cases the attackers were driven off by the Vietnamese 1st Marine battalion and National Police forces. There was speculation that the attacks on the eastern periphery of the city were diversions for the main attacks.

In the built-up areas of the city, small infiltration units surfaced, spreading havoc and confusion. Infiltration was accomplished using various means: wearing South Vietnamese army and marine uniforms,

219

traveling at night in small groups of 4 to 10 men, and hiding in commercial cargo vehicles. Upon arrival in the city, it was not difficult for the infiltrators to obtain weapons and military equipment. Secret caches of weapons and explosives were established throughout the Saigon area. Once again, Cholon was a primary assembly area for enemy infiltration units. That section of the city was rumored to have tunnels running from street to street and house to house. While the infiltrators were troublesome to the Vietnamese and US forces, the major threat was from main force VC and NVA units that were poised to attack the city from the west.

Most of the main attack units used invasion routes that traversed the open rice paddies, swamps, and pineapple plantations that lay to the south and west of Saigon. To the west, it was only thirty miles to the Cambodian border where the NVA base areas were located. Protecting the southern and western approaches to Saigon was difficult. In early April, Operation TOAN THANG was conducted by US and Vietnamese forces around the periphery of Saigon in an effort to prevent a reoccurrence of the Tet attacks. However, most of the main force Communist units were unaffected, since they were ensconced in their sanctuaries across the border.

In May of 1968, the residents of Saigon and surrounding areas were still reeling from the Tet attacks of January and February. Some 597 civilians had been killed and another 882 wounded during those attacks. Additionally, over 10,000 homes had been destroyed and 68,000 persons classified as refugees as a result of the fighting. The latter number swelled even higher as refugees from the surrounding countryside fled into the city's already crowded slums. To make matters worse, Saigon's economy had been crippled as a result of damage to the city's infrastructure and places of business. Commercial life was severely affected. Perhaps the worst impact of the fighting, however, was the people's loss of confidence in their government and its leaders. Saigon's residents, who once lived in relative peace and safety in their capital, were now filled with fear and uncertainty about the future. The May attacks would shake their confidence even further.

The attacks on the highway bridges that connected Saigon to Bien Hoa and Long Binh were meant to divert attention from the Communists' main objectives: the strategic Tan Son Nhut airbase and

Cholon. Initially, Saigon and its suburbs were defended by ten South Vietnamese combat battalions—three airborne, three marine, and four Ranger. The battalions were deployed within the city and along its periphery. When it became apparent that there were insufficient Vietnamese forces to defend the city, the US II Field Force Commander ordered US reinforcements into the capital region. Task Force Hay, led by Major General John Hay, was activated to command and control the US forces. The US 1st Division, 9th Division, 25th Division, and 199th Light Infantry Brigade were all placed under the operational control of Task Force Hay.

Fire Support Base Tri-Corners—0300 Hours, 5 May

Tri-Corners was on high alert. There were light contacts with enemy reconnaissance units on 1 and 2 May, but no one was sure of the exact location of several battalion-size units that were reported moving south along the Bien Hoa–Long Khanh Province boundary. Numerous reports from civilians and agents indicated that the enemy battalions had crossed Highway 1 east of Trang Bom, but no one knew where they headed next. Brigadier General Forbes thought they were headed for the Long Binh–Bien Hoa area, and planned to intercept them before they arrived. Consequently, the change in mission that he received on 4 May was unexpected.

The new mission was to become effective at 1200 hours on 5 May, and it called for the 199th LIB to move with all possible speed to the southwestern edge of Saigon where it would be under the operational control of Task Force Hay. Concurrently, the 1st Australian Task Force was designated to take over in AO Columbus. The movement of the Warrior and Cottonbaler battalions was scheduled to begin on the morning of 5 May.

At 0300 hours on 5 May, Specialists Oldenburg and Lambert were three hours into their radio watch shift in the Warrior TOC, when they heard a series of muffled explosions outside the sandbagged bunker. The TOC bunker sat in a 12-foot-deep bulldozed cut in the ground. On the firebase's outer perimeter, Captain Dabney's Delta Company grunts, at first, thought they were under mortar attack. No one spotted the bright orange rocket exhausts of the incoming 122mm rockets. Fortunately the Warriors were experts in bunker construction. The bunkers were dug several feet down into the earth with overhead cover consisting of a piece of corrugated steel half-pipe covered with a triple layer of sandbags. When the rockets began to fall, the men were sleeping or standing watch inside the bunkers. Only two Delta Company soldiers were wounded as the 122mm rockets exploded on the firebase.

A few minutes after the last rocket exploded, Charlie Battery, 2/40th Artillery's 105mm howitzers and the Warrior battalion's 4.2" mortars fired counter-battery missions at the suspected rocket launching sites. One of the Delta Troop, 17th Cavalry's platoons observed secondary explosions in the area of the counter-battery fires. Moments later the Warrior TOC was notified by brigade headquarters that Bien Hoa was also under heavy rocket attack. The May Offensive was underway.

AO Winchester

The new 199th LIB area of operations, AO Winchester, bordered the western and southwestern sides of Saigon and encompassed most of Binh Chanh District in Gia Dinh Province. The 4/12th Warrior battalion was assigned responsibility for the northern portion of the AO, and established FSB Stephanie just north of Highway 10. The 3/7th Cottonbaler Battalion moved into an area south of Highway 4 and established FSB Horseshoe-Bend just off Highway 4. A fishnet factory was located on the same property, and the factory building was used as as the 199th LIB's forward headquarters. Only three kilometers separated FSB Stephanie and FSB Horseshoe-Bend. When the 2/3d Infantry returned to brigade control on 7 May, the Old Guard battalion moved into an area to the south of the 3/7th Infantry. The brigade's fourth infantry battalion, the 5/12th Infantry, was placed under the operational control of the 101st Airborne Division.

The terrain in AO Winchester was generally flat and most of the area was cultivated in rice paddies and small farmsteads. Numerous canals crisscrossed the area with sparse vegetation along their banks. Most of the population resided in hamlets and villages that sat astride the highways and roads that ran through the area. The areas that bordered Saigon and Cholon were densely populated.

The local force units that normally operated in the area were in a high state of readiness and fully prepared for the May Offensive. In addition to attacking bridges, PF outposts, and other targets, the Local Force VC provided guides to lead the main force VC and NVA units through AO Winchester on their way to Saigon. The rapid deployment of the Warrior and Cottonbaler battalions to areas that straddled the enemy infiltration and withdrawal routes resulted in a week of intense and bloody combat.

Fire Support Base Stephanie—1800 hours, 5 May

The site chosen for Fire Base Stephanie was in a Vietnamese cemetery, four hundred meters north of Ap Tan Hoi. While the rice paddies that surrounded the site were dry in early May, the rice fields would be flooded with more than a foot of water before the end of the month. The monsoon season was fast approaching. The cemetery sat on the only ground higher than the flood plain. The villagers were dismayed about the new fire support base's location, but there were no suitable alternatives.

FSB Stephanie was ideally situated to protect Saigon's western boundary. The firebase straddled a primary VC and NVA infiltration route that led from the large pineapple plantation located some 15 kilometers west of the city directly toward the city's western suburbs. Intelligence reports, visual reconnaissance, and imagery interpretations revealed that the pineapple area contained in excess of 3,700 fortifications. Therefore, the pineapple area became the final staging area for Communist units marching from Cambodia to attack targets in the Saigon area. FSB Stephanie was located nine kilometers east of the pineapple area, and just six kilometers from the western perimeter of Tan Son Nhut Airbase. Having reconnoitered their invasion routes days prior to the offensive, the enemy units marching toward Saigon were totally surprised by the presence of US troops in the area on 5 May.

Three of the Warrior battalion's four rifle companies air assaulted into the area around the new FSB site during the afternoon of 5 May. Captain Dabney's Delta Company moved overland with the battalion

convoy to provide security en route. Lt. Colonel Mastoris selected
Captain Bob Tonsetic's Charlie Company to secure the new FSB.
Captain Tonsetic was Mastoris' most experienced company leader,
and the Warrior battalion commander was concerned about the secu-
rity of FSB Stephanie, particularly in its formative stages. With two
artillery batteries, Charlie Battery 2/35th (155mm), and Charlie
Battery 2/40th (105mm), Stephanie became a prime target for the
NVA battalions and sapper units operating in the area.

At 1800 hours, the 4/12 Infantry land convoy arrived at FSB
Stephanie after a harrowing five-hour road march. After departing
Long Binh, the convoy sped south on Highway 13 and crossed the
Newport Bridge under sniper fire. Changing routes to avoid road-
blocks, the convoy entered the congested traffic of Saigon and made
its way to the western side of the city. Passing through Phu Lam, the
convoy drove west on Highway 10 toward the village of Binh Tri
Dong about 4.8 miles west of downtown Saigon.

When the land convoy arrived just before dusk, ground guides
directed the vehicles into positions within the firebase. Captain
Tonsetic positioned the armored cav platoon's ACAVs where they
were most needed to bolster the perimeter defense with their .50 caliber and M60 machine guns. Two M42 Dusters also arrived with the
convoy, and these were position along the northern and western
perimeters. A 155mm howitzer battery from II Field Force artillery
was directed into firing positions by Lieutenant Colonel Myer, the
2/40th artillery commander. The mud-spattered trucks and tracked
vehicles rolled through the cemetery, in some cases knocking over
grave markers and headstones.

The Vietnamese cemetery was quickly transformed into a firebase,
as fortification materials were airlifted in by CH-47 helicopter. Charlie
Company grunts constructed sandbagged bunkers with overhead
cover on the perimeter. As the grunts began to dig in, the 105mm howitzers, slung beneath CH-47s along with boxes of howitzer rounds,
were lowered near their surveyed firing positions. Artillerymen quickly unhooked the slings from the howitzers and manhandled the guns
into firing positions, while other members of the gun crews rushed
around the artillery pieces placing aiming stakes and laying them in
for registration.

While Charlie Company secured the firebase perimeter, Alpha Company, commanded by Captain Pete Albers, moved west to establish a night defensive position two kilometers to the west in the vicinity of the small village of Ap Tan Hoi. The villages of Ap Tan Thanh and Ap Tan Hoi were situated just to the west of Binh Tri Dong. It was difficult to distinguish one village from the next, since all three had grown together along Highway 10.

Bravo Company, under Captain Lee Smith, was deployed four kilometers to the south of FSB Stephanie, and two kilometers south of Ap Tan Thanh and Highway 10. Most of the area around Bravo Company's position was cultivated in rice paddies.

When Delta Company arrived with the land convoy, LTC Mastoris ordered Captain Dabney to move his men to a position about a kilometer north of the base. The Delta Company position was surrounded by rice paddies, small groves of palm trees, and patches of swamp. Unbeknownst to the 4/12th commanders, NVA units were already infiltrating through the areas around FSB Stephanie, and moving into the villages of Binh Tri Dong, Ap Tan Thanh, and Ap Tan Hoi.

It had been a long day for the grunts of Delta Company. After the early morning rocket attack at FSB Tri-Corner, the company had been air lifted back to the brigade's main base at Long Binh. There, hopes for at least a shower, a few hours relaxation, and a night in garrison were dashed when the company was ordered to move south with the land convoy to the new AO. Arriving late in the day, the company had little time to reconnoiter the area north of FSB Stephanie. Captain Dabney selected the company's night defensive position in a grove of palm trees, and selected two ambush positions and three listening posts outside the perimeter.

At 2130 hours, the grunts manning one of Delta Company's listening posts were on high alert. Staring through the green glow of their Starlight Scopes, the men on the LP saw a squad of NVA regulars walking directly toward their position. The enemy soldiers were less than twenty yards away. As a listening post, the men were not supposed to engage the enemy, but instead radio back an early warning to the Company NDP. There was no time for that. The LP was about to be discovered, so the men opened fire on the unsuspecting NVA. They killed one and took two prisoners, but the rest of the NVA squad fled. Unsure if there were other enemy in the vicinity, the grunts hurriedly searched the body of the dead NVA and hustled their prisoners to another hiding position about a hundred meters away. They bound and gagged their prisoners and opted to wait for morning before moving back to the company NDP. No one slept, fearing the NVA who had escaped during the firefight would return with reinforcements.

AO Winchester—6 May

Shortly after midnight, an ACAV crew attached to Delta Company spotted another NVA squad a few hundred meters from the company's perimeter. The track opened up with .50 caliber machine-gun fire, scattering the group. Captain Dabney dispatched a patrol to check the area, but after sweeping the vicinity, the patrol leader reported finding only blood trails. Illumination rounds fired by the battalion's mortar platoon cast long shadows over the dry rice paddies and palm groves, as the patrol returned to the company's position. The weary infantrymen waited for the dawn.

Charlie Company's 1st Platoon, led by Lieutenant Howard Tuber, manned the bunker line on the northern perimeter of FSB Stephanie. The platoon heard firing and saw the muzzle flashes and tracer rounds from Delta Company's contacts during the night. As dawn arrived, an alert 1st Platoon grunt spotted a group of soldiers moving into a palm grove 300 meters north of the perimeter. There was not yet enough light to identify them as US or Communist soldiers. The report was radioed in to the Charlie Company CP bunker, and Captain Tonsetic directed Lieutenant Tuber to send out a patrol to check the area.

The Charlie Company patrol was about fifty meters from the palm grove when they were taken under fire by a dug-in NVA squad. Their fire was murderously accurate. Twenty-five year old PFC Dennis Dunsing was mortally wounded, and two more men were hit as well. The patrol pulled back toward the perimeter with their casualties, under covering fire from the base perimeter.

Captain Tonsetic and his first sergeant, George Holmes, ran to the 1st Platoon CP as the squad withdrew. A hasty plan of attack was developed. Two squads from 1st Platoon and two ACAV from D/17th Cav moved north from the perimeter to destroy the enemy. Captain Tonsetic, Lieutenant Tuber, and 1st Sergeant Holmes accompanied the patrol. David Douglas led one of the 1st Platoon squads. As the combat patrol neared the palm grove, the NVA opened fire. Sergeant Douglas was hit by the first burst of fire. Although he was painfully wounded, the sergeant moved forward and destroyed the nearest enemy position with a hand grenade. Following his example, the Charlie Company grunts moved forward and in a short but violent firefight killed nine of the NVA and captured two prisoners. The patrol searched the surrounding area, as First Sergeant Holmes took charge of the prisoners and marched them back to the firebase. Douglas was awarded a Bronze Star for his leadership and heroism during the firefight.

When Charlie Company's combat patrol returned to the firebase perimeter, the CO's RTO, Bob Archibald, was sent to the battalion aid station to check on the men who were wounded. According to Archibald, the medics were still treating them. He wrote, "The medics were trying to save someone. . . . One of our medics realized that they had lost him, and the medic was visibly upset by their failure to save the soldier." The day was just beginning.

A few hundred meters to the north, Captain Dabney redeployed his platoons to meet a new threat. Beginning at daylight, the company's observation posts had begun to report sightings of groups of 10 to 15 NVA marching toward Delta Company's position. Captain Dabney quickly readjusted his platoon positions to engage the enemy with maximum firepower. According to Pasqual Ramirez, a squad leader with 2nd Platoon, his platoon moved east to intercept the enemy groups as they emerged from a tree line. Sergeant Charles McGowen led one of the other 2nd Platoon squads.

Sergeant McGowen's squad was first to reach the new position and open fire on the NVA troops. As he moved forward to hurl a hand grenade at the NVA, McGowen was hit with a burst of fire and mortally wounded. His squad then advanced, killing seven enemy soldiers. They also captured a prisoner. ID cards and other documents found on the enemy bodies and prisoner identified the NVA as members of the

272d NVA Battalion and the C-100 Sapper Company, 9th NVA Division. During interrogation, the POW said that his unit had departed Cambodia six days earlier on a mission to attack Saigon.

In sweltering heat, Delta Company continued to sweep the dry rice paddies and palm groves north of FSB Stephanie for the remainder of the morning. At 1145 hours, a platoon-size force from Delta Company intercepted a platoon of NVA. A sharp fight broke out. During the initial burst of fire, three Delta Company warriors were wounded as they took cover and returned fire.

Specialist Harvey Cooley, a 19-year-old medic from Houston, Texas rushed forward and began to treat two of the wounded. The third wounded man, PFC Raymond Witzig, began to crawl toward Specialist Cooley's location. When Cooley saw that the man's wounds were too severe for him to move further, he ran forward and picked up the wounded soldier. As he carried Witzig back toward the cover of a rice paddy dike, the NVA opened fire. Both men were killed. Harvey Cooley received the Silver Star for his heroic actions to save the lives of his wounded comrades.

Specialist Cooley had only been with Delta Company for a week when he was killed in action. He had replaced medic Ramiro Chavez, who was reassigned to the battalion aid station. When Chavez saw Cooley's body at the aid station, he asked the battalion surgeon if he could return to Delta Company, even though he'd spent more than his share of time in the field. When the battalion surgeon approved his request, Chavez grabbed his aid bag and hopped on the next resupply chopper headed for Delta Company's location.

Captain Dabney ordered his attached ACAVs to reinforce the platoon that was still in contact. With the additional fire support from the ACAVs, the Delta Company grunts assaulted the NVA position, killing seven, and capturing two 60mm mortars. During the assault, one of the attached ACAVs was hit with an RPG-7, wounding two of the crew members. Dust-offs were called to evacuate Delta Company's seven WIA and the two wounded cavalrymen. It seemed as if the NVA were everywhere.

As the day wore on, fighting continued around FSB Stephanie. In addition, there was really no safe spot at the firebase itself. Sniper fire wounded a howitzer crewmember and a soldier from the Warrior battalion headquarters. Despite the sniper fire, the men at FSB Stephanie continued to work on the fortifications. The battalion requested a bulldozer to construct a berm around the firebase, but the only one available to the brigade was attached to the 2/3d Infantry, and would not be available for several days.

As dusk approached, the southeastern side of the perimeter began to receive heavy sniper fire. The fire came from the village 400 meters to the south of the firebase. It was later determined that a battalion of the 273d VC Regiment occupied a large bunker complex in the village. The bunkers were constructed under the houses, using the cement floors as overhead cover. Numerous tunnels were dug from each bunker to as many as eight firing positions. The fortifications had been under construction days before the offensive began. It would take a tremendous effort using ground troops, artillery, and air strikes to dislodge them. On the ground, the task would fall on the grunts of the Warrior and Cottonbaler battalions

AO Winchester—Night of 6–7 May

As darkness descended on the area around FSB Stephanie, the sniper fire continued. Charlie Company sent out three listening posts north, west, and southeast of the perimeter. The listening posts were meant to provide early warning if enemy infiltrators tried to penetrate the perimeter. LTC Mastoris ordered Alpha, Bravo, and Delta Companies to establish platoon-size ambushes throughout the Warrior battalion's AO. As night fell, the ambush patrols moved stealthily into their ambush sites to wait for the enemy.

One of Alpha Company's ambushes was sprung shortly after 2000 hours. Four enemy soldiers were killed. Less than an hour later, the Charlie Company LP on the southeastern side of the perimeter spotted three enemy slipping out of the village headed toward the perimeter wire. The infiltrators were driven back to the village by M79 fire from the perimeter. As the night progressed, enemy movement was also detected north of FSB Stephanie. Shortly before midnight, Delta Company killed an NVA machine-gun team as it moved to a position near their night defensive position. More groups of NVA were spotted moving east to west between FSB Stephanie and Delta Company's positions to the north. LTC Mastoris ordered a 100 percent alert at FSB Stephanie.

Captain Smith's Bravo Company was deployed a few hundred meters to the south of Tan Thanh/Binh Tri Dong village. Between 0100 and 0300 hours, 7 May, the company intercepted several enemy squads moving toward the village. Seven insurgents were killed, and four AK-47 rifles and a B40 rocket launcher were recovered. Meanwhile, intelligence reports received at brigade level confirmed that there was a large enemy force in Tan Thanh. The brigade S3, LTC Don Bolduc, alerted the 3/7th Infantry to a change in mission. The brigade commander ordered the Cottonbalers to move three rifle companies to the south of Tan Thanh village in preparation for an attack. Captain Smith's Bravo Company was placed under the operational control of the 3/7th Infantry until the village was cleared.

In the meantime, Captain Dabney's Delta Company was attacked in its NDP by an estimated 200 NVA regulars. The attack began just after 0300 hours. With four ambush patrols positioned outside the company's primary NDP, the NVA unit outnumbered Captain Dabney's force and was able to quickly establish fire superiority. Dabney radioed the battalion headquarters for assistance and a resupply of ammo while his FO adjusted the artillery and mortar DEFCONs. Battalion commander Bill Mastoris responded immediately, ordering five ACAV stationed at FSB Stephanie to reinforce Delta Company. A flareship, gunship team, and a FAC were also launched to support Delta, arriving overhead of the company's night defensive position by 0400 hours. As the Spooky flareship illuminated the paddies below, Cobra gunships blasted the enemy positions with rockets and mini-gun fires. Captain Dabney attempted to direct a medevac helicopter into his position to evacuate casualties, but the incoming fire was too intense.

With the arrival of the Armored Cav platoon and gunship strikes, the tide of battle began to shift. At 0500 hours, a USAF FAC radioed Dabney that two F-100s were on station. After marking his own positions with strobe lights, Dabney pinpointed the enemy locations for the FAC. Moments later, the F-100s roared through the night sky strafing the NVA positions. On each run, the high-performance aircraft dropped canisters of napalm and followed up with 20mm cannon fire before kicking in their after-burners and soaring off for another pass. The airstrike broke the back of the NVA attack.

As dawn broke over the smoke-covered battlefield, the enemy survivors began to withdraw. Dust-offs were finally able to land to evacuate Delta Company's 15 WIAs and one KIA. On a sweep of the area outside their perimeter, the Delta Company grunts found 56 NVA bodies and one man wounded. The prisoner later identified himself as a member of the 5th Regiment, 7th NVA Division. During interrogation the wounded soldier stated that his battalion had moved into the area during the night, but he had no knowledge of where it was headed or the nature of its mission. Delta Company acquitted itself well in the fight, but it was only a preview of what lay ahead for the Warriors.

FSB Stephanie continued to receive intermittent sniper fire from the village to the south throughout the morning of 7 May. An enemy 12.75 machine gun firing from the village poured fire into Charlie Company's bunkers on the southern perimeter. A Charlie Company soldier was severely wounded when a round from the heavy machine gun shattered the man's knee joint, nearly severing his lower leg. Artillery crewmen from Charlie Battery 2/40th Artillery and Charlie Battery 2/35th Artillery were particularly at risk as they manned their howitzers during fire missions. LTC Meyer, the 2/40th Artillery commander, ordered his battery commander to engage suspected enemy sniper locations in the village with direct fire.

Beginning at 1055 hours, Alpha, Charlie, and Delta Companies of the 3/7th air-assaulted onto LZs south of the villages of Binh Tri Dong, Ap Tan Thanh, and Ap Tan Hoi. During the airmobile operation, Bravo Company, 4/12th was in a hot firefight with the enemy force in Tan Thanh village. Advancing on the village from the south, the Bravo Company grunts were hit with a barrage of small arms, RPG, and mortar fire.

Twenty-five-year-old Staff Sergeant Johnny Velasquez was platoon sergeant of Bravo's 4th Platoon. The San Francisco native had joined the 199th LIB in February 1968 after a tour with the 101st Airborne Division. Velasquez wrote, "That morning we began to move out towards the village. We all knew that we were going to be in a firefight. However, we didn't realize how bad it was going to be, and how hard we were going to get hit."

Caught in the open rice paddies, the Bravo Company Warriors hit the ground and began to return fire. According to Johnny Velasquez, his friend and fellow platoon sergeant, Sergeant First Class Lloyd Tribbett of 2nd Platoon, "stood to pull down two brand new sergeants, and all three were killed by machine-gun fire."

Bill Hill from Columbus, Georgia was a member of Velasquez's platoon. When the platoon was pinned down in the open, Hill hit the dirt and opened up with his M60. After engaging a house where most of the fire was coming from, he yelled to his buddy Johnny Chambers to engage the house with a LAW. As Chambers zeroed in on the house, Hill provided the gunner with covering fire. The pair then moved to another location and repeated the action. After Hill spotted a target, he shouted the location to Chambers using a "direction on the clock." Chambers would then fire a LAW at the target from the kneeling position while Hill provided covering fire with his M60.

Taking advantage of Hill and Chambers' covering fire, Bravo Company pulled back and took cover behind a series of dikes south of the village. As his men returned fire, Captain Smith called for artillery, gunship, and TAC air support to suppress the enemy fire. The fire was so intense that it was not possible for a medevac chopper to land near Bravo's positions.

When he received the order to pull back, Sergeant Bobby Hill and his platoon fell back and took cover behind a rice paddy dike about 100 yards from the southern edge of the village. From the new position, Hill's platoon began to deliver a heavy volume of fire on the insurgents' positions in the village. Platoon Sergeant Hill, a lanky North Carolinian, had bagged a POW earlier in the day, but had no way to evacuate the man. Fearing that the enemy soldier would attempt to escape during the firefight, Hill grabbed the VC and held him in a headlock with one arm while he fired his M16 with his free arm. The VC was determined to escape his captor, and reached for Sergeant Hill's holstered .45 caliber pistol. The two wrestled for the loaded pistol in a life-and-death struggle. Hill grasped the weapon by the barrel, wresting it away from the VC. Then he slammed the butt of the pistol into the VCs head, fracturing the man's skull. Still under heavy incoming enemy fire, Sergeant Hill grabbed his M16 and resumed firing on the enemy positions.

Alpha, Bravo, and Delta companies from 3/7th Infantry were on the ground by 1315 hours, and headed north toward positions around the Tan Thanh village. Heavy fighting continued throughout the afternoon in the Bravo, 4/12th sector. Despite gunship and air strikes on their positions, the enemy resistance continued. Attacking again across flat open rice paddies, the Bravo Company grunts were unable to gain a foothold in the village. Two more Bravo Company soldiers, Staff Sergeant Roger Ackerman of Lowell, Wisconsin, and PFC Gary Howard of Quincy, Florida were killed, and eight men, including the Bravo Company CO, Captain Lee Smith, were wounded. Smith refused medical evacuation, opting to stay with his men.

When Bravo Company's ground attacks faltered, a platoon of ACAVs from Delta Troop, 17th Cav moved through the company toward the village. As they drove into the village, the ACAVs were met with a barrage of machine-gun and RPG fire. The lead ACAV was struck by an enemy anti-tank rocket and burst into flames. Three of the crewmembers were seriously wounded and needed help. Specialist Leonard Sargent, a Bravo Company fire team leader, dashed across the paddies to rescue the wounded troopers who were in danger of being burned alive in the track. After carrying one of the troopers to safety, Specialist Sargent again exposed himself to intense enemy fire and returned to rescue another wounded crewman. When he reached the burning ACAV, three VC charged the vehicle, firing their AK47s as they ran. Sargent opened fire on the trio with his M16, dropping all three. As he placed the wounded trooper on his shoulder, another VC charged toward him. Repeating his previous action, Sargent shot the VC with his M16 rifle. Returning to his fire team's position, he then administered first aid to the wounded troopers. Specialist Sargent was awarded the Silver Star for his heroism in rescuing the wounded cavalrymen.

Tan Thanh village was a well-prepared defensive position, and every avenue of approach was covered by anti-tank and automatic weapons fire. The enemy was fully prepared to die defending their positions. After an aerial reconnaissance, LTC Hall was convinced that daylight ground assaults against the heavily fortified positions without additional air and artillery support were doomed to failure. The Cottonbalers needed overwhelming air and artillery support. Hall put his artillery LNO and S3 Air to work preparing requests for additional artillery and air strikes. The Cottonbaler commander ordered a full-scale attack on Tan Thanh village on the following morning.

Fire Support Base Stephanie continued to receive fire from the northern perimeter of the village throughout the afternoon, despite the direct artillery fire, gunship strikes, and air strikes. Three men were hit by sniper fire on the firebase, including the Charlie Company First Sergeant, George Holmes. Holmes was hit with a ricocheting AK-47 round and was not seriously hurt. After treatment at the battalion aid station he was returned to duty.

As dusk fell, fires started by the air strikes on the village illuminated the night sky, and smoke drifted from the destroyed houses. To the northeast, fires could be seen burning in Saigon. The Warriors and Cottonbalers prepared for night operations. The Cottonbalers established positions both east and west of Tan Thanh village, while Bravo Company held its position to the south. The enemy occupying the village were cordoned off, since FSB Stephanie was located directly to the north. Ambush positions and listening posts were established throughout the area to prevent any enemy from reinforcing or escaping from the village. Additionally, Spooky flareships orbited the area and provided illumination for the ground troops. Lieutenant Colonel Hall and his staff continued planning and preparations for the final assault on Tan Thanh village.

While LTC Hall and his Cottonbalers focused on Tan Thanh village, LTC Mastoris' main concern was the area to the north and west of FSB Stephanie. The Warrior commander continued to receive reports of enemy units transiting the area to reinforce their forces fighting around Tan Son Nhut Airbase. Mastoris was also concerned with enemy attempts to reinforce units in Tan Thanh village. An enemy platoon-size force was spotted moving about 300 meters from the southeastern edge of the firebase perimeter headed for the village. The enemy was engaged with mortar and M79 fire that killed several of the insurgents and scattered the rest before the platoon reached the village. The remainder of the night passed without any major contacts in the Warrior AO.

Tan Thanh Village—8 May

At dawn on 8 May, Bravo Company, 4/12th, still held positions behind the paddy dikes south of Tan Thanh. Before the sun was totally above the horizon, the company was hit with a barrage of mortar and RPG fire that killed one man and wounded fourteen others.

Johnny Velasquez wrote, "After yelling 'incoming,' I dove into the large hole we had dug. However, a mortar round exploded in front of our Chu Hoi (former VC), who was killed instantly. Lieutenant Nixon (4th Platoon leader) was standing next to him and was severely wounded." It was an odd twist of fate that Nixon was nearly killed that morning.

Lieutenant Dan Nixon had completed his six months as a rifle platoon leader in Bravo Company at the beginning of May. The men of his platoon were disappointed when their lieutenant was reassigned to advise an ARVN unit. In their opinion, his replacement just didn't measure up. Lieutenant Nixon was surprised when a several men from his former platoon showed up at the ARVN compound and asked him to return to Bravo Company. Nixon hitched a ride back to his company where he spoke with Captain Lee Smith, Bravo's newly assigned commander. Smith agreed to let Nixon return to the company, but not to his old platoon. Lieutenant Nixon returned as Bravo's 4th Platoon leader just in time for the fight for Tan Thanh village.

After Nixon was patched up by the company medics, his platoon sergeant, Johnny Velasquez, carried the young lieutenant to the medevac chopper, assuring him that they would meet again someday. They did, 32 years later.

Nixon was not the only officer wounded in the mortar attack. The Bravo CO, Captain Lee Smith, was wounded by shrapnel for the second time in two days. Ignoring his painful wounds, Smith called for gunship and TAC air support to suppress the enemy fire. He then radioed for two dust-offs to evacuate the wounded and KIA.

When the dust-off ships arrived on station, gunships covered the evacuations with rocket and machine-gun fire. Eight litter patients and nine ambulatory patients along with the KIA were loaded aboard two medevac helicopters. Captain Smith and those with minor wounds were flown to FSB Stephanie for treatment at the battalion aid station. The others were flown directly to 3d Field Hospital in Saigon.

Captain Smith was the third Bravo Company officer to be wounded and evacuated. Two platoon leaders, Lieutenants Dan Nixon and Jim Macy, were also out of the fight. LTC Mastoris called upon Captain Bob Tyson, the Echo Company commander, to fill in for Smith as temporary commander of Bravo Company. Tyson hopped on the battalion resupply Huey that was hauling a supply of ammunition out to the company and took command. In addition to the officers, all of the Bravo medics were wounded in action, and only one was able to stay with the company. It was a bad day for Bravo Company.

At 0845 hours, the first in a series of six air strikes hit the enemy positions in Tan Thanh village. A pair of F100 fighters dropped four 500 lb. bombs, and four napalm canisters on the enemy positions. Eight structures were destroyed and five were damaged. Prior to the air strikes, psychological warfare aircraft dropped leaflets and used loudspeakers to warn all civilians to vacate the area. Between the air strikes, artillery and 106mm recoilless rifles pounded the enemy positions in the village.

When the air strikes were complete, Alpha, Bravo, and Delta Companies of the 3/7th, and Bravo 4/12th launched a coordinated assault on the village to dislodge the enemy. The day was blistering hot as the Cottonbalers and Warriors moved out under the midday sun. Bravo and Delta Companies of the Cottonbaler battalion began their assaults from the western side of the village, while Alpha 3/7, and Bravo 4/12 attacked from the south.

Captain Fred Gentile had flown in to Alpha Company's night defensive position the night before the attack with battalion commander LTC Hall. Gentile had been newly promoted to Captain and LTC Hall asked Gentile if he would "stay the night with Alpha Company." Gentile, who was wearing his first set of clean jungle fatigues in months, and had no field gear with him, understood what his battalion commander meant. He was giving him command of Alpha Company on the spot. First Sergeant Ford, the Alpha Company top kick, welcomed Gentile aboard. He knew Gentile was one of the most experienced officers in the battalion. The new Alpha CO had some big shoes to fill. His predecessor, Captain Tony Smaldone, had been one of the best company commanders in the 199th LIB.

When Captain Zimmerman's Delta Company entered the village, it immediately ran into stiff enemy resistance. Captain Frank Slaughter's Bravo Company moved forward to support Delta. After more than an hour of heavy fighting to dislodge the enemy from their underground bunkers and fighting positions, Delta Company had eight men WIA and one KIA, Sergeant Michael Connolly.

Twenty-one-year-old Sergeant Mike Connolly, a native of Woodside, New York, had been walking point for his platoon as it advanced into the village. Connolly was a fire team leader and not required to walk point, but he had volunteered. As he moved forward, he sensed that his platoon was headed directly into an enemy ambush kill zone. Looking around, he spotted an enemy machine-gun barrel protruding from a bunker hidden beneath a pile of rubble. Rather than diving for cover, he turned and shouted a warning to his comrades. Then he threw his body into the line of fire of the machine gun, absorbing the initial burst of fire. Sergeant Mike Connolly was posthumously awarded the Silver Star for gallantry in action.

By 1530 hours, all three Cottonbaler companies and Bravo 4/12 were still struggling to take control of the village. Taking cover behind piles of rubble, the grunts tried to isolate the enemy fighting positions and take them out with hand grenades and small arms fire. It was tough going. In addition to casualties from hostile fire, heat casualties became a major problem as the temperature soared into the high nineties. Among the heat casualties was the interim Bravo 4/12 commander, Captain Tyson. Tyson was evacuated due to heat stroke and a ruptured eardrum. Captain Lee Smith, who was under treatment for shrapnel wounds at the battalion aid station at FSB Stephanie, flew back to his company to reassume command.

Fighting in the village was sheer hell for the grunts. The earth shook beneath their feet as 500-pound bombs exploded a few hundred meters from their positions, and the powerful shock waves knocked some off their feet. The Cottonbalers and Warriors felt the searing heat of burning napalm as canister after canister was dropped near their positions. Most of the structures that were still standing after the bombings were consumed by leaping orange tongues of fire. Despite the blazing infernos, the enemy who were dug-in beneath the concrete slabs of the houses continued to fire on their attackers. An intricate tunnel system dug weeks before the offensive allowed the insurgents to move undetected from position to position. Progress was slow and costly for the grunts.

LTC Hall orbited overhead in his C&C ship directing the battle. When he was notified that a Delta Company solider had been seri-ously burned by a white phosphorus grenade, Hall ordered his pilot to land to evacuate the injured man. As the C&C ship touched down, it was hit with a burst of machine-gun fire that mortally wounded Hall's artillery liaison officer, Captain David Rodman. Despite the withering fire directed at the helicopter, the Delta Company grunts carried the badly burned soldier to the C&C ship, where he was lifted on board. While the C&C ship flew toward 3d Field Hospital, LTC Hall request-ed more air strikes to break the stalemate on the ground.

The air strikes continued until 1900 hours, but stiff enemy resis-tance continued. As darkness approached, LTC Hall ordered his men to pull back to their cordon positions around the village. The exhaust-ed infantrymen established ambush positions to seal off all enemy routes of withdrawal. It had been a frustrating and confusing day for the grunts. Despite heavy losses, and multiple air and artillery strikes on the enemy positions, they could only confirm six enemy dead. Undoubtedly, there were many more who were either buried beneath the rubble or pulled back into the underground bunkers by their com-rades. Nonetheless, the enemy still held most of the village. The setting sun brought some relief to the nearly unbearable heat as the Cottonbalers and Warriors dug in for the night.

AO Winchester—9–10 May

Specialist Dave Taylor of Charlie 4/12 was standing watch on a night LP some three hundred meters north of FSB Stephanie. Peering through the eyepiece of a Starlight Scope, Taylor saw a startling sight. Silhouetted against the night skyline were several long columns of NVA moving slowly westward across the open rice paddies. Taylor wrote in a letter home a week later that, "The line of NVA was over 3,000 meters long. Some soldiers were carrying wounded on stretchers . . . they were walking out of Saigon at a measured pace. Even as artillery was called in on them, I don't remember them scattering or changing pace dramatically. I recollect that there must have been easily a thousand troops in that column."

Taylor radioed his platoon CP to report the sighting. The NVA and VC were withdrawing from Saigon, heading west across the northern portion of AO Winchester toward their sanctuaries in Cambodia. The NVA columns were on a collision path with the night defensive positions of the Warrior battalion.

A few minutes before 0100 hours, Delta Company 4/12 radioed the battalion TOC to report that their T-shaped ambush had made contact with three separate groups of NVA. An estimated 60 enemy were taken under fire as they approached the southern tip of the "T." The western tip of the ambush engaged another group of 60 at a range of 200 meters, and a third group of approximately 30 enemy were taken under fire as they moved past the eastern tip of the "T." Each group returned a half-hearted fire and then withdrew out of small arms range. As the enemy withdrew they were pounded with 81mm mortar fire, and when a gunship team arrived over the scene the survivors dispersed in all directions. Delta Company then dispatched patrols to sweep each contact area.

While Delta sprung its ambush north of FSB Stephanie, Charlie Company's 1st Platoon manning the bunker line on Stephanie spotted a column of 100 NVA moving east to west about 800 meters north of the perimeter. This was one of the columns spotted by Specialist Taylor's LP. Charlie Company's 81mm mortars opened fire on the column, scattering some, but the NVA soon regrouped. Carrying their wounded, the NVA continued their westward trek through the rice paddies north of the fire base. They moved toward a gap between the FSB Stephanie and Delta Company ambushes.

Moments later, Captain Tonsetic hastily organized a combat patrol to intercept the NVA column. The Charlie Company CO led his men through the perimeter wire on the northwestern side of FSB Stephanie. The patrol moved north through the darkness for several hundred meters and then turned east to intercept the enemy column. Their course led them directly toward it. When the enemy was in sight, Tonsetic deployed his men behind a rice paddy dike, and the patrol opened fire when the enemy was fifty meters from the dike. Taken completely by surprise, the head of the enemy column was cut to pieces with M16, M60, and grenades. Fourteen NVA were killed and three badly wounded prisoners were taken. The remainder of the enemy force dispersed in small groups fleeing northward.

Leaving a security force behind to guard the prisoners, Captain Tonsetic set off in pursuit of the fleeing enemy. The patrol overtook a group of about fifteen NVA who decided to make a stand behind a rice paddy dike. Charlie Company's patrol took cover behind another dike and returned fire. Opting not to assault across the open rice paddy, Captain Tonsetic radioed his 81mm mortar platoon for fire support. Moments later the patrol heard the *thunks* of 81mm rounds being fired back at firebase. Seconds later, the rounds were blowing the NVA to pieces behind the paddy dike.

When the fire mission ended, the Charlie Company grunts moved forward in an assault line firing from the hip. Four NVA bodies, all riddled with shrapnel wounds, lay strewn behind what was left of the dike. The patrol also recovered a US PRC-25 radio, set to one of the frequencies used by the control tower at Tan Son Nhut Airbase. Intelligence analysts later concluded that this group of NVA were from the assault force that had attacked Tan Son Nhut. After recovering weapons and documents from the fallen enemy soldiers, Tonsetic's patrol returned to the site where the POWs were under guard and remained at that location until first light.

While Charlie and Delta Companies of the Warrior battalion intercepted NVA units moving through the darkened rice paddies and palm groves north of FSB Stephanie, small groups of VC holed up in Tan Thanh village attempted to break out of the Cottonbaler cordon. Between 0200 and 0500 hours, small groups of insurgents attempted to slip between the Alpha 3/7 and Bravo 4/12 positions, taking full advantage of the moonless night. Using Starlight Scopes, the alert Cottonbalers spotted the fleeing enemy and opened fire. The survivors dispersed, each man fleeing on his own. Unit cohesion had completely broken down. Gunship teams orbiting the area hunted down the fleeing enemy like hungry sharks. Those who chose to stay and fight at Tan Thanh, or who were too badly wounded to flee, were about to experience the full weight of US air power.

Lieutenant Colonel Hall requested and received authorization for a total of 18 air sorties on 9 May. His intention was to break the back of the enemy resistance before continuing the ground attack. Unlike the previous day's strikes, LTC Hall requested 750-lb. bombs with delay fusing. The instantaneous fused bombs dropped during the prior day's missions had resulted in little damage to the underground bunkers in Tan Thanh.

At daybreak, the bright morning sunlight promised another scorching day in the parched rice paddies southwest of Saigon. Fires still smoldered in the village of Tan Thanh, and the smell of cordite and already decaying flesh of man and beast permeated the dewy morning air. At FSB Stephanie, Captain Tonsetic's sleep-deprived patrol entered a gap in the razor sharp concertina wire with two badly wounded prisoners. A third had died of his wounds during the night. One of the wounded prisoners was identified as an officer, but was incapable of speech. Interrogation at the firebase was not an option. The pair was dusted off for treatment at 3d Field Hospital.

While the Cottonbaler battalion stood by for the air strikes at Tan Thanh, Captain Dabney's Delta Company grunts swept the areas of their previous night ambushes, finding 36 bodies and a number of weapons, documents, and a radio made in Communist China. Identity cards found on a number of bodies indicated that the KIAs were from the 246th NVA battalion. Delta Company also captured a prisoner who stated that his unit was to attack FSB Stephanie that night, but unexpectedly ran into Delta Company's ambush and Charlie Company's patrol, completely disrupting the attack. It was apparent that FSB Stephanie was a "thorn in the side" of the enemy commanders who were attempting to withdraw their units from the Saigon–Tan Son Nhut areas. The FSB was not in the equation when they planned for the attacks.

The air strikes on Tan Thanh village began shortly after 0800 hours. Pairs of F-100s swooped down from the sky like birds of prey releasing their payloads of 750-lb. high-drag bombs. Thunderous explosions shook the earth as the bombs burrowed into the earth and detonated. Earthquake-like tremors shook the ground a kilometer away. Clods of dirt, pieces of concrete, and rocks shot upward like a volcanic eruption, then showered down on the ground below. Huge craters were created after each explosion. Troops on the cordon and at FSB Stephanie pulled their steel helmets down over their faces and crouched low in their fighting positions. The final air strike was completed at 1000 hours. It was inconceivable that anyone could have survived the bombings, but there were some who did.

Platoon Sergeant Johnny Velasquez wrote, "The following morning after the airstrikes there was movement in the rice paddies next to the village. This person came towards us yelling in Vietnamese that he was not armed and wanted to surrender. I told the Captain that I would go and get him, and to cover me. I went towards him, which was approximately 200 meters. I grabbed him by the arm and escorted him back with our Vietnamese translator. The prisoner . . . was an officer with the NVA. He pointed out where many enemy positions were, and said they took heavy casualties during those three days."

The Cottonbaler companies and Captain Smith's Bravo Company 4/12 began their sweep of the village shortly after the air strikes ended. Only sporadic enemy fire was encountered as the grunts began to pull dead and wounded VC from the wreckage. The work was nonetheless dangerous. PFC John Kirchner of Lancaster, Pennsylvania was killed in action, and six men were wounded during the mopping-up operation. Two more US personnel were wounded during the air strikes. In all, 70 enemy bodies were pulled from the wreckage and tunnel complex, and a number of dazed POWs were taken.

Battlefield interrogation of the prisoners by the Cottonbaler battalion's Kit Carson scouts revealed that the POWs were members of the 7th and 8th VC Battalions of the 9th VC Division. Others were members of the 264th NVA Battalion that was attached to the 9th VC Division. An officer POW said that his unit had marched to Tan Thanh from Cambodia. His battalion consisted of a light weapons company, an automatic weapons company, a machine gun company and a mortar company. The prisoner also said that there were still many men buried in the ruins and tunnels beneath the village. It was impossible to get them all out.

The costly battle to dislodge the enemy from Tan Thanh village was over by dusk on 9 May. Fires continued to smoulder throughout the village, and the stench of death permeated the dank tropical air. War had come to Tan Thanh like a whirlwind and destroyed it in two days. Fifty-four structures were completely destroyed, and another twenty-seven were damaged. Tan Thanh would be rebuilt in time, but memories of the fighting would live on in the minds of the men who fought there. Meanwhile, as darkness descended, another deadly struggle was about to begin north of FSB Stephanie.

Delta Company of the Warrior battalion spent the daylight hours of 9 May sweeping the rice paddies and palm groves north of FSB Stephanie, finding four additional enemy bodies and recovering nine AK-47 rifles, an RPD light machine gun, and a B40 rocket launcher apparently abandoned by fleeing enemy soldiers during previous contacts. Captain Dabney scouted the area for a new position for the company's night operations. He selected an area approximately 800 meters southwest of the previous night's ambush position.

Delta Company arrived at their new defensive position by late afternoon. Captain Dabney order his platoons to dig in for the night. He paid particular attention to the 81mm mortar position. He wanted the crew to dig a pit deep enough to fire the mortar without exposing themselves to incoming fire. Dabney also managed to acquire a .50 caliber machine gun. This weapon was not found on a light infantry company's TO&E. The .50 caliber had proved its worth in the previous night's ambush, but the gun had subsequently jammed. Replacement parts were needed to put it back in service. Just before dark, four ACAVs arrived at Delta Company's CP to deliver a resupply of ammunition, and the Cav platoon leader was able to supply the parts Dabney needed for his .50 caliber.

At dusk, Captain Dabney went up and down the line, checking the fields of fire of all his machine guns and insuring that each fighting position had at least two Claymore mines placed to the front. Trip flares were placed on all approaches to the company's defensive positions. After inspecting his perimeter, Dabney called his platoon leaders to the CP for final instructions. The Captain warned that he expected an attack before midnight, and he ordered his platoons to 100 percent alert. Dabney's premonition was right on target.

At 2020 hours, a small group of NVA probed Delta Company's position, trying to identify crew-served weapons emplacements. Dabney's riflemen and grenadiers opened fire, driving off the enemy. Delta's machine gunners wisely held their fire, waiting for the main attack. Captain Dabney ordered a patrol to sweep the area. The patrol found five enemy dead, an AK-47 assault rifle, and a Chicom pistol fifty meters forward of the perimeter.

An hour later, a major attack was launched against Delta Company's NDP from the north. One heavy and two light machine guns began to rake the Delta Company positions. The enemy machine guns were firing from positions about 100 meters from the perimeter. Dabney ordered his 81mm mortar crew to fire on the enemy positions. One of the first rounds knocked out one of the enemy light machine guns. Moments later, artillery rounds fired from FSB Stephanie destroyed the 12.75mm heavy machine gun, but the company continued to take fire from the darkened paddies and hedgerows.

As the fighting continued, Captain Dabney requested gunship and flareship support, while his platoons returned the enemy fire. Two Delta Company grunts were wounded in the initial exchange. Delta's machine guns and Claymores mowed down more NVA before they could reach the perimeter. The NVA then moved to the southwest in an attempt to encircle Delta Company's positions.

Captain Dabney was up and down the firing line all night, encouraging his men and directing their fire. At one point, he personally manned a machine gun to kill three enemy soldiers who were less than 25 meters from the perimeter. RPGs began to slam into Delta Company's perimeter, spraying shrapnel throughout the area. An Australian correspondent spending the night with Delta Company caught a piece of shrapnel in the head, but the wound was not fatal. A dust-off arrived to evacuate Delta's wounded, but was unable to land due to heavy incoming fire.

The situation began to improve when a Spooky flareship and a gunship team arrived over the battlefield to provide illumination and fire support. Captain Dabney had the gunships fire to the west of his perimeter, making their runs from north to south. Simultaneously, Charlie Battery, 2/35th Artillery fired close defensive 155mm fires north of Delta's positions, while Charlie Battery, 2/40th Artillery launched blocking fires to the northeast and northwest. When the gunships departed the area to rearm and refuel, the Spooky took over, laying down a curtain of fire around Delta Company with its mini-gun.

Colonel Davison, who was monitoring Delta Company's fight, ordered a Forward Air Controller to the scene. It was 2300 hours when the FAC arrived overhead. Captain Dabney requested air strikes to the north and northeast of his positions. Minutes later, the fighters arrived and began dropping napalm on the enemy troops. One of the napalm canisters landed dangerously close to the Delta Company positions. The uniforms and web gear of several men were scorched, but none of the grunts were seriously burned. The air strikes were complete shortly before midnight, all but ending the NVA attack on Delta Company. After his company was resupplied with ammunition, Captain Dabney ordered his platoons to sweep the areas in front of their positions. The patrols reported a total of 24 enemy bodies and an assortment of small arms and crew-served weapons. The Delta Company commander was cited for extraordinary heroism for his valorous actions during the period 6 to 10 May, and was awarded the Army's Distinguished Service Cross. Delta Company was awarded the Presidential Unit Citation for the May Offensive.

While small unit actions continued to occur around FSB Stephanie over the following days, Delta Company's night defensive battle on 9–10 May was the last major contact for the Warrior battalion during the Communists' May Offensive of 1968. By the 10th it was evident that the enemy had largely withdrawn from Saigon, and by 12 May there were indications that the enemy was withdrawing troops from the surrounding areas. Nonetheless, the Communists maintained a capability to launch highly lethal attacks against US and Vietnamese forces. During the period 12–14 May 1968, the 199th Infantry Brigade's 2/3d Infantry, under the command of Lieutenant Colonel William Carper, fought a bloody series of offensive and defensive battles with the VC 6th Local Force Battalion and elements of the 271st, 272d, and 273d Regiments in an area southwest of Cholon and north of Binh Chanh.

CHAPTER 16

THE OLD GUARD HOLDS ON

AO Winchester-South—12 May 1968

The 2/3d Infantry, nicknamed the "Old Guard," is part of the oldest regiment in the US Army. Organized in 1784, the Old Guard participated in the Indian expedition under Anthony Wayne and fought at the battle of Fallen Timbers in 1794. During the War of 1812, the regiment participated in the Canada, Chippewa, and Lundy's Lane campaigns, and during the Mexican War the regiment fought from Palo Alto to Monterrey and all the way to the climatic battle at Chapultepec, where it was given the honor of leading the Army into Mexico City. The Old Guard also distinguished itself during the Civil War, plains Indian Wars, and the Spanish American War, when it saw action both in Cuba and the Philippines. World War II saw the regiment earning a campaign streamer for Northern France after its deployment from the American Theater in 1945. Assigned to the 106th Division, the regiment fought its way through France into Germany by the war's end. The 2nd Battalion of the 3rd Infantry was again activated at Fort Benning, Georgia on 1 June 1966 and assigned to the 199th Infantry Brigade that was about to deploy to Vietnam.

After deploying with the Redcatcher brigade to Vietnam, the 2/3d Infantry gained extensive experience fighting in the area around the southern and southwest approaches to Saigon. By May 1968, the Old Guard battalion had more experience conducting operations in rice paddies, mangrove swamps, and nipa palm groves that covered southern approaches to Saigon than any of the Redcatcher battalions.

During Operation FAIRFAX (12 January–14 December 1967), the 2/3d Infantry operated continuously in this type of terrain south of Saigon, and then returned to the area in February 1968. From 18 February 1968 until 7 May, the Old Guard battalion was under the operational control of the 9th US Division, gaining even more familiarity with the terrain of the northern Mekong Delta.

When the 199th Light Brigade's 3/7th, 4/12th, and 5/12th Infantry Battalions deployed south from AO Colombus on 5 May 1968, the 2/3d was already deployed in the southern portion of AO Winchester. The Old Guard battalion sector straddled Highways 4, 233, and the Kinh Sang canal. Highways 4 and 233 connected Saigon and Cholon to the Mekong Delta, and the Kinh Sang canal led directly to the large pineapple plantation west of Saigon. Thus, the 2/3d was deployed astride major infiltration and withdrawal routes used by enemy units during the May Offensive. It was during the withdrawal phase of the enemy's offensive that the 2/3d fought its toughest battles.

The 2/3d Headquarters was located at FSB Zindernuef northwest of Binh Chanh, along with Bravo Battery 2/40th Artillery (105mm). Two 81mm mortar firebases, Hun and Attilla, were also established in the area to support the battalion's operations. Two rifle companies operated from each of these bases. During daylight hours, Hun and Attilla were secured by a minimum number of personnel, usually just the members of the mortar platoons. At night, the bases were defended by those platoons not deployed on night ambushes.

On Sunday, 12 May, LTC Carper's 2/3d Infantry, reinforced by Alpha Company 5/12th Infantry, conducted daylight reconnaissance-in-force operations east and west of Highway 4 in the vicinity of the Binh Dinh bridge. The 5/12th rifle company was attached to Carper's battalion to give it an added punch. The 5/12th Infantry battalion had joined the 199th Brigade a month earlier when it arrived from Ft Lewis, Washington. What it lacked in experience, the battalion made up for in aggressiveness, and Alpha Company was no exception.

The Old Guard reconnaissance-in-force operations on 12 May were intended to locate and destroy a number of enemy units that had been spotted moving east to west through the area during the previous night. Those units were fired upon by artillery, helicopter gunships, and a C-47 gunship before dispersing into the surrounding countryside. During the daylight operations on 12 May, several enemy bodies, ammunition, and documents were found, but no contact was made with enemy forces. That same evening, Alpha and Charlie Companies returned to FSB Hun, and Bravo, Delta, and Alpha 5/12 moved back to FSB Atilla. Local ambushes were established in the vicinity of the two bases. The battalion's Echo Company reconnaissance platoon was forward deployed to an ambush position along a stream some three kilometers northwest of the Binh Dinh bridge.

Beginning around 2200 hours, the recon platoon began to report enemy movement near their position. The VC were carrying heavy packs, with individual and crew-served weapons. Not wanting to disclose their position, the recon platoon called in artillery fire on the enemy troops. The fire mission was devastatingly accurate. Five105mm howitzer rounds exploded in the middle of the VC formation. An estimated 30 VC were killed in the barrage. The remaining VC dispersed in small groups and kept moving. As the night wore on, more groups of VC moved past the recon platoon, and more artillery was fired. It was apparent that the recon platoon's position was directly in the path of an enemy withdrawal route. Concerned that the platoon would be spotted by the VC once daylight broke, the Old Guard commander alerted Alpha Company 5/12th to move to reinforce the recon platoon at first light. Arrangements were made for two South Vietnamese RAG boats to transport the relief force from Alpha 5/12. An airmobile lift company was also requested, but none was available before mid-day. The recon team's best chance of reinforcement was Alpha 5/12.

At 0715 hours, two platoons from Captain Robert Ward's Alpha Company 5/12 departed FSB Atilla, mounted on five ACAVs from Delta Troop 17th Cav. The Cav vehicles transported the infantrymen as far as the Binh Dinh Bridge where they boarded the RAG boats that would ferry them to an area close to the recon platoon's position.

While the slow-moving WWII-era RAG boats moved downstream toward the drop-off point, the recon team spotted an enemy force moving 50 meters northeast of their position. The VC spotted the recon team and opened up with machine-gun fire. Thirty-one-year-old SFC Charles Sandberg was mortally wounded, and two other members of the patrol suffered serious wounds. The recon team knew they were in a bad situation. They returned fire, and called for gunship support and an urgent dust-off. At 0905, a helicopter gunship team arrived and began a series of gun runs that suppressed the enemy fire, but did not silence it. The recon team's situation became more serious by the minute.

After turning north on a tributary of the Rach Lam, the RAG boats slowed their speed as they negotiated the twisting waterway. Dense foliage covered both banks of the muddy stream. The noisy grind of their vintage diesel engines could be heard for hundreds of meters upstream. Concealed in positions along the west bank, the VC waited patiently for the slow-moving craft. When the RAG boats entered the kill zone, RPGs slammed into their hulls, and the soldiers in the boats received a hail of machine-gun bullets. Two Alpha Company troopers were KIA and one man was WIA as the boats returned fire. The Vietnamese Navy coxswain of the lead boat was also wounded, but he stayed at the helm and steered his boat through the kill zone. Thirty minutes later, the Alpha 5/12 relief force disembarked from the RAG boats. They were still about 1500 meters south of the recon team's location, but fearing another ambush, the Captain wisely opted to move overland. After calling in a dust-off to evacuate his casualties, the resolute Alpha 5/12 Commander ordered his platoons to move out. Moving rapidly through muddy paddies, the exhausted Alpha Company grunts reached the beleaguered recon team's location at 1130 hours.

Under heavy incoming fire, Alpha Company grunts took cover behind a large rice paddy dike, while helicopter gunships pounded the VC position with rockets and machine guns. Undaunted, the insurgents kept up a steady fire from their sturdy concealed bunkers in a nipa palm grove 200 meters away. Three heavy machine guns were slamming rounds into the rice paddy dike that shielded the 5/12 grunts and the recon team. Behind the dike, Alpha Company's grenadiers attempted to suppress the machine-gun fire by firing well-aimed 40mm grenades into the bunker complex. It was a standoff, but the Old Guard commander had more reinforcements on the way.

A few minutes before noon, Captain Jerry Romine's Bravo Company 2/3d air-assaulted into an area about one kilometer north of the contact area to establish blocking positions, while Delta 2/3d, led by Captain Bill Danforth, were slogging through the muddy paddies to reach the scene. Taking up positions on the right flank of Alpha 5/12, Delta Company reported spotting 35 to 40 newly constructed bunkers occupied by an estimated reinforced company. The Old Guard commander requested air strikes to soften up the bunker complexes before launching ground assaults. The Alpha 5/12 platoons and Delta 2/3 were ordered to pull back in preparation for the air strikes.

During the air strikes, Alpha 5/12 captured a prisoner who had fled the bunker complex. The prisoner identified himself as a member of the 3d Battalion, 1st Regiment, 9th VC Division. Under interrogation, the enemy soldier said that there were still 60–70 VC holding the complex, and that the battalion's four companies were spread throughout the area. He further estimated that his battalion had lost some 31 killed and 50 wounded by artillery fire during the previous night.

With the detailed information provided by the POW on the VC position, the Alpha 5/12 platoons and Delta Company launched assaults on the bunker complex. The Alpha 5/12 troops quickly overran the first line of bunkers. Unsure if the enemy had pulled out, 22-year-old Specialist Four Kenneth Olson from Paynesville, Minnesota cautiously moved forward with a fellow grunt to investigate a second line of bunkers. The pair were ten meters from one of the bunkers when the VC opened up. Reacting immediately, Specialist Olson grabbed a frag grenade from his web gear, pulled the pin, and tossed it toward the bunker. The grenade exploded but did not silence the hostile fire. Olson armed a second grenade as he prepared to assault the position. As he rose to hurl the grenade, he was wounded by enemy fire, causing him to drop the armed grenade. According to the award citation, "Realizing that it would explode immediately, Sp4c. Olson threw himself upon the grenade and pulled it into his body to take the full force of the explosion. By his unselfish action Sp4c. Olson sacrificed his own life to save the lives of his fellow comrades-in-arms." For his courageous actions, Specialist Kenneth Olson became the second member of the 199th Infantry Brigade to earn the Medal of Honor.

Inspired by Specialist Olson's actions, the Alpha and Delta Company grunts continued their attack, overrunning the bunker complex, killing or capturing the remaining VC and capturing intact an enemy heavy machine gun. Casualties in the two Alpha 5/12 platoons were one KIA and 10 WIA, eight of whom required medical evacuation, while Delta Company had one man wounded. Having completed their mission, the Echo recon team survivors were flown back to the battalion fire support base.

As darkness approached, the 2/3d and 5/12th companies began to dig in for the night. Dark rain clouds began to build up on the horizon, and flashes of lightning danced in the dark purple sky. A steady rain began to fall as the grunts wrapped themselves in their ponchos and hunkered down in their fighting positions, staring across the slowly flooding paddies. No one looked forward to the long night ahead.

Lieutenant Colonel Carper's 2/3d Infantry was spread thin during the night of 13–14 May. This situation did not go unnoticed by VC, who though badly mauled during the fighting in Saigon and Cholon, remained combat effective and dangerous. While most of the main force enemy battalions were withdrawing to the west intent on reaching their sanctuaries in Cambodia, the 6th Local VC battalion continued to contest US and ARVN forces for control of the area on the southwest outskirts of Saigon. This local force enemy battalion was based in the area, and had an extensive intelligence and support network to facilitate its operations. When an opportunity presented itself, units of the 6th Local Force Battalion remained prepared to strike. Opportunities in the 2/3d AO were not hard to come by on the night of 13–14 May.

Construction of the two small 2/3d fire support bases, Hun and Attilla, was still in progress on 13 May. The troops of the Old Guard battalion had had little time to improve their positions at the firebases due to the continued high tempo of operations. Between daylight sweeps and reconnaissance-in-force operations and night ambush patrols, the grunts had been kept too busy to work on the fortifications of the small firebases. Generally, the bunker line was thinly manned at the bases when most rifle platoons were out on night ambush patrols. The night of 13–14 May was no exception.

Captain Fred Wallenborn's Alpha Company and Captain Vesa Alakulppi's Charlie Company of the Old Guard operated from Fire

Base Hun. The companies' 81mm mortars were set up within the perimeter, and the outer perimeter bunkers were manned by soldiers not deployed outside the base on operations. Fire Base Attilla was similarly home to Captain Jerry Romine's Bravo Company, Captain Bill Danforth's Delta Company, and Captain John Hume's Echo Company. As a result of the heavy contacts on 13 May, both Hun and Attilla were both undermanned as the darkness of night descended.

Captain Vesa Alakulppi's Charlie Company CP group, along with the mortar platoon and a few soldiers from Alpha Company were the only forces defending firebase Hun that night. Captain Wallenborn's Alpha Company was on operation northeast of Hun, and Alakulppi's three rifle platoons were also deployed outside the base. Two of the Charlie Company rifle platoons were deployed on night ambushes, and the third rifle platoon was securing the Binh Dinh bridge with an ACAV platoon from Delta 17th Cav. In all, this left only around 40 men to defend Firebase Hun.

Firebase Hun was situated between a road on its west side and an unfinished railroad bed on the east. There were twelve sandbagged bunkers in various stages of construction on the outer perimeter. Alpha Company usually manned the bunkers on the western and northern portions of the perimeter, but on the night of 13–14 May only a handful of Alpha Company grunts who were unable to deploy with the company were on the bunker line. Squad leader Jim Clark from Alpha Company was one of those who remained. Clark, who along with his RTO had just returned from R&R that day, recalled that C Company grunts manned about half of Alpha Company's bunkers, leaving every other bunker unoccupied. Clark and his RTO moved into one of the unoccupied bunkers along with a forward observer. Alpha Company's mortars were set up behind the bunkers, but the mortar crews had accompanied the rest of the company on operation.

On Charlie Company's side of the perimeter, some of the bunkers were also unoccupied that night. Charlie Company's mortar pit and the FDC were located in the center of the base along with the Charlie Company CP. The CP was set up in an abandoned Vietnamese hooch in the center of the perimeter.

Captain Vesa Alakulppi, the Charlie Company CO, was a rising star in the Old Guard battalion. Upon his arrival in Vietnam, the Captain had been assigned as the battalion's S2, and in March he was selected by the battalion commander to take command of Charlie Company. Alakulppi had all of the qualifications for combat command. The son of a career officer, he had graduated from the United States Military Academy in 1963. After completing the Armor Officer's basic course and Airborne School, he was assigned to Germany where he served as a company commander in the 3/35th Armor. In 1967, Captain Alakulppi received orders for Jungle Warfare School in Panama, and a subsequent assignment in Vietnam.

Fire Base Hun—Early morning hours, 14 May

The month of May in the Mekong Delta region of Vietnam is a transitional month between the dry and summer monsoon seasons. The dry season lasts from December through April when the area receives almost no rainfall. By June the full blast of the summer monsoon arrives. Torrential downpours are not, however, uncommon in mid- to late-May, and such a downpour occurred on the night of the 13th. This act of nature leveled the playing field for the Viet Cong and set the stage for an attack on Charlie Company's isolated outpost.

The summer monsoon hit with full force around midnight, and the rains began with devastating force. About an hour later, the 6th VC Local Force Battalion launched its attack in the blinding rainstorm. As torrents of rain blew across the rice paddies, the VC crawled along the unfinished railroad bed that paralleled the eastern side of the base until they were within a few meters of the bunker line. The attack began when a salvo of 15 RPGs blasted the perimeter. The incoming fire was murderous. Several bunkers were hit, along with the Charlie Company mortar platoon's FDC. The grunts who occupied the targeted bunkers were immediately killed or wounded, or suffocated beneath the wreckage.

In the ensuing confusion, the VC who had crept into the abandoned railroad bed assaulted the bunkers on the east side of the perimeter. A corner M60 machine-gun bunker was captured almost immediately and its occupants killed. The VC then turned the machine gun on the inner perimeter and CP. Simultaneously, groups of VC hidden behind the rice paddy dikes close to the perimeter opened up on the other bunkers and CP with automatic weapons, small arms, and rocket fire, pinning down the grunts. As Alakulppi's men returned the fire, more enemy infiltrators slithered through the muddy paddies toward the bunker line. After cutting their way through the perimeter concertina wire, they crawled forward in the pouring rain to lob hand grenades into the perimeter before rushing forward with satchel charges. Within minutes, four of the base's twelve bunkers were either knocked out or captured.

Twenty-five-year-old Specialist James Kline from Philadelphia was an assistant machine-gunner in Charlie Company. Kline's bunker was hit with an RPG that wounded the occupants, but they managed to continue to hold the bunker. According to his award citation, Specialist Kline "left his position to aid his injured comrades. Moving through withering enemy machine-gun and rocket fire, he carried one casualty after another from the battle area to safety. After having removed six men from the line of fire, he began checking bunkers for other wounded personnel. He discovered that two American casualties were trapped in an enemy-held bunker. Disregarding his safety, Specialist Kline courageously assaulted the position, killing two insurgents and silencing their machine gun. As he continued to advance . . . he was mortally wounded." For his extraordinary heroism that night, Specialist James Kline was posthumously awarded the Army's Distinguished Service Cross.

When Captain Alakulppi saw that the VC had penetrated his perimeter and captured four of the perimeter bunkers, he directed his men to shift their fires to contain the enemy penetration. Leaving his command post he moved toward the fighting along the perimeter, intent on leading a counterattack to recapture the enemy held bunkers. As he moved toward the enemy-held bunkers, encouraging his men and directing their fire, he fell mortally wounded from a burst of enemy fire.

Twenty-one-year-old PFC Tim Moore was acting squad leader of one of Charlie Company's mortar squads. Moore and the other members of his squad—Robin Hickenlooper, Allen Newland, and Gary Schuetzle—were all asleep when the assault began. Reacting immediately, they ran to their mortar pit and began firing close defensive fires, alternating between HE rounds and illumination rounds. Moore recalled that they kept firing until the mortar overheated and a round became lodged in the tube. With his mortar out of action, Moore and his squad moved to assist the platoon's other mortar crew. That second mortar was firing on the VC who still held the corner machine-gun bunker. The squad leader was aiming and adjusting by sight. Moore replaced a wounded gunner and kept up the fire until the bunker was knocked out, killing all of the VC intruders. Moore and his men then moved to take over an unmanned Alpha Company mortar on the western side of the base, where they continued to fire on the attackers. The fight inside the perimeter continued as small groups of FSB Hun defenders, including some of the wounded, battled to regain control of the base.

Jim Clark of Alpha Company and his RTO were asleep in a bunker when the VC began their attack. Clark wrote, "We came out of the bunker and saw the fighting on the other side of the mortar pits. Taylor [Clark's RTO] and I saw that the weapons bunker on our side had been taken over, and the enemy was firing the M60 toward the C Company side. Taylor and I worked our way around and up the moat-like ditch that our bunkers were built on and took back the bunker. We manned the bunker until daylight hours and fired lots of rounds from the M60."

Fighting continued all along the bunker line as the grunts fought to kill the invaders and take back their base. It was close combat of the most savage type. Charging through the pelting rain, the Charlie Company grunts used rifle butts, pistols, and bayonets to kill the intruders. In some instances, the combat was hand-to-hand inside the dark bunkers, as wounded men grappled with invading VC. No quarter was asked or given.

The attack on Fire Base Hun was observed by other 2/3d units in the vicinity. Sergeant Bob Himrod, a scout dog handler, accompanied one of Charlie Company's platoon ambushes that night. The ambush site was about a kilometer east of Charlie Company's base in some nipa palm growth on the edge of a rice paddy. Himrod later wrote, "Around one in the morning, it started to rain very heavy. . . .The rain made a lot of noise as it came down on the vegetation around us. Without the aid of a night vision device the view was otherwise pitch black. Off in the distance came a couple of loud explosions followed by automatic weapons fire. I could see the telltale green tracers of the enemy firing into Elvira [Hun]. It looked like the Fourth of July. . . . We could make out distant shadows of people moving around the firebase. Bright flashes followed by loud explosions echoed across the rice paddy. Pink and green tracers seemed to be flying everywhere."

Steve Perkins was with an Alpha Company platoon ambush patrol some three kilometers south of Firebase Hun. Perkins recalled that a large VC force passed their platoon's night ambush position around midnight, headed in the direction of the firebase. According to Perkins, the platoon leader radioed for artillery and gunship support, but was told the support was not available. The platoon leader decided not to open fire as his platoon was badly outnumbered. Two and a half hours later, the platoon heard the explosions and firing at FSB Hun. The patrol was ordered to hold their position until daylight.

A helicopter gunship team and Spooky flareship finally arrived over the besieged firebase around 0330 hours. The adverse weather and communications problems had slowed the response. Many aircraft were grounded because of the storm, and according to the 2/3d Daily Staff Journal, the battalion command frequency "seemed to be jammed." As the Spooky flareship illuminated the rain-soaked rice paddies surrounding Fire Base Hun, the Cobra gunships raked the VC positions around the base with rockets, 40mm, and machine-gun fire. Encouraged by the arrival of the gunships, the Old Guard grunts managed to kill or seriously wound all of the VC who had penetrated the base. According to the battalion S2/3 Journal, the perimeter was reported as "restored" by members of Charlie Company at 0445 hours. However, the base was still under sporadic fire from outside the wire. The defenders were relieved when told that help was on the way. Second Platoon, Delta Troop, 17th Cav was ordered to reinforce the defenders of Fire Base Hun. It was still pitch black as the Cav troopers cranked-up their ACAVs, and rumbled down the road headed for Hun.

Bob Himrod wrote, "At around four a.m., two APCs came roaring across the bridge. As they cleared the bridge, they opened up with their .50 caliber machine guns. The lead track pulled up off the northern perimeter and the second stopped short of the south end. The Viet

Cong were trapped in a deadly crossfire. I could see the fleeing enemy having their bodies torn apart by the murderous fifty fire."

Staring through the hazy gray twilight, the defenders of Fire Base Hun surveyed the paddies around their base. Jim Clark described the scene: "As morning came, the enemy was laying in the paddies in front of us and every now and then one would pop up and try to run for it. It reminded me of a circus shooting booth. . . . Also, I crawled out in front of the bunker . . . to check the enemy dead and another jumped up and ran. I picked up an AK47 and fired at him, but the AK had a hole in the barrel and flames shot out and scared the shit out of me. I believe the hole was from a grenade that I had thrown earlier." After the remaining VC were killed or captured, the defenders began to count their losses.

When the grunts emerged from their bunkers shivering from the cold dampness of the morning air, they were shocked by the carnage around them. Slowly, those who were able began to pull their dead and wounded comrades along with the enemy dead from the wrecked bunkers. Of the 40 or so men who defended Fire Base Hun, six were killed, including the company commander, Captain Alakulppi, and 29 others were wounded. Dust-off ships continued to land at the base until 0830 that morning, when all of the dead and wounded were evacuated. Twenty enemy bodies were strewn among the wreckage inside the perimeter, and two wounded VC were taken prisoner. Before the day was over, another 89 enemy bodies were recovered from the rice paddies and nipa palm bogs around the firebase.

On their way back to Charlie Company's base, Bob Himrod's ambush patrol found two VC medics who had been cut down in the crossfire of the ACAVs' .50 calibers. According to the scout dog handler, "The paddy water was stained red with their blood." The patrol moved on until they approached the Charlie Company perimeter. Concerned that his men might be mistaken for enemy, the patrol leader halted the patrol north of the perimeter until he established radio contact with the base. Himrod described the scene when the patrol arrived.

"There were two Viet Cong prisoners squatting sharing a cigarette. They had obvious bullet wounds but seemed oblivious to their injuries. Another soldier who had survived that hellish night was being restrained from harming the prisoners. Half the bunkers had been overrun and a number of Americans had been killed. A pit was dug and the enemy bodies were thrown in it and covered with dirt." The fight for Firebase Hun was over, but it was not the only desperate fight that night.

Both Alpha, 5/12 and Delta, 2/3 came under attack during the early morning hours of 14 May. The companies were in night defensive positions close to the scene of the previous day's contact. Alpha Company's perimeter was hit at 0250, and at 0310 Captain Danforth's Delta Company radioed the 2/3d TOC to report that their perimeter was surrounded and the situation was critical. Gunship and flareship support was requested along with artillery fire. Captain Danforth later described his situation in an article in the Redcatcher Yearbook.

"They crawled up behind the dikes of rice paddies around us. With the heavy rain, we didn't see them until they were 20 meters from the perimeter and had started firing. We knew they were all around us. The men let go with all we had and held them. They were so close that they were throwing grenades at us. After 90 minutes of that, we started to conserve ammo some, and called in artillery, 360 degrees around us."

Alpha Company, 5/12 and Delta Company, 2/3 both successfully fought off the attacks against their perimeter, but not without loss. Delta Company had two men KIA and eight wounded, and Alpha Company reported one man KIA and eight WIA. The enemy also paid a high price. The paddies were strewn with enemy bodies and weapons. The Old Guard's fights on 13–14 May were the last major contacts of 199th Light Infantry Brigade units during May Offensive.

Although the May offensive had failed to achieve its objectives, and the VC and NVA suffered enormous losses in men and equipment, the Communist units remained highly lethal and capable of inflicting heavy losses on US and South Vietnamese forces. The month of May 1968 was the bloodiest month of the war for the 199th LIB. Forty-two members of the brigade were killed in action, and hundreds more were wounded, yet there was no end in sight for the war. It appeared that the enemy was prepared to fight on forever. As unrest erupted on the home front, and politicians negotiated for a way out of the war, the troops, with warrior stoicism, continued to fight and die for a cause that no one could adequately explain or justify.

EPILOGUE

On October 11, 1970, some twenty-nine months after the end of the Communist May Offensive of 1968, an honor guard composed of officers, warrant officers, and enlisted soldiers representing the units of the 199th Light Infantry Brigade stood at attention on a muddy field at Camp Frenzell-Jones. It was raining, just as it had rained on the day of the arrival of the brigade in Vietnam some forty-seven months earlier. That short departure ceremony marked the end of the Redcatcher Brigade's service in the Vietnam War. The US Army was in the process of withdrawing its combat units from Vietnam at an accelerated pace.

The fierce battles described in the preceding chapters were the bloodiest of the war for the Redcatcher Brigade, but the battles of 1968 should not overshadow the difficult days that followed. In the aftermath of the May Offensive, sharp encounters with VC and NVA units continued through August and September of 1968. In June 1968, the highly respected commander of the Cottonbalers (3/7th Infantry), LTC Ken Hall, was killed along with several members of his staff. Two months later, the 199th Light Brigade commander, Brigadier General Franklin Davis, departed the command after he was wounded in action during an operation in the Rung Sat Special Zone. The 2/3d commander, LTC Herbert Ray, was wounded in the same action. Casualties in all ranks remained high, as infantrymen of the brigade continued to pursue VC and NVA forces into their sanctuaries.

On April 1, 1970, just five months before the Brigade's withdrawal from Vietnam, Brigadier General Bond, the 199th LIB Commander, was killed in action. Undaunted, Warriors of the brigade's 5/12th

261

Infantry crossed the Cambodian border a month later and distinguished themselves at LZ Brown. There were countless acts of heroism and valor during the Brigade's final months in Vietnam that are not recounted in this book, but perhaps someday those stories will be told as well.

On October 15, 1970, the 199th Light Infantry Brigade was inactivated in a ceremony at Fort Benning, Georgia, from whence it had come almost four years earlier. The 199th LIB's colors were furled, cased, and placed in storage, and its tattered combat journals and after-action reports were boxed and shipped off to the National Archives repository in Maryland, where they are safeguarded in perpetuity with the records of the nation's other wars.

The men who served in the Light Brigade, with the exception of the 753 brave men who fell in battle, returned for the most part to civilian life. A few remained in the Army to pursue a career. Those who returned got on with their lives. Some resumed their education, while others went to work. Most married and raised families. Few spoke or wrote of what they had experienced in Vietnam. Unlike veterans of earlier wars, their service was never honored. Rather, their service was viewed with indifference and in some cases disrespect. For the most part they turned the other cheek and led productive lives. Their stories of heroism, courage, and sacrifice remain mostly untold. This book recounts a few of their stories.

NOTES

PROLOGUE

Cliff Kaylor was the author's radio operator from January through April 1968, and is currently a VA counselor in Eugene, Oregon. His perspective on the December 1967 battles near Fire Base Nashua was extremely helpful.

Colonel (Retired) Wayne Morris, was the senior platoon leader with Alpha Company, 4/12 Infantry during the December 6 battle. While working in Prague, Czech Republic, he provided the author with detailed emails describing the fighting on December 6, 1967, and answered a number of the author's questions. While Colonel Morris stays in contact with several members of his platoon, this is the first time he has written his recollections and thoughts about the battle.

Roberto Eaton currently living in his native country of Paraguay provided details on Bravo Company's actions on December 6, in email responses to the author's interview questions.

CHAPTER 1: WHAT CAME BEFORE

Lineage and historical information concerning the 12th Infantry, 7th Infantry, and 3d Infantry were derived from Lineage and Honors Information, Organizational History Program, Force Structure and Organizational History Branch, US Army Center of Military History, and the Redcatcher Yearbook published in May, 1969.

Colonel William Schroeder, US Army Retired, provided detailed information concerning the 4/12 Infantry's role in Operation FAIRFAX in personal and telephonic interviews. He also provided the author with copies of his Commander's Notes, After Action Reports, as well as his personal maps and overlays from his tour as battalion commander.

Biographical information on Brigadier General Robert Forbes was summarized from the Abbreviated History of the 199th Infantry Brigade prepared by the 199th Infantry Brigade Historian. The author also had the privilege of having several one on one personal conversation with Major General Robert Forbes, US Army Retired, before his death in 2002.

The action on November 29, 1967 involving Charlie Company 4/12 Infantry was described in detail to the author by Colonel Schroeder, Jim Pittman, and George Hauer. Pittman and Hauer were both recommended for the Silver Star, however, the paperwork was lost and the men never received their awards. When Colonel Schroeder was notified in 2005 that the men had never received the awards, he reconstructed from his own war records the events of the firefight and resubmitted the recommendations for the Silver Stars. The awards were subsequently approved by the Department of the Army and Colonel Schroeder arranged an awards ceremony in Melbourne, Florida on March 11, 2005, some 37 years after the battle.

CHAPTER 2: ACROSS THE SONG DONG NAI

Details on the LRP operations described in this chapter were obtained from the F Company (LRP) After Action Report, Operation Kickoff, 3–5 December 1967. The report is on file at the National Archives. Additional information was found in Don and Annette Hall's compelling book, *I Served*.

CHAPTER 3: THE BLOODIEST DAY
CHAPTER 4: VICTORY AT NIGHT

General and specific information describing of enemy units, base camps, and tactics was derived from multiple sources including Michael Lanning and Dan Cragg's book, *Inside the VC and NVA* for general information, and Appendix 1 (VC Order of Battle) to Annex A (Intelligence) to II Field Force After Action Report for the Tet Offensive for Order of Battle information. Specific information was derived from 199th Infantry Brigade INSUM 337–342. 031800 to 081600 December 1967, and Headquarters

4/12 Letter dated 6 January 1968 to Commanding General, 199th Infantry Brigade, Subject: VC Base Camps.

Details and descriptions of the December 6, 1967 battle were derived from multiple sources including official documents, periodicals, on-line web pages, and personal interviews and email correspondence. Official documents included the 4/12 Infantry After Action Report, for 6-7 December 1967, Daily Staff Journals of the 4/12 Infantry for 6 and 7 December 1967, and II Field Force and 199th Infantry Brigade General Orders for personal awards for Valor. Larry McDougal's October 2003 article, *Day of Valor*, published in the periodical *Vietnam* was also used as a source. On line sources used were Norman Reeves website, 199th Light Infantry Brigade Republic of Vietnam, and Phil Tolvin's website 199th Light Infantry Brigade Redcatcher-A Vietnam Vet.

Background information on Chaplain Liteky and his actions on December 6, were obtained from his citation for the Medal of Honor, and from Colonel Schroeder and others, as well as articles published in the Redcatcher, 199th Light Infantry Brigade newspaper, December 15, 1968, and an article published in the *Witchita Beacon* on February 7, 1969.

Individual accounts of the battle and its aftermath were obtained from the following individuals: Colonels Retired, William Schroeder, and Wayne Morris, Roberto Eaton, James Pius, Wayne McKirdy, Marv Stiles, Jim Choquette, Dennis Castaldo, George Hauer, Frank Paoicelli, and Cliff Kaylor.

The source of information for 12th Infantry Regiment casualties on D-Day was obtained from Stephen Ambrose's book, *D-Day, June 6, 1944, The Battle for the Normandy Beaches* (page 292).

CHAPTER 5: THE ENEMY LIES LOW

Official documents used in writing this chapter included 4/12 Infantry After Action Reports for 19 and 27 December, dated 20 and 30 December 1967, respectively, and Daily Staff Journals of the 4/12 Infantry for the period 8 through 28 December 1967.

II Field Force General Orders for the award of the Silver Star and 199th Infantry Brigade General Orders for the award of the Bronze Star for valor, and Purple Heart were also sources of information.

Individual recollections and descriptions of the combat actions were provided by Colonels Retired William Schroeder and Paul Viola, First Sergeant Retired George Holmes, William McClean, Bob Archibald, Gary

Coufal, Cliff Kaylor, Larry Norris, and David Taylor.

CHAPTER 6: THE GATHERING STORM

General background information on the VC/NVA preparations for the Tet Offensive was found in Don Oberdorfer's book, *Tet*.

Official documents used in preparing this chapter included the II Field Force Combat After Action Report-Tet Offensive, 31 January-18 February 1968, the199TH Infantry Brigade Combat After Action Report for Operations MANCHESTER, UNIONTOWN/STRIKE AND UNIONTOWN I covering the period 1 December 1967-2February 1968, and the 199th Infantry Brigade After Action Report, Long Binh/Saigon, TET CAMPAIGN, 12 January-19 February 1968.

The author was also provided critical information on intelligence gathering during this period by Dave Parks and Major Retired Ken Welch.

CHAPTER 7: A BATTLE JOINED
CHAPTER 8: FIGHTING ON ALL SIDES

All sources for Chapter Six are also applicable to this chapter.

Keith Nolan's book, *The Battle for Saigon-Tet 1968*, was also a valuable source of information in writing this chapter. Shelby Stanton's book, *The Rise and Fall of an American Army—U.S. Ground Forces in Vietnam, 1965–1973*, provides a summary of the fighting in the Long Binh/Bien Hoa and Saigon areas (pages 215–229), but lacks the detail and first person accounts found in Nolan's book.

Additional documents used in writing this chapter include the following:

4/12 Infantry Combat After Action Report (OPERATION UNION-TOWN) 14 January-17 February 1968.

Daily Staff Journals of the 199th Infantry Brigade, 30 January through 2 February 1968.

Daily Staff Journals of the 4/12 Infantry, 30 January through 2 February 1968.

Daily Staff Journals of the 2/47 Infantry 31 January through 2 February 1968.

199th Infantry Brigade Operational Report-Lessons Learned for the quarterly period ending 30 April 1968.

3d Ordnance Battalion Operational Reports-Lessons Learned for the quarterly periods ending 31 January and 30 April 1968.

Valorous Unit Award, 199th Infantry Brigade.

The following periodicals were also sources of information for this chapter:

The Hurricane: A Publication of II Field Force Vietnam, April 1968 issue.

Octofoil, 9th Infantry Division in Vietnam, article by Arnauld Fleming, "Widows Village: VC Graveyard," Vol. 1, No. 2.

Redcatcher, 199th Light Infantry Brigade, article by Michael Swearingen, "Redcatchers Smashed Enemy's Tet Attacks," December 15, 1968.

Vietnam magazine, article by LTC (Ret), "The Tet battles of Bien Hoa and Long Binh," February 2006.

Individual recollections and descriptions of the combat actions described in this chapter were provided by the following individuals: Colonel Retired William Mastoris, Lieutenant Colonel Retired Jim Dabney, Major Ken Welch Retired, First Sergeant Retired George Holmes, Larry Abel, Robert Archibald, Nick Schneider, Jim Choquette, Cliff Kaylor, Mike Raugh, and Gary Coufal.

CHAPTER 9: ASSAULT ON SAIGON
CHAPTER 10: A DAY AT THE RACES

General background on the fighting in Saigon and Cholon was found in Don Oberdorfer's book, *Tet*. Keith Nolan's book, *The Battle for Saigon—Tet 1968*, was also a useful reference particularly in regard to the enemy attack on Tan Son Nhut and the firefight at the U.S. Embassy, and other key targets in Saigon. Nolan's book also documents the initial response to these attacks by the 716th MP Battalion, as well as the deployment of the 3/7 Infantry to Cholon, and the establishment of Task Force Ware.

John C. McManus' article, "Battleground Saigon", in the periodical *Vietnam*, February 2004, was also a useful reference. Major R.E. Funderburk's article, "Delta Unit Fought in Saigon" in the 9th Infantry Division's publication, *The Old Reliable*, February 1968, was also used as a reference in describing the role of the 5/60 Infantry in the battle to secure Cholon.

Official US Army documents used as references for these chapters included:

Combat After Action Report—TET OFFENSIVE, Headquarters, II Field Force Vietnam, 31 January–18 February 1968.

After Action Report, Long Binh/Saigon, TET CAMPAIGN, 199th Infantry Brigade (Separate) (Light), 12 January–19 February 1968.

Daily Staff Journals of the 3d Battalion, 7 th Infantry, 31 January–4 February 1968.

Task Force Ware Combat After Action Report, 31 January–18 February 1968.

Task Force Ware Briefing Notes, Battle of Tan Son Nhut (VC Tet Offensive).

Lieutenant Colonel MacGill, US Army Retired, provided the author with an eyewitness account of the 3/7 Infantry's attack to recapture the Phu Tho Racetrack and secure Cholon. MacGill was the S3 Operations officer of the 3/7 Infantry and as such directed and controlled and directed the deployment of the battalion's ground units during the fighting including the reinforcements from the 5-60th Infantry. Doug McCabe provided a detailed account of the fighting from the perspective of a frontline infantryman.

Colonel William Schroeder, US Army, Retired, provided a detailed account of the establishment and deployment of Task Force Ware. As G3 of the Task Force, Schroeder was a key player in controlling the deployment of US combat units into Saigon/Cholon and assignment of missions to US forces.

CHAPTER 11: NIGHT OF FIRE:

US Army documents pertaining to the 4/12 Infantry, 199th Infantry Brigade listed in Chapter 7 are applicable to this chapter.

The author's own recollections and notes on this phase of the Tet fighting near Long Binh was the basis for this chapter. Several members of C Company 4/12 Infantry shared their own memories including First Sergeant George Holmes, Robert Archibald, Cliff Kaylor, and Gary Coufal.

CHAPTER 12: COTTONBALER HOT LZ

The 3/7 Infantry Daily Staff Journal for 4–5 February 1968, provided the framework for this chapter in regard to the sequence of events and time frames for the airmobile assault and subsequent ground actions. Award citations for heroism were useful in documenting individual actions in the air and on the ground.

Lieutenant Colonel Jim MacGill, US Army Retired, was the planner for the airmobile assault, and was overhead controlling the assault from the battalion C&C ship.

His recollections and perspectives on the airmobile assault were essential in the preparation of this chapter. Bill Trotter, one of two platoon leaders, on the initial assault provided a detailed account of the assault and subsequent defense of the landing zone. Ron Whelan's memorable account of airmobile assault was essential to the chapter. Whelan was a Sergeant in the first platoon to land on the hot LZ.

CHAPTER 13: TO SNARE A GENERAL

US Army Documents cited as references in Chapters 8–10 are also applicable to this chapter.

Colonel William Schroeder who was G3 for Task Force Ware provided the author an account of how this operation was conceived and assigned to the 3/7 Infantry, rather than to ARVN forces. Lieutenant Colonel MacGill's input was vital since he controlled the execution phase of the operation initially from the air and later on the ground during the mop-up phase. Retired Lieutenant Colonel Trotter, who was a platoon leader in Bravo Company, observations on the operation and his newly assigned company commander was also helpful. Chester Porter, Brad Huffman, Ron Whelan, and Bill Plains all provided unique descriptions of the fighting through the eyes of the combat infantryman.

CHAPTER 14: APRIL 1968—A CRUEL MONTH

Annex B (Intelligence) and Annex C (Operations) to the 199th Infantry Brigade Operational Report-Lessons Learned for the period ending 30 April 1968, provided the best official summary for the operations described in this chapter. Daily Staff Journals for the 3/7 Infantry and 4/12 Infantry provided specific details on unit locations, engagements, and time frames. Individual award citations were used to describe individual acts of heroism.

As S3 for the 3/7 Infantry, retired Lieutenant Colonel MacGill provided the best input on the fighting from the battalion level. He was also able to provide valuable information on the personalities of his newly assigned battalion commander, Lieutenant Colonel Ken Hall, as well as the company commanders of the 3/7. Frank Auer, Doug McCabe, Ron Whelan, Glen Pagano, Bill Plains, and Bob Himrod all provided vivid eye witness descriptions of the close combat on the ground. There are no apparent contradictions in their descriptions of the battles described in this chapter.

CHAPTER 15: THE MAY OFFENSIVE

Ronald Spector's book, *After Tet: The Bloodiest Year in Vietnam*, was used as a general reference in writing this chapter. Chapters 7 and 8 of Spector's book provide an overview of the May Offensive at the country-wide level. The amount of information and detail on the fighting in and around Saigon is limited.

US Army documents used as references in preparing this chapter included:

Daily Staff Journals of the 199th Infantry Brigade (SEP) (LIGHT), 4-31 May 1968.

Daily Staff Journals of the 4th Battalion, 12th Infantry, 4-31 May 1968.

Daily Staff Journals of the 3d Battalion, 7th Infantry, 4-31 May 1968.

Feeder Report for After Action Report. Company D, 4th Battalion, 12tth Infantry, May 1968.

INSUM 126–68. 05001 to 052400 May 1968. 199th Infantry Brigade (SEP) (LIGHT).

Operational Report-Lessons Learned for the quarterly period ending 31 July 1968. 199th Infantry Brigade (SEP) (LIGHT).

Presidential Unit Citation, Company D, 4th Battalion, 12th Infantry, 199th Infantry Brigade

Task Force Hay Combat After Action Report, 05–16 May 1968

Task Force Hay G3 Briefing Notes, VC Offensive, 5 May 1968

Air Liaison Report for TF HayAfter Action Report. Air Liaison Office, Headquarters II Field Force, 18 May 1968.

II Field Force and 199th Infantry Brigade General Orders for individual acts of heroism performed during May 1968 Offensive.

Colonel William Schroeder, US Army retired, contributed valuable input on the role played by TF Hay in directing the US units involved in countering the enemy offensive in the Saigon/Cholon area.

Colonel William Mastoris, US Army retired, provided important insight into the 4/12 Infantry's role in the May Offensive from the battalion commander level. His insight on air and artillery support coordination issues was especially helpful.

Lieutenant Colonel Jim Dabney, US Army retired, was an invaluable source of information on Delta Company's role in the May Offensive. Dabney's description of the tactics he employed to defeat a numerically superior force is a credit to this brave officer.

Jim Dabney continues to identify men his company who deserved awards, but were overlooked when he left the company shortly after the May Offensive. He spends considerable time resubmitting award recommendations for these men. Pasqual Ramirez of Delta Company provided important information on the fighting before he was wounded and evacuated. Pasqual was also able to organize a reunion of 4/12 veterans in 2005, at Columbus, Georgia where the author was able interview a number of veterans who shared their experiences for this book. Gunter Bahlaq shared the journal he kept during the May Offensive during the reunion.

In addition to the Delta Company veterans interviewed at the 2005 reunion, the author was able to gather information from a number of Bravo Company veterans in attendance. Information provided by Roberto Eaton, First Sergeant (retired) Bobby Hill, Dan Nixon, William Hill, and Johnny Velasquez was essential to the preparation of this chapter.

Charlie Company's role is the May Offensive is based on the author's own recollections and those of several veterans of Charlie Company including Colonel retired Paul Viola, First Sergeant George Holmes, Bob Archibald, Mike Hinkley, and Dave Taylor. Taylor's report from his night listening post on 9 May was of particular interest to the author, since Taylor recorded the event in a letter he wrote shortly thereafter. The report described an NVA column of some 1,000 men stretching for some 3,000 meters on the horizon north of Fire Base Stephanie. Taylor's reported sighting never reached the author who was in command of Charlie Company at that time. Dave Taylor, who earned a PhD in Paleontology after the war, made a return visit to Vietnam in 2004 with his wife and daughter. He toured the areas north of Saigon where Charlie Company fought during December and January 1968, and the area where the company fought during the May Offensive. He was unable to identify the area where Fire Base Stephanie was located. Urban sprawl has overtaken most of areas where the battles described in this chapter were fought.

CHAPTER 16: THE OLD GUARD HOLDS ON

The following US Army documents were useful in preparing this chapter:

Operational Report-Lessons Learned for the quarterly period ending 31 July 1968. 199th Infantry Brigade (SEP) (LIGHT).

Daily Staff Journals of the 199th Infantry Brigade (SEP) (LIGHT), 4–31 May 1968.

Daily Staff Journals of the 2d Battalion, 3d Infantry, 4-31 May 1968.

II Field Force and 199th Infantry Brigade General Orders for individual acts of heroism performed during May 1968 Offensive, Medal of Honor Citation Specialist Kenneth Olson.

Chapter Sixteen was the most difficult chapter of this book to write. The existing documentation is limited in detail, and it was difficult to locate veterans who were willing to share their stories with the author. There are relatively few survivors of the attack on the seriously under-manned Fire Base Hun. Since it was such a traumatic event in their lives, a number of these men prefer to remain silent, or communicate solely with other survivors. Tim Moore of Charlie Company and Jim Clark of Alpha Company, who shared their experience with the author, are two exceptions. Their vivid recollections of what happened at Fire Base Hun are both chilling and disturbing. Both men fought valiantly with their comrades to defend the fire base and recapture the enemy-occupied bunkers. Bob Himrod, a scout dog handler, who observed the attack from an ambush position some distance from the fire base and was one of the first to enter it after the attack provided another unique perspective. Steve Perkins, who was on an Alpha Company ambush near Fire Base Hun, recalled that a large VC force passed nearby the ambush position headed in the general direction of Fire Base Hun. Speculation that this force was in fact the same enemy unit that attacked Fire Base Hun could not be substantiated by the author's research. There was constant night movement of enemy troops throughout the 2/3d Infantry's area of operation during this period.

SOURCES & BIBLIOGRAPHY

FIRST PERSON SOURCES

This book relies heavily on input provided by numerous Vietnam veteran who were willing to describe and share their personal stories and recollections of their combat experience. In addition to providing their eyewitness accounts in personal conversations, interviews, correspondence, and emails, many of those listed below also shared personal letters, diary entries, photographs, and web-site descriptions of their experiences that were relevant to the story. The following individuals, listed by unit, contributed details of the combat actions described in the book.

4/12th Infantry: *Headquarters*, Colonels William Mastoris and William Schroeder (Ret.); Alpha Company: Colonel Wayne Morris (Ret.), Dennis Castaldo, James Pius, Norman Reeves; *Bravo Company*: Roberto Eaton, First Sergeant Bobby Hill (Ret.), William Hill, Dan Nixon, Phil Tolvin, Johnny Velasquez; *Charlie Company*: Larry Abel, Robert Archibald, Gary Coufal, George Hauer, Michael Hinkley, First Sergeant George Holmes (Ret.), Cliff Kaylor, Larry Norris, Jim Pittman, Michael Raugh, Dave Taylor, Colonel Paul Viola (Ret.); *Delta Company*: Gunter Bahlaq, Lieutenant Colonel Jim Dabney (Ret.), Robert Fromme, Ken Kussy, Pasqual Ramirez.

3/7th Infantry: *Headquarters*, Lieutenant Colonel James MacGill (Ret.), William Starrett; *Alpha Company*: Fred Gentile, Douglas McCabe, Frank Paoicelli; *Bravo Company*: Glen Pagano, Bill Plains, William Trotter, Ron Whelan; Delta Company: Frank Auer, Brad Huffman, Chester Porter.

273

2/3d Infantry: *Alpha Company*: Jim Clark, Larry McDougal, Steve Perkins, Jay Vorhees, Charlie Company: Tim Moore

2/40th Artillery: Paul Lange, Wayne McKirdy, Marv Stiles. **Delta Troop 17th Armored Cavalry,** Jim Choquette. **179th MI Detachment,** Major Ken Welch (Ret.).

856th Radio Research Detachment, Dave Parks. **40th Public Information Detachment,** Mike Swearingen. **49th Infantry Platoon (Scout Dog),** Bob Himrod.

BOOKS

Ambrose, Stephen E. *D-Day June 6, 1944.* New York: Simon and Schuster Inc., 1994.

Ebert, James R. *A Life in a Year, The American Infantryman in Vietnam.* New York: The Random House Publishing Group, 1993.

Gouge, Robert J. *These are my Credentials.* Bloomington, IN: Authorhouse, 2004.

Hall, Don and Annette. *I Served.* Bellevue, WA: A.D. Hall Publishing, 2001.

Nolan, Keith W. *The Battle for Saigon—Tet 1968.* New York: Pocket Books, 1996.

Lanning, Michael L. And Cragg, Dan. *Inside the VC and NVA.* New York: Ivy Books, 1992.

Oberdorfer, Don. *Tet.* Garden City, NY: Doubleday & Company, Inc., 1971.

Palmer, General Bruce Jr. USA. *The 25- Year War: America's Military Role in Vietnam.* New York: Simon & Schuster Inc., 1994.

Spector, Ronald H. *After Tet-The Bloodiest Year in Vietnam.* New York: Vintage Books, 1993.

Stanton, Shelby L. The Rise and Fall of an American Army, U.S. Ground Forces in Vietnam, 1965-1973. Novato, CA: Presidio Press, 1985.

Summers, Harry G. Jr. *The Vietnam War Almanac.* Novato, CA: Presidio Press, 1985.

Tonsetic, Robert L. *Warriors.* New York: The Random House Publishing Group, 2004.

Westmoreland, William C. *A Soldier Reports.* Garden City, NY: Doubleday & Company, 1976.

PERIODICALS

"Valorous Unit Award Given to 199th, The Full Account of the Redcatchers in the Tet Battles." *Redcatcher, 199th Light Infantry Brigade* (bi-weekly newspaper of the 199th LIB), December 1, 1968, 1–7.

"Medal of Honor for Chaplain."*Redcatcher, 199th Light Infantry Brigade*, December 15,1968, 1.

"1Lt Morris Won DSC with 4/12." *Redcatcher, 199th Light Infantry Brigade*, February 1, 1969.

Devitt, Lt. Col. J.W. ed. The Hurricane; A Publication of II Field Force Vietnam, April 1968.

Draper, Wayne. "Infantryman Thrives on War." Times Staff Correspondent, News clipping date unknown.

"DSC for CPT Dabney." *Redcatcher, 199th Light Infantry Brigade*, March 1, 1969, 3.

Fleming, Arnauld, "Widows Village: VC Graveyard." *Octofoil, 9th Infantry Division in Vietnam*, Vol. 1, April, May, June (68) No.2, 10–12.

Funderburk, R.E. Major. "Delta Unit Fought in Saigon." *The Old Reliable*, February 21, 1968.

Gross, John E. LTC (Ret). "The Tet Battles of Bien Hoa and Long Binh." *Vietnam*, February 2006, 18–26.

McDougal, Larry. "Redcatchers' Day of Valor." *Vietnam*, October 2003, 20–25 & 53.

McManus, John C. "Battleground Saigon." *Vietnam*, February 2004, 26–33.

Mulligan, Hugh. "No Time for Prayers when Priest Trades Bible for M16." *The Wichita Beacon*, February 7, 1969.

Swearingen, Michael D. Jr. "Redcatchers Smashed Enemy's Tet Attacks." *Redcatcher, 199th ight Infantry Brigade*, December 15, 1968, 4–5.

Tour 365, *Magazine of U.S. Army Vietnam*, Spring-Summer 1968, 46–51.

Wixon, Coleen. "Retired colonel still taking care of his men." Press Journal- Indian River, March 15, 2005.

DOCUMENTS

After Action Report, Long Binh/Saigon, TET CAMPAIGN; 199th Infantry Brigade (Separate) (Light), 12 January–19 February 1968.

After Action Report, 4/12th Inf., 6-7 December 1967. Headquarters, 4th Battalion, 12th Infantry, 8 December 1967.

After Action Report, Company E, 4/12th Inf., 19 December 1967. Headquarters, 4th Battalion, 12th Infantry, 20 December 1967.

After Action Report, 4/12th Inf, 27 December 1967. Headquarters, 4th Battalion, 12th Infantry, 30 December 1967.

After Action Report, Company F (LRP) Operation Kickoff, 3–5 December 1967. Undated

Air Liaison Report for TF Hay After Action Report. Air Liaison Office, Headquarters II Field Force, 18 May 1968.

Combat Operations After Action Report, Operation FAIRFAX/ RANG DONG, 12 January–14 December 1967. Headquarters, 199th Infantry Brigade (SEP) (LIGHT), 3 January 1968.

Combat Operations After Action Report, Operations MANCHESTER, UNIONTOWN/STRIKE and UNIONTOWN I, 1 December 1967 - 2 February 1968." Headquarters, 199th Infantry Brigade (SEP) (LIGHT), 8 February 1968.

Combat After Action Report— TET OFFENSIVE, Headquarters, II Field Force Vietnam, 31 January–18 February 1968.

Combat After Action Report (Operation Uniontown). Headquarters, 4th Battalion, 12th Infantry, 199th Infantry Brigade (Sep) (Light), 14 January–17 February 1968.

Daily Staff Journals of the 199th Infantry Brigade (SEP) (LIGHT), 1 December–31 May 1968.

Daily Staff Journals of the 2d Battalion (M), 47th Infantry, 31 January–2 February 1968.

Daily Staff Journals of the 3rd Battalion, 7th Infantry, December 1967–May 1968.

Daily Staff Journals of the 4th Battalion, 12th Infantry, December 1967–May 1968.

Department of the Army, Lineage and Honors, Headquarters and Headquarters Company, 199th Infantry Brigade.

Department of the Army Pamphlet, No. 550-40, U.S. Army AREA HANDBOOK for VIETNAM, September 1962.

Feeder Report for After Action Report. Company D, 4th Battalion, 12th Infantry, May 1968.

Headquarters, DEPARTMENT OF THE ARMY, General Orders No. 77, Award of THE MEDAL OF HONOR—Chaplain (Captain) Angelo J. Liteky. 10 December 1968.

Headquarters, DEPARTMENT OF THE ARMY, General Orders No. 22, Award of THE MEDAL OF HONOR—Specialist Four Kenneth L. Olson. 23 April 1970.

Headquarters, UNITED STATES ARMY VIETNAM, General Orders No. 3687, Award of THE DISTINGUISHED SERVICE CROSS—Tonsetic, Robert L. 1 August 1968.

Headquarters, II FIELD FORCE VIETNAM, General Orders No. 1468, Award of The Silver Star—Pretty, Robert A. 26 December 1967.

Headquarters, II FIELD FORCE VIETNAM, General Orders No. 1476, Award of The Silver Star—Hahn, Gary G. 28 December 1967

Headquarters, II FIELD FORCE VIETNAM, General Orders No. 1479, Award of The Bronze Star Medal—Lindsey, Daniel H. 29 December 1967.

Headquarters, II FIELD FORCE VIETNAM, General Orders No. 1481, Award of The Silver Star—Whitton, Teddy G. 30 December 1967.

Headquarters, II FIELD FORCE VIETNAM, General Orders No. 1482, Award of The Silver Star—Sognier, John W. 31 December 1967.

Headquarters, II FIELD FORCE VIETNAM, General Orders No. 2, Award of The Silver Star—Finley, Guy M. 2 January 1968

Headquarters, II FIELD FORCE VIETNAM, General Orders No. 18, Award of The Silver Star—Clark, Gary R. 9 January 1968.

Headquarters, II FIELD FORCE VIETNAM, General Orders No. 60, Award of The Silver Star—Martinez, Rogelio M. 21 January 1968.

Headquarters, II FIELD FORCE VIETNAM, General Orders No. 125, Award of The Silver Star—Tinker, Norman L. 10 February 1968.

Headquarters, II FIELD FORCE VIETNAM, General Orders No. 162, Award of The Silver Star—Harper, Richard W. 20 February 1968.

Headquarters, II FIELD FORCE VIETNAM, General Orders No. 196, Award of The Silver Star—Garrison, Daniel E. 5 March 1968.

Headquarters, II FIELD FORCE VIETNAM, General Orders No. 311, Award of The Silver Star—Burkhart, Ronald W. 19 April 1968.

Headquarters, II FIELD FORCE VIETNAM, General Orders No. 331, Award of The Silver Star—Collier, Junius, 26 April 1968.

Headquarters, II FIELD FORCE VIETNAM, General Orders No. 340, Award of The Silver Star—Drees, Donald B. 29 April 1968

Headquarters, II FIELD FORCE VIETNAM, General Orders No. 342, Award of The Silver Star—Walker, Billy D. 29 April 1968.

Headquarters, II FIELD FORCE VIETNAM, General Orders No. 348, Award of The Silver Star—McLaughlin, Stanley A. 30 April 1968.

Headquarters, II FIELD FORCE VIETNAM, General Orders No. 354, Award of The Silver Star—Mason, Arthur, 2 May 1968.

Headquarters, II FIELD FORCE VIETNAM, General Orders No. 358, Award of The Silver Star—Dalrymple, Bobby S. 2 May 1968.

Headquarters, II FIELD FORCE VIETNAM, General Orders No. 366, Award of The Silver Star—Bohrer, Albert H. 4 May 1968.

Headquarters, II FIELD FORCE VIETNAM, General Orders No. 371, Award of The Silver Star—Oakes, Allen R. 4 May 1968.

Headquarters, II FIELD FORCE VIETNAM, General Orders No. 382, Award of The Silver Star—Acevedo, Jose A. 10 May 1968.

Headquarters, II FIELD FORCE VIETNAM, General Orders No. 398, Award of The Silver Star—Wyers, Orville D. 14 May 1968.

Headquarters, II FIELD FORCE VIETNAM, General Orders No. 399, Award of The Silver Star—Jaynes, Clifford L. 15 May 1968.

Headquarters, II FIELD FORCE VIETNAM, General Orders No. 478, Award of The Silver Star—Boyles, Jerry L. 1 June 1968.

Headquarters, II FIELD FORCE VIETNAM, General Orders No. 495, Award of The Silver Star—Cooley, Harvey L. 5 June 1968.

Headquarters, II FIELD FORCE VIETNAM, General Orders No. 561, Award of The Silver Star—South, John H. 19 June 1968.

Headquarters, II FIELD FORCE VIETNAM, General Orders No. 563, Award of The Silver Star—Vetter, Ernest Jr. 20 June 1968.

Headquarters, II FIELD FORCE VIETNAM, General Orders No. 569, Award of The Silver Star—Connolly, Michael D. 22 June 1968.

Headquarters, II FIELD FORCE VIETNAM, General Orders No. 631, Award of The Silver Star—Rangel, Roberto, 5 July 1968.

Headquarters, II FIELD FORCE VIETNAM, General Orders No. 735, Award of The Silver Star—Key, Phillip O. 21 July 1968.

Headquarters, II FIELD FORCE VIETNAM, General Orders No. 751, Award of The Silver Star—Doiron, Gerald C. 24 July 2968.

Headquarters, II FIELD FORCE VIETNAM, General Orders No. 778, Award of The Silver Star—Sargent, Leonard W. 29 July 1968.

Headquarters 199th INFANTRY BRIGADE (SEP) (LT), General Orders 834, Awarded: The Bronze Star Medal with AV" Device (Posthumously)—Midcap, David M. 24 December 1967.

Headquarters 199th INFANTRY BRIGADE (SEP) (LT), General Orders 835, Awarded: The Bronze Star Medal with AV" Device (Posthumously)—Reynolds, Joseph L. 24 December 1967.

Headquarters 199th INFANTRY BRIGADE (SEP) (LT), General Orders

837, Awarded: The Bronze Star Medal with AV" Device (Posthumously)—Pruitt, William H. 24 December 1967.

Headquarters 199th INFANTRY BRIGADE (SEP) (LT), General Orders 838, Awarded: The Bronze Star Medal with AV" Device (Posthumously)—Limbacher, Durward A. 24 December 1967.

Headquarters 199th INFANTRY BRIGADE (SEP) (LT), General Orders 851, Awarded: The Bronze Star Medal with AV" Device (Posthumously)—Zeigler, Eugene 30 December 1967.

Headquarters 199th INFANTRY BRIGADE (SEP) (LT), General Orders 20, Awarded: The Bronze Star Medal with AV" Device (Posthumously)—Harper Thomas O. 6 January 1968.

Headquarters 199th INFANTRY BRIGADE (SEP) (LT), General Orders 21, Awarded: The Bronze Star Medal with AV" Device (Posthumously)—Filippi, John C. 6 January 1968.

Headquarters 199th INFANTRY BRIGADE (SEP) (LT), General Orders 22, Awarded: The Bronze Star Medal with AV" Device (Posthumously)—Buckner, Robert O. 6 January 1968.

Headquarters 199th INFANTRY BRIGADE (SEP) (LT), General Orders 28, Awarded: The Bronze Star Medal with AV" Device (Posthumously)—Bawal, Robert J. 10 January 1968.

Headquarters 199th INFANTRY BRIGADE (SEP) (LT), General Orders 30, Awarded: The Bronze Star Medal with AV" Device (Posthumously)—Moreu-Leon, Mario. 11 January 1968.

Headquarters 199th INFANTRY BRIGADE (SEP) (LT), General Orders 31, Awarded: The Bronze Star Medal with AV" Device (Posthumously)—Puhi, Daniel K. 11 January 1968.

Headquarters 199th INFANTRY BRIGADE (SEP) (LT), General Orders 41, Awarded: The Bronze Star Medal with AV" Device (Posthumously)—Dehart, Solomon W. 12 January 1968.

Headquarters 199th INFANTRY BRIGADE (SEP) (LT), General Orders 52, Awarded: The Bronze Star Medal with AV" Device (Posthumously)—McLoud, Douglas L. 15 January 1968.

Headquarters 199th INFANTRY BRIGADE (SEP) (LT), General Orders 52, Awarded: The Bronze Star Medal with AV" Device (Posthumously)—McLoud, Douglas L. 15 January 1968.

Headquarters 4th Battalion 12th Infantry, Letter to Commanding General, 199th Infantry Brigade (Sep) (Lt), Subject: VC Base Camps, dated 6 January 1968.

Headquarters 4th Battalion 12th Infantry, Commanders Notes #22, dated

31 December 1967.

INSUM 337–42. 031800 to 081600 December 1967. 199th Infantry Brigade (SEP) (LIGHT).

INSUM 36–68. 05001 to 052400 February 1968. 199th Infantry Brigade (SEP) (LIGHT).

INSUM 126–68. 05001 to 052400 May 1968. 199th Infantry Brigade (SEP) (LIGHT).

Letter from Major General Robert C. Forbes to 1LT James G. Lindsay. 3 January 1970.

Operational Report—Lessons Learned for the quarterly period ending 31 January 1968. 199th Infantry Brigade (SEP) (LIGHT).

Operational Report—Lessons Learned for the quarterly period ending 30 April 1968. 199th Infantry Brigade (SEP) (LIGHT).

Operational Report—Lessons Learned for the quarterly period ending 31 July 1968. 199th Infantry Brigade (SEP) (LIGHT).

Operational Report—Lessons Learned for the quarterly period ending 31 January 1968. 3rd Ordnance Battalion.

Presidential Unit Citation, Company D, 4th Battalion, 12th Infantry, 199th Infantry Brigade (SEP) (LIGHT).

Press Release 2/5, Lt. Mike Swearingen, 40th PI Det., 199th Infantry Brigade, 5 February 1968.

Press Release 2/11, Lt. Michael Vaughan, 40th PI Det., 199th Infantry Brigade, 5 February 1968.

Press Release 2/23, Spc. Weldon Dupuis, 40th PI Det., 199th Infantry Brigade, 17 February 1968.

Redcatcher 32d Reunion and Memorial Dedication, 199th Light Infantry Brigade. Booklet compiled by Larry McDougal, Redcatcher Association Historian. May 1998.

Redcatcher Yearbook." Information Office, 199th Light Infantry Brigade, May 1968.

Task Force Hay Combat After Action Report, 05–16 May 1968.

Task Force Hay G-3 Briefing Notes, VC Offensive, 5 May 1968.

Task Force Ware Combat After Action Report, 31 Jan–18 Feb 1968.

Task Force Ware Briefing Notes, Battle of Tan Son Nhut (VC Tet Offensive).

Valorous Unit Award, 199th Infantry Brigade (SEPARATE) (LIGHT).

ON LINE SOURCES/WEB SITES

After Action Reports. http:25th aviation.org/history/After Action
    Reports.
Ramirez, Pancho. 4th Battalion, 12th Infantry Regiment, 199th Infantry
    Brigade. http:pancho199th freeservers.com.
Reeves, Norman, 199th Light Infantry Brigade Republic of Vietnam.
    http:www.bloody1.com.
Silver Spurs, A Troop, 3/17th Air Cavalry. http: members.aol.com/bear
    317/spurs.htm.
The Vietnam Veterans Memorial. http:the wall-usa.com.
Tolvin, Phil, 199th Light Infantry Brigade Redcatcher—A Vietnam Vet.
    http:members.aol.com/phil6135.
199th Light Infantry Brigade Vietnam. http:www.redcatcher.org.
The Tet Offensive—1968—716 MP Battalion. http://home.mweb.co.
    za/re/redcap/tet.htm
5th Battalion, 60th Infantry Association http://members.tripod.com/
    5thbattalion/index.html
Vesa Juhani Alakulppi. http://www.virtual.org/da/AlakulppivJol.htm

INDEX